AF228195

PORTUGAL'S BUSH WAR IN MOZAMBIQUE

PORTUGAL'S BUSH WAR IN MOZAMBIQUE

AL J. VENTER

Foreword by Brigadier-General Nuno Lemos Pires,
National Defense Policy Deputy Director at the
Portuguese Ministry of Defense in Lisbon and Force Commander of the
European Union Training Mission in Mozambique (EUTM-MOZ)

CASEMATE

Philadelphia & Oxford

Published in the United States of America and Great Britain in 2022 by
CASEMATE PUBLISHERS
1950 Lawrence Road, Havertown, PA 19083, USA
and
The Old Music Hall, 106–108 Cowley Road, Oxford OX4 1JE, UK

Hardback Edition: ISBN 978-1-63624-110-4
Digital Edition: ISBN 978-1-61200-937-7

A CIP record for this book is available from the British Library

Printed and bound in the United Kingdom by TJ Books

Typeset in India by Lapiz Digital Services, Chennai.

For a complete list of Casemate titles, please contact:

CASEMATE PUBLISHERS (US)
Telephone (610) 853-9131
Fax (610) 853-9146
Email: casemate@casematepublishers.com
www.casematepublishers.com

CASEMATE PUBLISHERS (UK)
Telephone (01865) 241249
Email: casemate-uk@casematepublishers.co.uk
www.casematepublishers.co.uk

Contents

Acknowledgements

Portugal's Bush War in Mozambique is to be my last book on Lisbon's colonial conflicts in Africa. There have been quite a few, beginning with *The Terror Fighters*, which covered the time I spent with the Portuguese Army in Angola in the 1960s.

Portugal's Guerrilla Wars in Africa was written much later and was subsequently translated, along with other titles, into Portuguese. To date, that work has gone into five editions in both English and Portuguese, indicating a growing interest in how Portugal survived its distant conflicts in Africa in the 1960s and the first half of the 1970s.

Gaining access to the three Portuguese territories in Africa was always difficult, because unlike the Americans—then fighting a war of their own in Southeast Asia—Lisbon rarely encouraged media coverage, especially if the approach came from an *estrangeiro*, a foreigner. Some journalists (using our own connections) made the grade, but that was a rare achievement; one of the reasons why these African struggles rarely made the news.

My access was due to one man, then a Portuguese Army colonel whom I'd first met at the London Embassy where he served as military attaché. This was the same man, General José Manuel Bettencourt Rodrigues who, among other achievements, was appointed Minister of the Portuguese Army (1968–70), Commander of Angola's eastern military zone (1971–73) where he trounced his guerrilla opposition, and finally appointed as Governor General of Portuguese Guinea (1973–74), today Guiné-Bissau.

The colonel had invited me to his office at the embassy to chat about some of my experiences while traveling overland from Cape Town to Dakar, the Senegalese capital. Along the way I'd spent time in the Republic of Guinea, a former French possession that had transmogrified from a colony into a Marxist state and by the time I arrived there, was in solid support of a guerrilla army fomenting revolution in Portuguese Guinea.

I was stuck for some time in Koundara, a small town in northern francophone Guinea which lay adjacent to the Senegalese frontier, having been told that my papers "were not in order." They were, of course, because I'd used the same passport to traverse a dozen other African states as I headed towards London.

In the process, thanks to a couple of Peace Corps volunteers who were teaching there, I was able to observe a lot of what was going on at the time in Koundara, much of it linked to what was happening militarily only a couple of hundred kilometers to the west. In particular, there was a Soviet radio relay station functioning in a house close to where I was staying.

After I'd arrived in London a few weeks later, I mentioned this in passing to some of my South African friends and someone must have sent it on to Pretoria. They, in turn, alerted Lisbon, which was why Colonel Bettencourt Rodrigues asked me to join him for coffee.

Axiomatically, one good turn deserves another, and it was to the good colonel that I turned when I wanted to visit Angola a year or two later to cover that war. His response: "Send me your passport." I did the same again when I wanted to get into the ongoing war in Portuguese Guinea, at the time the most demanding of Lisbon's three African conflicts.

In contrast, I didn't need his authorization to get to Mozambique's "Sharp End." I simply went straight in from where I was living in South Africa—as I had done many times in the past. The only difference was that I'd already published several books on Portugal's wars in Africa and the authorities in Lourenço Marques, Tete and elsewhere were astonishingly supportive.

They actually went a lot better. Tete's regional governor, a military man, put his plane along with an air force pilot at my disposal so that I could visit the site of the Cahora Bassa Dam, then under construction on the Zambezi River. He was being cautious, he told me, because the road between Tete and the dam was regularly ambushed. In fact, he confided later over a bottle of Aguardiente, "the entire Zambezi Valley is thick with the bloody enemy."

That trip to Tete, as well as subsequent journeys—many in military convoys that took me further north—form the basis of this book. The convoy trip between Tete and Mwanza in Malawi's south (Chapter 14) was not only instructive, but offered a series of insights as to how ordinary people in Mozambique were coping with the guerrilla struggle, of which landmines were only one of the problems.

As with all conflicts, as I was to discover over time, the closer you are on the ground to where things are happening, the better you understand what is really going on…

I have many others to thank for helping me to bring this work to fruition including numerous Portuguese friends who were, or still are, involved with that East African country. Dr John P. Cann, a former U.S. naval aviator who made captain and is now retired, heads the list. Jack, as we all know him, has published widely on Portugal's colonial wars and has permitted me to use some of his observations within these covers.

Professor Ian F. W. Beckett, in his day a leading light at Britain's Royal Military Academy Sandhurst, warrants special thanks. His observations feature prominently in Chapter 6. So too with Tom Cooper, whose grasp of modern air forces fringes on the encyclopedic and has published volumes on the subject, came to the rescue when I asked him to write the chapter on the role of the Portuguese Air Force in Mozambique. That appears in Chapter 9.

Neall Ellis, whose biography *Gunship Ace—The Wars of Neall Ellis* has gone into another edition, and about whom various books have been written (*Mercenary*, as well as *The Chopper Boys*), needs special thanks. (Neall and I first flew together operationally in Angola 40 years ago.) So too with Douw Steyn, a 4 Reconnaissance Regiment veteran, who is still held in high regard by his former Soviet enemies.

A most esteemed contact in Maputo (not for the first time) has been João Paulo Borges Coelho, whose seminal *African Troops in the Portuguese Colonial Army, 1961–1974* placed the role of Black soldiers serving in Lisbon's forces in Africa in true perspective, all of which needs a chapter on its own. Thank you again, João. I also appreciate the help I got from Stephen Dunkley who came up trumps with the background and story to one of the finest unconventional fighters to emerge from the Mozambique war: Daniel Roxo.

A final word is essential for me to commend the two people who went to considerable lengths to get this book published. The first is David Farnsworth, Casemate's head honcho and a very dear friend; and no less important, Madelon Venter, who bust an editorial gut in putting it all together.

It was a devil of a job across three continents, but we did it!

Foreword

During 1995 and 1996, as an officer in the Portuguese Army, I served in Mozambique. For more than a year, with the rank of captain, I had the opportunity to travel the length and breadth of that country in my Portuguese Army uniform and there was nowhere that the local people did not treat me with affability and respect. Those Mozambicans I encountered along the way were both friendly and helpful and they made the posting one of the best missions of my life.

I had the opportunity to repeat that experience in Angola at the turn of the new millennium and I must confess that there were familiar times in both African countries when it felt almost like home.

To anybody looking at these African experiences, it is difficult to explain the strong feelings of respect between the Portuguese and the Mozambican people, especially among the military. I was always comfortable in the Mozambican barracks where I spent good time, working shoulder-to-shoulder with the Special Forces School in Nacala (in the north), the Military Police in Machava and again with Special Forces groups in Matola (both near Maputo, the country's capital, called Lourenço Marques in the Portuguese epoch).

It was the same each day with that East African country's army and military leadership in Maputo itself. We had fought a long and bitter war decades before, but now we were comrades. Loyalty, friendship and deep respect as brothers-in-arms predominated.

There are those, I am sure, who will read these lines and find this difficult to appreciate, but you need to delve further into this book to understand why this was so.

The Portuguese bush war in Mozambique (1964–74) followed many trends that were present during World War I (1914–18) after it had expanded into Africa. To a considerable extent, these trends remain there to this day. In fact, neither conflict was ever a simple two-sided conflict because there were always numerous other issues involved—including tribalism, which in Africa is always rampant—coupled with various internal factors (in Mozambique's case, more than a dozen).

In what our forefathers called the "Great War," there were numerous extraneous interests that came into play. These included Kaiser Wilhelm's Imperial Germany, Imperial Britain, South Africa, Belgium and of course Portugal. Nor can one ignore large private commercial concerns (such as the enormous Niassa Company) and ethnic revolts like multiple Jihadist appeals clandestinely promoted by the Germans and led by the wily Lieutenant-Colonel von Lettow-Vorbeck who remained ensconced in Tanganyika for almost the duration of World War I.

The German Army—in East Africa it consisted mostly of White-officered, Swahili-speaking, Black Askari squads—twice invaded Mozambique during that period. Moreover, a century ago, conflict in Mozambique was all about local and territorial ambitions, linked perceptibly to internal political chaos that emanated from Lisbon—and a lot else besides—much of which is dealt with in detail in Chapter 2.

All of which begs the question: Was any of this different from what is going on in that faraway country today?

More pertinent, the colonial wars of the 1960s and 1970s need to be understood through the prism of the Great Powers' influence during the so-called Cold War, neatly encapsulated in a line in the Introduction which reads: "Portugal—a brave but indigent country—could not muster the resources required to effectively take on the might of the Soviet Union and its many collaborators."

Things have moved on to the present era and it is difficult to understand what exactly is taking place right now in Cabo Delgado, Mozambique's northernmost province: impossible in fact, if one does not identify a multitude of Russian, United States, Chinese, French and other European interests that are set off against fundamental Islamic movements. Never mind adding to that mix a constant series of ongoing internal Mozambican disputes, corruption, rampant north–south tribalism, disputes over natural resources in addition to a variety of concepts that constitute the multiple elements of a somewhat fractious state.

War in Mozambique has always been about the people—the same great society that is still today largely ignored in the ongoing north–south disparity. In the past, curiously, it was the masses who were really the most influential element that led to relatively stable situations in the end, for the simple reason that the locals fought more, endured more, died a lot more often and essentially, made the seminal difference as to what did or did not happen.

It was also the people who chose their allies, as well as when and how things were achieved. In 1918 for instance, when so many locals in the north supported the Germans against their British-South African-Portuguese opponents, local folk stood alone, just as they did during the 1960s and 1970s guerrilla conflict. They did so again during the horrific civil war from 1977 to 1993 where many more died violently than during the colonial period.

Or now, against ruthless, sometimes mindless Jihadist groups that have made it clear in a succession of recent insurgent skirmishes that they intend to disrupt traditional ways of life—developed over centuries—and will murder as many innocents as it takes to achieve their aims.

When one looks at Chapter 6: "How Others Viewed Mozambique's War," we begin to see what we did not appreciate before and—dare I say it—nowadays people still don't get it either. What is happening in the north's Cabo Delgado Province at present, in a region that has become a disputed area with massive international ramifications, shows that issues are never clear-cut, now additionally compounded by religious strife.

Conflict in Mozambique has always involved a great measure of turmoil, not only for all the soldiers and different types of combatants that fought there, but for the local folk as well, sometimes even more so. Under terrible conditions, the military often operated with little effective rear support and almost always in an openly hostile environment. The troops endured long-term commitments year after year, the majority looking forward to political solutions that either never arrived, or when they did, invariably came much later than promised.

In Chapter 9, which deals with the role of the Portuguese Air Force in Mozambique, we sense the terrible isolation that the troops on the ground endured. If not for the exceptional work of hundreds of helicopter and fixed-wing aviators, that outcome of the war would almost certainly have been even worse, catastrophic possibly.

For the thousands of soldiers mobilized to Mozambique—in 1973 the Portuguese Army had about 70,000 men deployed there—life was tough. Conditions were most times harsh and quite often painful; the majority of troops were more than 11,000km from home, most stuck with two-year postings in an Africa that they had never experienced before. As a consequence, the heart of this book lies within Mozambique's 10-year counter-insurgency war which lasted from late 1964 until the army mutiny in Lisbon in April 1974.

All military actions on the ground—at all times, as might be expected in a colonial environment—had a strong political flavor, with constant attempts to ensure unity of effort between the various civilian and military participants.

That was also the case in Angola, as well as Portuguese Guinea (later Guiné-Bissau). And while fairly comprehensive civilian-military efforts were achieved in other counter-insurgency wars—such as the Malayan Emergency (it was never categorized as a war) or Kenya's Mau Mau Rebellion against British forces—hostilities in Lisbon's colonial empire in Africa, because of distance and other factors, were on a far more expansive scale and also lasted longer.

However, the consistency between specific policies adopted in Lisbon and those which the military commanders on the ground actually carried out, gradually tended to erode, both policies having shifted in opposite directions to the extent that they would reach breaking point in 1974 with the army coup d'état.

In a counter-subversive war, as explained in the final chapter, the reality boiled down to objectives that were almost impossible to achieve, and that in spite of all the efforts made, coupled to a comprehensive view in conducting the war through the convergence of the partial strategies taken in the military, political, economic and diplomatic fields. One also has to take into account the fact that from north to south, Mozambique's coastline is 2,470km long, or further than the distance by air between London and Athens.

Nor can one ignore the fact that the country is roughly twice the size of California, none of which made things any easier when fighting a dirty, distant guerrilla war.

At the end of the day, Portugal's bush war in Mozambique was a conflict that has barely been recognized for what it truly was: a tiny European nation battling insurmountable odds, totally alone and with almost no allies against an enemy backed by all the resources offered by the Soviet Union and China.

Following political wrangles at home, Lisbon decided to withdraw from Africa, but what an incredible legacy she left behind, something which today's generation has only recently discovered: a fulfilling tradition and indeed, a proud nation and people who did marvelously when called upon to do so.

Brigadier-General Nuno Lemos Pires

Nuno Lemos Pires, Portuguese Army Brigadier-General, is currently assigned as National Defense Policy Deputy Director at the Ministry of Defense and Professor at the Portuguese Military Academy in Lisbon. He holds a PhD in History, Defense and International Relations, served in several units including as platoon and company commander in Infantry School; Military History and Strategy Professor at the PRT War College; Intelligence Officer in NATO Rapid Deployable Corps—Spain; MA to the Commander at NATO Joint Command Lisbon; Mechanized Battalion Commander in the PRT Mechanized Brigade; Training Director at the Combined Arms School and Commander of Cadets at the Military Academy. During his assignments he participated in missions in Mozambique, Angola, Pakistan and Afghanistan. He has published 10 books and cooperated in more than 100 publications written in Portuguese, Spanish and English, the majority focused on military history, strategy and international relations. The general is currently based and in command of all European forces deployed in Mozambique.

It is of interest that the author, while covering Portugal's colonial war in Angola half a century ago, spent time with Brigadier-General Lemos Pires's father, then serving in a senior position in the war in the *Dembos* (jungle) north of Luanda.

Introduction

This book is about a war that is almost forgotten, rarely grieved and took place in one of the most beautiful countries in the world. It was fought in Africa by one of the smallest European nations which, in the final analysis, was ranged against the most formidable of odds.

The effort on both sides was valiant, but in the end Portugal—a brave but indigent country—could not muster the resources required to effectively take on the might of the Soviet Union and its collaborators from whom its opponents received almost all of the support they needed. Lisbon's adversaries included every single communist country on the planet and almost all of free Africa. Yet, all things considered, Portugal did not actually lose the war: it was radical domestic politics that heralded the end.

Portugal's three wars in Africa—in its former colonies of Angola, Mozambique and Portuguese Guinea—have, with time, become examples of remarkable staying power on the part of the *métropole*, enmeshed as it was in the kind of imponderables that have surrounded every conflict since the beginning of time. It is a tribute to the country that it managed to hold on for as long as it did: World War II—though on a much larger scale—lasted only six years, roughly the same time that the United States Army was "officially" deployed in South Vietnam.

Even today, few of the younger generation in Portugal are aware of the enormous scale of difficulties that faced its army in fighting these wars, many thousands of kilometers from home and spread across the extremities of the world's second largest continent. The distance from Bissau, the Guinean capital, to Maputo in Mozambique is almost 7,000km. While war raged, most troops were sent to Africa by sea and it could take more than a month to travel from Lisbon to Lourenço Marques. How different to the way the Americans fought in Vietnam: almost all their movements were by air.

For all that, the Portuguese Army by 1973 had tens of thousands of men of all races on the ground, in a vast country where there was a single reasonably maintained road that stretched from north to south. Most of the rest weren't tarred, which perfectly suited the opposition's minelayers.

In effect, Lisbon's wars in both Mozambique and Angola centered on the use of landmines, laid wherever possible by the guerrillas in the vast interior of this African country. While the Portuguese struggled for years to find an answer to these bombs that were customarily buried in the sand and which made the guerillas' task relatively easy because there were—and still are—very few surfaced roads, the weapon was ideally suited for purpose.

Moscow provided a variety of landmines, both anti-personnel and anti-tank. The latter were most commonly deployed: the TM-46 (since superseded by the TM-57), both of which contained charges of roughly six kilograms of TNT and enough to render any large vehicle, armored or otherwise, into scrap. As a consequence, most of Lisbon's casualties stemmed from landmine blasts.

The continuing scourge of landmines in Mozambique was to prove just one of the bitter legacies of a long and arduous war.

***

Portugal's empire came into being as a consequence of the successful efforts of Lisbon's Prince Henry the Navigator in the first half of the 15th century to discover a trade route to India, something dealt with in more detail in a later chapter.

While other European nations had previously preferred the more ponderous and dangerous overland road to the east, through the Levant and age-old Persia, the Portuguese, to give them their due, looked at the alternative option. That was by sea, around the Cape of Good Hope. To take this giant step—which, in its day, was every bit as momentous as man's first flight to the Moon—the explorers needed a succession of supply stops along the route for fresh victuals and water, which is why they established overseas trading stations in Angola and Mozambique. These overseas colonies, provinces, call them what you will, eventually expanded and were ultimately settled by Portuguese nationals who, by the time the colonial war ended in 1974, numbered more than 300,000.

Putting down roots in Africa—after having first to placate it—was never easy. Tribal leaders were traditionally suspicious of strangers bearing trinkets, and for good reason. Africa had always been a ready source of slaves: East Africa was the first region to be subjected to this pernicious exploitation, mainly Arab-perpetrated to start with—many centuries before any Europeans arrived (though few historians have been, or are willing even today, to lay that charge against the Islamic world). Once the first early Portuguese settlers had put down roots, they, too, started their own slave-raiding missions.

Consequently, there were vigorous attempts by some African leaders—if not to prevent the establishment of a permanent European presence, at least to limit it, especially on the periphery of their tribal kingdoms. But the early Portuguese explorers were a resolute lot and they persisted.

Once the first colonists had settled along the coasts of both Angola and Mozambique in the late 1400s and early settlements like Luanda and Lobito became towns, Black leaders not yet under the "protection" of Lisbon would do what they could to prevent these newcomers from taking more land. Attempts at countering the settler influence went on for centuries, especially in Angola.

Distance proved an enormous disadvantage to the early settlers prior to the arrival of the internal combustion engine and before enzootic and epizootic diseases had been partially eradicated. Even today, tsetse, rinderpest and many tick-borne diseases still affect some areas, particularly in the north and along sections of the Zambezi, but it was really severe in the old days when a community would depend on horses to move about.

Early history about Mozambique discloses some interesting developments over the centuries. For instance, there are few people in metropolitan Portugal today who are aware that parts of this vast East African country were once dominated by the Austrian crown, a situation that held for six years from 1777 to 1783. The Austrians also occupied Lourenço Marques for a lengthy period.

Before that, in 1719, the Dutch East India Company took control of Lourenço Marques and instructions to that effect were sent to the Castle in Cape Town, even though Portugal had already occupied the entire East African coast between what is today Maputo and Mombasa. All the harbors and consequently, all exports as well, were dominated by Portuguese interests.

In both cases gold and other precious metals and stones, as well as ivory, were clearly motivating factors. Gold mined in the African interior reached the coast in such quantity that many European countries set up trading posts such as Sofala in Mozambique. Even after the 17th-century decline in the gold trade, Portugal along with the other colonial powers continued to settle, trade and exploit their African possessions.

They did not do so, however, without encountering resistance. In Southern Africa there were numerous uprisings among the tribes; first by the Xhosa and their allies and subsequently by the Zulus against the might of the British Army (which proved that it was not as formidable as had been anticipated). Insurrections later spread northwards into the Matabeleland and what became known as Rhodesia.

It was a time of uprisings in Africa: in the Gold Coast, in Benin, Nigeria, in some of the French colonies and against newly arrived Europeans in German

South West Africa (Namibia today) and in the *Kamerun*. The bloodiest clash might well have been the notorious *Maji Maji* Rebellion in German East Africa (later Tanganyika, Tanzania today) which went on for well over a year.

Disputes broke out too between the colonial powers, and eventually the frontiers of the various states were formally drawn up in Berlin at a negotiating table by all the European countries with interests in the continent. These included Britain, France, Portugal, Belgium and Spain; Amsterdam's colonial interests having long ago been superseded by London. All gathered in Berlin in 1884–85 under the auspices of the German Chancellor Otto von Bismarck to regulate any border disputes, effectively formalizing Europe's "Scramble for Africa."

***

The intent of Portuguese policy in Africa seemed always to have been to preserve the status quo and, in this respect, tradition rested heavily in the Portuguese African world. Over the centuries, the colonial structure (and the attitudes that went with it) gelled and these began to dominate political and domestic Portuguese life among the settler community and the making of overseas policy in Lisbon. It was not always negative.

Attitudes among those Lusitanians who had their homes in Africa included a kind of racial tolerance, a self-acknowledged Christian paternalism toward the African, suspicion of outside interference in the colonies, the notion that the African must be obliged to work as well as the simple faith that the Portuguese way was "the right way, perhaps the only way."

At one time or another, especially in the last two centuries, these concepts were recorded into Portuguese colonial legislation, and to a large extent while Lisbon still ruled, explained the state of affairs in the territories immediately prior to the start of hostilities in what became known as the *Guerra de Libertação*.

There is no question that the administration of the African colonies was paternalistic, something which the Portuguese themselves admit, even today. The chain of authority passed in unbroken succession from the sclerotic Overseas Ministry in Lisbon down to a minor army of hand-picked village chiefs.

For all that, political rights for Africans—an issue that became crucial in later years once Portugal was fighting for survival in Africa—did not exist. Nor had the kind of paternalism that Lisbon liked to espouse brought any kind of measurable material benefits to the largely Black population. The war caused

Lisbon to raise standards among the broader populace but because Portugal was then the poorest nation in Europe, it was a marginal improvement. In fact, the imbalance between the cost of living in Angola and Mozambique and the average wage (about US$6 month in the early 1960s) was extreme.

The same was true of education for African people, of whom fewer than three percent were literate; the prospects of an African child achieving more than three years of rudimentary education were remote. Beyond the cities, large towns and several mission stations, health services scarcely existed. Partly from necessity but also by intent, the majority of the country's African people were left in a world of medieval ignorance and isolation.

The Portuguese admit that such conditions did exist. However, they always maintained, rightly or wrongly, that the spiritual advantages of their traditional policies more than compensated for material shortcomings. They would refer repeatedly to the goodwill and understanding between the races, boasting that there were no real political or racial problems in Portuguese Africa and in the later phase, making an issue of their belief that independence had led to communism in Ghana and Guinea, to bloody chaos in the Congo, and to African racism in the rest of the continent.

The average visitor saw Portugal's vaunted colonizing mission as another attempt in the history of European colonialism in Africa to "solve the recurring problems of native policy, disease and a frequently hostile terrain, White settlement, evangelization, and the exploitation of natural resources."

More to the point, many believed, quite justifiably, that Portugal had not been entirely successful. While admitting the validity of Lisbon's claims to racial tolerance in its colonies, the question must be asked whether this attitude was sufficient compensation for the ignorance, apathy, and continuous exploitation of the African population which had long characterized Portuguese policy.

Dr James Duffy, author and Professor of Spanish at Brandeis University, writing only a few months after Angola had been invaded from the Congo in 1961, had his own take on those early developments, assessments that would eventually affect all of Portuguese Africa.[1] His comments about Lisbon's administration of its possessions were insightful:

> As the Portuguese themselves acknowledge, the problems [in 1961] which must be solved have never been greater and the room for maneuver has never been less.
>
> The relative tranquility of Angola, Mozambique and Portuguese Guinea is not necessarily an accurate indication of political reality. But it is certain that outside the colonies, Portuguese African opposition groups, particularly those in Leopoldville and Conakry, grow daily in size and influence. [Tanzania was to become a major player not long afterwards.]
>
> Elsewhere in the continent African national sentiment is united against the continuing presence of Portugal in Africa. Abroad, Asian and Communist nations, with the support of

anti-colonial groups elsewhere, have taken up the attack against alleged Portuguese repressions, and each United Nations session rings with denunciations of Portuguese policy.

This concerted opposition lost Portugal a seat on the UN Security Council last December [1960]. There is also a question how much longer Portugal may count on even qualified support by Britain and the United States.

Finally, in Portugal itself, where there are unrest and dissent and the Salazar era may be coming to an end, the turn of political events could have unpredictable repercussions in Africa. To devise an African policy which can meet even several of these challenges will test the capacities of any Portuguese Government.

Duffy goes on to document the efforts of the Portuguese regime to create a sense of solidarity between the *métropole* and its colonies: "A steady diet of colonial news is fed to the controlled press and radio. Street rallies are organized to demonstrate popular support for Portuguese colonial solidarity." It was not enough.

In Mozambique in 1962, there began the third of Lisbon's guerrilla wars in Africa: an uprising preceded by the launching in Dar es Salaam of a local political party headed by Dr Eduardo Mondlane, an American-educated academic. He called his movement the Mozambique Liberation Front, or in Portuguese, the *Frente de Libertação de Moçambique* (FRELIMO).

Curiously, not all Mozambicans desired independence, and fewer still sought change through armed revolution; but from the start, FRELIMO was no lightweight. A fair proportion of its cadres had been trained abroad, many in the Soviet Union and still more in China and Cuba. In Africa, Algeria, Sekou Toure's Guinea Republic, Ethiopia and several other independent states hosted thousands of youthful Mozambican hopefuls in their bid to become combatants.

Unlike Angola in 1961, Lisbon was ready, if not for the full invasion, then for a limited unconventional war along its northern extremities. The Portuguese secret service had by then managed to penetrate the revolutionary movement's hierarchy in Dar es Salaam, with the result that military headquarters in Lourenço Marques had a fairly good idea of what to expect and when.

The final crunch came in September 1964 when the FRELIMO movement initiated its first military campaigns in northern Mozambique, having spent several years working secretly with many tribal leaders to foment revolt: in the process, bringing across the Rovuma River that formed the frontier with Tanzania, enough war materiel to ensure success against the colonial establishment.

A thoroughly unconventional, fairly low-key insurgency, it followed similar patterns to those Lisbon had experienced a few years before; first in Angola in 1961, followed a year later by the uprising in Portuguese Guinea (today Guiné-Bissau).

In all three military confrontations, hostilities were preceded by a period of clandestine infiltration, always from one or more neighboring states. With Mozambique's war, Tanzania—which chose a strong socialist line after this former League of Nations Mandate had been granted independence by Britain—became the launch pad.

It was not long before the main road southwards out of Dar es Salaam became East Africa's effective Ho Chi Minh Trail, the only difference being that Lisbon never plucked up the courage to tackle that problem at source, either by attacking the Tanzanian capital or by attempting to neutralize the route as the Americans had done in Southeast Asia.

For almost the full duration of the hostilities that followed in north and central Mozambique, the only real change came when President Kenneth Kaunda of Zambia decided to take his country into the war by offering full support to the guerrillas, which involved opening a second front in areas where Mozambique and Zambia shared common borders. It also included regional command posts in several Zambian towns in the east of his country, with a fully-fledged headquarters in Lusaka itself, manned not only by Mozambique expatriates but by Russian as well as Cuban advisors and specialists.

I would often spot these individuals whenever I visited Lusaka as the war progressed, usually during grand Sunday lunches offered on the main verandas of the Ridgeway and the Intercontinental hotels, both since renamed. A disparate bunch that included quite a few South Africans who became prominent in their own country after Nelson Mandela came to power. They were very much as aware of my presence, as I was of theirs and we sort of left it at that. I doubt whether that would happen in today's harsh political climate.

In the Mozambique war itself, hostilities were largely of a high-maintenance, low-contact nature, with the Portuguese Army launching the occasional large-scale search mission such as General Kaúlza de Arriaga's controversial Operation *Gordian Knot*. For their part, the insurgents did their best to stymie those efforts by laying as many landmines as they could rush to the ill-defined front line, almost always on the backs of porters who had been shanghaied into the roles of human carriers.

With hostilities covering an area probably half the size of France and with few surfaced roads—and three-quarters or more of Mozambique totally undeveloped—the war plodded on. It didn't help the revolutionary cause that the guerrillas had no vehicular transport of their own (they would use bikes when they could get them) but it did result in most things moving ponderously at what we scribes would declare was at a "bum-numbing boring pace."

Hostilities stepped up a level or two towards the end of the war when the guerrillas sensed that the Portuguese nation, battling three full-scale wars in faraway Africa, was becoming war weary; casualties were mounting and needs in a dirty distant war were steadily becoming more urgent.

By then, too, a new generation of youngsters from the metropolis had entered the fray, every one of them conscripted and the majority not nearly as subservient as their fellow countrymen had been early on when they were first drafted to Africa. Evidence of this change came with the iconic circular peace or freedom symbol of the Vietnam War which many young Portuguese soldiers wore around their necks.

***

After more than a dozen years of armed struggle, a military coup that toppled the Portuguese government also brought an abrupt end to its centuries as a colonial power. With independence in 1975, Mozambique and its politics swung hard left and with the Portuguese Army out of the way, the result was a civil war that ended with many more dead than during the colonial period.

The civil war statistics are staggering. Armed conflict between the FRELIMO government and the anti-government guerrilla movement, the Mozambique National Resistance Movement (*Resistência Nacional Moçambicana* or RENAMO), began in 1977, two years after independence, and lasted for 16 years. Hostilities during this period resulted in around one million deaths, 1.5 million cross-border refugees and 4.5 million domestic refugees.

Even to this day, the RENAMO war is remembered as one of the world's most tragic conflicts of the final years of the last century.

***

While the colonial war ended almost half a century ago, not much has changed in Mozambique. The Average Joe in the streets of the major cities is just as poor, the government remains totalitarian, stifling any opposition and economically, all attention has been focused on the south, though that was about to change with the discovery of gas deposits in the extreme north. But these days, even that is threatened since a new player threatens the country.

It took a while for Lisbon's war to lapse—two generations in fact—before another range of hostilities entered the picture, once again in the northern Cabo Delgado Province where another group of revolutionaries kicked off with their war against the forces of a now-independent Mozambique. Islamic State, all but dislodged from the regions it dominated east of Suez only a few years ago—and from which it was largely ousted by the governments of Syria and Iraq—has since turned its attention to Africa. It started by fomenting a new insurgency in West Africa's Saharan underbelly in the late 2000s and focused largely on Mali in the Sahel.

Islamic State then linked up with a veteran dissident bunch of guerrillas in Somalia, who call themselves al-Shabaab, as well as with Nigeria's Boko Haram terror movement.

In late 2017, Islamic State again realigned its priorities and, very much like FRELIMO had done before, these Jihadists sent agents into northern Mozambique to subvert such authority as existed of the ruling hierarchy in Maputo, more than a thousand miles to the south. That insurrection has gradually gathered strength and, by many on-the-spot accounts, so has the new generation of fighters who some locals like to refer to as al-Shabaab, for no other reason than that most of the revolutionary cadres currently operating in Mozambique were trained in Somalia.

What is significant about these developments is that while there are many factors in Mozambique's new war that compare with what took place half a century ago with the Portuguese, nothing seems to have halted the progress of Islamic State to move ahead in its conquests. That Islamic guerrilla force even managed to capture several ports north of the great harbor of what was once called Porto Amélia (today Pemba).

That, in a nutshell, is the situation as we go to press. Possibly a careful examination of how Lisbon fought its East African campaign—all detailed in this volume—will offer not only a few solutions to the Islamic State conundrum, but also answer some of the questions which have since emerged.

CHAPTER I

Mozambique Today

Mozambique is a remarkable country. Beautiful almost beyond compare as it lies on the Indian Ocean, undisturbed almost forever and, in the days before the colonial war, regarded by many who made their lives in that part of Africa as a minor paradise.

This is a country that I and my family have visited many times and often enthused about. My father was a regular visitor between the wars, to the point that he was to lose his first wife to malaria, contracted during a 1930s visit to Lourenço Marques. She died while still on the train on their way home to Johannesburg, something that my dad never quite got over.

My own movements throughout this former Portuguese territory have been extensive, from the country's Ponto do Ouro "deep south," all the way north through Xai Xai, Inhambane, Vilanculo, Beira, Quelimane and on to the present-day Pemba, not to be confused with Tanzania's Pemba Island of 1960s revolutionary fame. In between we also have Mozambique Island, a sanctuary for those looking for a remote corner of Africa to which to escape, along with Ibo Island and the stunning Quirimbas: I have scuba-dived off many of these still-exotic locations.

***

Stroll around the streets of modern Maputo—it was called Lourenço Marques not all that long ago—and the military presence remains manifest. There may not be as many roadblocks as there were when the colonial war ended almost half a century ago but the visitor is left in little doubt as to who is in charge.

As one heads north along Mozambique's relatively recently surfaced EN1 highway, it is impossible to avoid noticing that the military presence becomes more obtrusive. That stems largely from an Islamic-backed insurgency that has been troubling parts of the north of the country.

This insurrection—which the guerrillas liked to refer to as *Guerra de Libertação*—had nothing to do with the civil war of old that was linked to RENAMO. It is something quite new and those involved are radical Jihadists linked to Somalia's al-Shabaab. For now, Mozambique's military is trying to deal with the insurrection but without much success. There are people getting killed and nobody in the capital can lay a finger on how this debacle escalated to the extent that the country now faces a full-blown civil war in the north.

Nor does it seem that anybody in the capital is losing any sleep about the insurrection because killings are mainly Black-on-Black and the tourists keep coming to what was once one of the most beautiful wildlife parks in Africa, the Lugenda Wildlife Reserve, or quite simply, "Luwire."

Everything changed in the entire region once Islamic State started sending its recruits southwards into Mozambique from Tanzania.

The almost 2,000km-long road runs from Maputo to the city of Pemba not far from the Tanzanian frontier. It can take several days to cover the distance or, if you have the time, a month; apart from the north and their troubles, there is so much to do along the way.

The drive is an experience: part good, part bad, because conditions can be unpredictable, especially in the start-of-year rainy season which can end with cyclones.

Contrasts along the way—tiny villages that almost always have makeshift booths that offer their own versions of chicken *peri peri*, along with varieties of palm wine—are part of an astonishingly varied fare. Much of what is available is customarily set alongside the road, usually on the way in or out of town and almost always offset by the local clinic and school (both almost always squeaky clean and running efficiently). And, of course, the roadblocks, which rarely stop tourists for questioning and become more prevalent the further north you go.

More salient, you are never far from the sea and impromptu fresh fish dishes cooked over open fires alongside the road. And there is always time for a dip either in the local lagoon or surf, having parked your car in an adjacent village in perfect safety. A small clutch of meticals, the local currency, always does the trick. You need to watch for stonefish if you are strolling in bare feet in the shallows though: they are commonplace in most tidal waters.

Traveling about the country, what often impresses visitors from other African countries is the number of schools, all reasonably efficient and running to strict schedules. The schoolchildren in Mozambique are almost always immaculately clad in their spotless uniforms—it says a lot that this homogeny is achieved in a country where a man has to work several days in order to buy his son or daughter a new shirt and, sometimes a week for a new pair of shoes.

Cheek by jowl with these measures of privation are many larger towns that make for the unusual: like the seaside resorts of Xai Xai, Inhambane, Tofo (with magnificent shoals of whale sharks—dozens of them, many times of the year) and that remarkable backpacker's hideaway, Vilanculo, historic gateway to the Bazaruto Archipelago. The irrepressible Martha Gellhorn spent memorable times swimming alone off the shore in Bazaruto, nobody plucky enough to stop her.

You can stop almost anywhere along the way and find a place to stay—unlike Maputo—safe enough not to have to lock your bedroom door at night. And it's not expensive, because Mozambique is the one African country where the marketplace is one gigantic souk. If the price of a meal, or even of hotel rooms, is too high, no blinks if you try to barter your way downwards…

Beyond the great Save River bridge, sometimes only partially in use because of structural problems, is Beira—to my mind still a drab and dusty place and to be avoided if possible—even if not everybody agrees with me. After that come Quelimane and Nacala—with their gently sloping crystal-white sand beaches—and finally Pemba, now pivotal to a burgeoning oil center in the north. Along the way, there are any number of small seaside hotels and pint-sized lodges waiting, and the diving is always great.

For all that, it needs more than a modicum of courage to tackle the distance, but then Mozambique—even in colonial times—has never been taken lightly, nor should it. Nor can political instability be ignored. In recent times political tensions have triggered a series of attacks on civilian vehicles, even overland buses, some quite close to Beira, the country's second city.

Shortly before the new Islamic-linked war started in the north in 2017, one traveler reported, "I arrived in Beira after an enormous delay following a holiday in the stunningly beautiful region around Vilanculo." The reason was simple, or was it? Somewhere on the road, he explained, his bus had to wait for a military convoy to cross a particularly dangerous district…

The truth is that while there is some banditry—there is not a country in Africa that is not faced with similar problems—there is rarely loss of life. People steal, and you might be pick-pocketed, as happens everywhere, but local criminals (except in the Islamic-orientated far north of the country) really do respect human life.

What is astonishing is that with the country's open roads, wildlife reserves where there are animals in abundance and more stopping points along the way than can be imagined, is that Mozambique has never quite caught on with the youthful transient communities of either Europe or America.

Kerouac and his friends across the United States, had they been alive, would have loved the place. It's cheap, it's friendly and accessible and while there is palm wine just about everywhere, so is weed. And if you are not averse to "going native" for a spell, at prices that would buy you a pair of hamburgers in other parts of the world, you've got it made.

Obviously, it helps if you *fala português*.

***

In reality, life in present-day Mozambique—the country that produced Eusébio da Silva Ferreira, one of the all-time greats in world football (more commonly known, quite simply as Eusébio)—is both interesting and, depending on your predilections, can be rewarding. Like any country, it also has its quirks.

Big money from abroad—much of it brought in illegally to acquire private real estate—has come into the country in recent years, a good deal of it from South Africa, and there has been a proliferation of luxury homes built along one of the most exotic coasts in the world. The names on exclusive show-pages in some major international newspapers include Praia da Barra, Tofo, Ponta do Ouro, Bilene, Pomene Bay and others.

On pristine Bazaruto Island, perched on the coast between Beira and Maputo—and still very much like it was in the colonial epoch, except for the luxury resorts and its own air strip connecting it to Vilanculo—speculators have built a succession of exclusive estates where the price for a simple two-bed single-story house starts at several hundred thousand dollars.

But that is the reverse side of the coin in a country, where earning US$20 a day suggests a good measure of success in the run-down shanty towns that surround every significant conurbation. Most don't even have running water or sewage systems and here we're talking of homes to millions of locals, almost all Black or *Mestiço*. There are so many people of mixed ancestry in Mozambique that the country even has its own *Dia do Mestiço*, celebrated on June 27 each year.

Mozambique's downside can be severe, as we saw with Cyclone Idia that roared in across the Indian Ocean from Madagascar in early 2019 and not only leveled thousands of villages and towns (Beira suffered exceptionally badly) but caused more deaths than anybody is ever likely to know. Should it happen, it will take years to organize a proper census to establish exactly how many died, the majority indigent tribal people in the interior.

Bad weather apart, there has been very little attention given to the infrastructures of almost all of the county's residential areas: sidewalks, Maputo especially, collapsed decades ago and in some areas the potholes are so numerous that residents sometimes make their own tracks alongside main roads to avoid damage to their vehicles. There was a maxim doing the rounds during my last visit that suggested that if you saw the ears of a rabbit in a pothole on the road ahead, take care because it could be a donkey…

That said, Mozambique is not always gloom and doom. Take this blog from an Austrian aid worker based in Beira, employed by an NGO and enjoying the expat life. It is one of hundreds, perhaps thousands of similar comments on the Web, but the writer imparts something personal, even intimate about it.

In her report, titled "A Day in the Life of Someone Out There—in Mozambique," she provides us with a handful of unbiased insights to community life within the society where she lives. I quote:

> Mozambique is wonderful. But not everything is pleasant. Abstract problems deploy visible impacts. Take diseases: Mozambique has an HIV prevalence of more than ten percent; it was even higher in the past. The enormous shortage of teachers is not unique, but to an important extent a tragic result of the AIDS epidemic: Teachers get terminally ill and die and the same goes for other professional guilds.
>
> In contrast to most other lethal diseases, AIDS mainly affects young to middle-aged adults—parents of young children, an economically highly productive age group. 'Double Recruitment' is a common strategy in companies: Two people are hired and trained for one job—because chances are that one of them will pass away prematurely.
>
> But at times, I feel like a stranger, an alien from a different world. Most of the time, I know that I stick out, but every now and then I feel like a part of the ecosystem here.
>
> I have never been made unwelcome and I do accept that there are situations where I will never ever blend in. I did learn very quickly that my necessities and ideas of a fulfilled life do not fundamentally differ from those of my friends and acquaintances here—we all want to wake up in a good mood, we all have people we care about, we like to laugh and sometimes simply relax.[1]

It wasn't always so, especially during the colonial war that started in 1964 and lasted ten years, when a group of radical young officers in Lisbon ousted the government and ordered all the troops fighting in Africa to return.

Though the Portuguese colonies had become far more multiracial than before—of necessity, because the government needed the manpower to fight the guerrillas—race invariably dictated policies of state and it was usually with the Whites at the top of the pile.

All that changed dramatically when Samora Machel's ragtag (and often barefoot) army won the day and most of the White Portuguese that had made the country their home, some for centuries, fled back to Europe.

Change, when it came, was cathartic for many, but for a time the government seemed to make it work. David Ottaway, one of the *Washington Post*'s best-known foreign correspondents, reported while traveling in recently independent Maputo, on December 18, 1977, in an article headed "Races Mix Well in Mozambique."

He wrote his piece 30 months after the country had become independent and though there was much strife and bitterness when Machel began his tenure, things improved with time, though almost all private business had been nationalized by the state as part of RENAMO's program of divesting the people (which meant people with money) of their assets. Almost overnight thousands of businesses, factories and enterprises were stripped, a prelude to what has been happening in Venezuela in recent years. Yet, he maintains:

> For the 20,000 to 25,000 new and old Portuguese now living here [but only if they accepted the government's Marxist policies, if only nominally] a new, more peaceful era in race relations seems to be dawning.
>
> The sight of whites mingling easily with blacks and mixed-blood *Mestiços* in the bars, restaurants and even in many homes in Maputo is a common one … the exclusive Polana Hotel serves afternoon tea and cakes indiscriminately to chic Portuguese women wearing the latest fashions and to impeccably dressed black Mozambicans.
>
> In addition to the highly visible community of *Mestiços*, there is a surprisingly large number of "white Mozambicans." Indeed, the new high society of independent Mozambique is becoming a broad mixture of races including a small number of highly influential Indian Goans.

For a while, the Maputo government turned to outsiders to replace those Portuguese who had "taken the gap" (as the majority of White Angolans had done). The Luanda government resorted to bringing in Cubans by the thousands (which didn't work), even though the initial focus, as might have been expected, was on education and medicine. What resulted in Maputo was that the regime used its Lisbon Embassy to recruit thousands of badly needed teachers, doctors, civil servants and technicians.

Sadly, Ottaway made no mention of the rebel RENAMO movement, an offshoot of another colonial war in Rhodesia (Zimbabwe today). The organization was founded in 1975 as part of an anti-communist backlash against the country's ruling socialist hierarchy and partly fueled by incipient tribalism and corruption that had its roots in Maputo's new command structure. The civil war that followed ended up as one of the worst in Africa and only ended at the negotiating table decades later. It is still festering in isolated pockets in the interior.

***

That part of northern Mozambique where the colonial war was at its most intense—because of the proximity of a hostile Tanzania—must be one of Africa's most beautiful wildlife regions—which says a lot, because the Luwire game reserve spans almost the distance between Lisbon and Madrid and is twice as big as the Kruger National Park in South Africa.

This is a wild, primeval, half a million hectares that was remote even during colonial rule and where the Portuguese Army fought some of its most harrowing battles of the 1960s and mid-1970s. And with the great Rovuma River forming a natural boundary in the north of the country, Niassa Province and the adjacent Mueda Plateau were almost custom-made for laying Soviet anti-tank mines.

Yet today there is little evidence of that conflict. The mines are "certified" as having all been lifted (though I spoke to people living there who still spoke of isolated patches that they considered as dangerous) and the region contains some of the most remote and isolated bush country on the continent.

Travel by road from Pemba Harbor and it takes a good-quality all-terrain 4×4 more than half a day to cover the 400-something kilometers, and several hours more when it rains. It is a tough, bone-rattling journey and certainly not for everybody.

Most people fly, which is expensive: it costs US$500 to travel the distance in a small plane from Pemba to Luwire (and almost as much to get to Pemba from Johannesburg, in large part because of the gas industry), so tourists who go there are mostly from Europe and America.

That said, the experience of flying from Pemba to Luwire is like few others on the continent, usually at fairly low level to take in the scenery. Much of the terrain is dotted by tall granite mini-mountains, some a thousand meters or more high. There are few towns or settlements along the way, which is presumably one of the reasons why a tourist magazine recently suggested that visiting the place was like "following in the footsteps of David Livingstone" (who recorded visiting the place in his diaries).

***

Much has happened in Mozambique since both the colonial and civil wars ended, but the violence is not yet over, in part because of the country's natural wealth.

The vast natural gas reserves discovered off Mozambique's shores were meant to herald a new era of peace and prosperity for one of Africa's poorest nations. However, as London's *Financial Times'* Southern African correspondent, Joseph

Cotterill, told us in June 2018, a spate of beheadings and torched villages blamed on a shadowy insurgency has exposed the gulf between Mozambique's gas ambitions and the grim reality for many in the isolated and poor north.

At the time of his report, at least 39 people had been killed since the start of the previous month by a mysterious group apparently seeking to impose a militant form of Islam in Cabo Delgado (which was once furiously contested by the Portuguese Army). He said that the Mozambican armed forces had launched a crackdown in the region, but that the group has evaded capture, as they had done most times in the past. He continued:

> The rapid growth of an insurgency about which little is known has sparked alarm. The United States Embassy advised citizens to leave Palma, where an onshore LNG terminal is being built. To which Alex Vines, the Africa director of London's Chatham House, the Royal Institute of International Affairs added, "Mozambique is the weakest state in Southern Africa."

Vines declared in a paper published by Chatham House that "the Maputo government had not been able to contain a [recent] rebellion of middle-aged RENAMO fighters [FRELIMO's old civil war foes], and it is now unable to prevent this emerging threat."

More recently, after further attacks in the extreme north of the country in which dozens were killed, the "unknown enemy" was given a name when Somalia's notorious al-Shabaab terror group claimed responsibility. In a press release issued in Europe, the Jihadist group declared that it had not only launched a new civil war, but had done so under the auspices of Islamic State (see Epilogue).

Adding to Maputo's woes has been the exposure recently of an enormous financial fraud within the government and which was deliberately hidden from the country's parliament. Totaling something in excess of US$500 million which were labeled "loans," the money was diverted and remains unaccounted for.

When the hidden debt was revealed, Mozambique—which relies on donor aid and is one of the world's poorest countries—was plunged into the worst financial crisis in its history. Washington very outspokenly alleged that at least US$200 million was spent on bribes and kickbacks, including US$12 million for former finance minister Manuel Chang, who originally signed off on the debt guarantees.

As somebody in Maputo's Clube Naval was heard to comment, with something that resembled a disconsolate shoulder shrug when the news was first released: "*C'est l'Afrique.*"

Portugal's Illustrious Maritime and African History

There are many factors that ended up playing significant roles in Portugal's historical legacy, not only of colonialism but also its valiant early years of exploration southwards and towards Asia. Undeniably, these proud exploits were every bit as important to Europe as were Spain's efforts to create a legacy in the New World. Indeed, it was Lisbon that tentatively opened Africa's ancient portals to legions of European explorers and settlers, but sadly, as with Spain, the record became tarnished.

The ships that took Europe's navigators to these distant lands were diverse—from as little as 100 tons, and perhaps 18 to 20 meters—to the leviathans of their age. They ranged from minuscule three-masted *naos* or carracks (and before that, caravels) to cumbersome wooden East Indiamen over 1,000 tons.

That would have placed them almost in the same gross tonnage bracket as some of the naval frigates deployed by Britain during World War II. It says a great deal for the remarkable expertise and skill of the men who constructed these fragile ships five centuries before.

Portuguese historian Filipe de Castro provides an excellent analysis of that period in his fine book titled *The Pepper Wreck*. He deals specifically with Portuguese East Indiamen,[1] though there was not much difference on board any of the ships that plied this route, except that the Dutch and the English generally treated their crews better than their Lusitanian counterparts. Notwithstanding, British discipline on board was severe and seamen could be court-marshaled for willfully disobeying orders.

The maritime records that are available for inspection at most maritime museums in London, Madrid, Amsterdam and London reveal a good deal about those early times, including the fact that several elements motivated the early navigators to explore beyond Europe's borders.

The first was the knowledge that, somewhere beyond the horizon, there were other civilizations and cultures—remote, mysterious and sometimes (as with China and Japan) more advanced in some respects than their own societies—that were not only enormously enticing but had much to offer. The dictum was fundamental: make contact with those far-flung societies, and fortunes might be made.

Until these intrepid seafarers arrived, all trade with the East had been by land. Eastern goods had been reaching Europe from the East for a thousand or more years, including silks, spices, medicines, gemstones and a wide variety of trade goods favored by wealthy Europeans. The one drawback was that all movement was overland, a good deal of the journey traversing the vast stretch of semi-desert historically referred to as Asia Minor and its legendary Silk Road. It would undoubtedly have included present-day Iran, Syria and Iraq.

In that early period, Lisbon was the first to take the initiative. Prince Henry's navigators forged alliances and trading pacts: first with leaders along the coast of Africa, then with the Indians, the Ceylonese, Javanese and others. In time, more alliances followed and it wasn't long before these links were extended to the fringes of the Pacific Ocean, which was when China and Japan came into the picture.

However, to do that, the Portuguese—bold and forward-looking initially— needed stopping points along the way. Their ships had to be assured of safe anchorage where they could be resupplied (and sometimes repaired), crews rested and the sick left in comparative safety to await craft heading back to Lisbon.

One of the first so-called "halfway houses" was at the port of Sofala, one of the oldest harbors documented in Mozambique, situated on the edge of a wide estuary called *Rio de Sofala* on older maps. Somali merchants had established a colony there to extract precious metals from the goldfields in Great Zimbabwe, home of the legendary Monomotapa. This prompted Portuguese chronicler Thomé Lopes to identify Sofala with the biblical Ophir and its ancient rulers with the dynasty of the Queen of Sheba.

In those parts of Africa—after something of a toehold had been achieved— notably in Mozambique and Angola—things were extremely difficult in the early days, and they continued to be arduous for the majority of Europeans who sought to prosper on what became known as the "Dark Continent."[2]

Nevertheless, over the centuries, much has changed. One only needs to look at antiquarian maps of the West Coast of Africa produced a century or two ago; many showed a paucity of detail relating to Africa's interior.

The first major war with Germany forced the pace of progress in Africa, both for Britain and France and, to a lesser degree, Belgium, Spain and Portugal. Lisbon, in that first Great War, was a staunch military ally of the British. It did not take long for hostilities to move southwards, and for this, the European combatants needed to know if they were to be involved.

A more comprehensive understanding of Mozambique's earliest days comes from a remarkable book originally published some years ago in Japan. Titled *The Origins of War in Mozambique—A History of Unity and Division*, the book is a mammoth and enormously insightful work by Sayaka Funada-Classen and first published in English by a South African company, African Minds.[3]

Funada-Classen tells us: In 1505—only a few years after the first Black slaves were shipped to the Spanish colony of Santo Domingo in the Americas, and only months after Leonardo da Vinci painted his Mona Lisa—Antonio Fernandez, a Portuguese convicted criminal or *degredado* was sent into the East African wilderness in search of gold and local knowledge in return for a pardon. Traveling into the interior from Sofala, which lies south of present-day Beira, he walked to the Odzi River and up to the Zambezi, keeping meticulous records along the way.

Fernandez survived his grueling journey and returned to Portugal a decade later. Fifty-six years later, Gonçalo da Silveira, a Jesuit who had followed Fernandez's journey into the interior, was to meet an unexpected end. No sooner had he converted ranking members of the royal establishment ruling the Kingdom of Monomotapa to Christianity than Arab Moslems—fearing infidel inroads into what they regarded as a lucrative slave, gold and ivory trading catchment—deliberately generated suspicion and hostility towards the Jesuit priest among his new converts and had him murdered.

Eight years after Gonçalo da Silveira's death, a punitive mission against the already-disintegrating Kingdom of Monomotapa was mounted at the behest of the teenage king of Portugal and his advisors. The expedition was led by Francisco Barreto, the newly appointed governor of what was to become the Province of Mozambique.

He left Lisbon with three ships and 1,000 men and arrived in Africa after a harrowing sea voyage during which many lives were lost. But still worse was to come. Almost all of Barreto's contingent, unaccustomed to local conditions and hampered by their archaic regalia, which included armor, soon succumbed to the stifling tropical heat and the scourge of malaria. Only a handful returned home.

Their stories were horrific and had a lasting effect on their compatriots who ventured to East Africa in later years. The few soldiers who had not died from disease were either killed by wild animals or, in some instances, slaughtered and eaten by cannibalistic tribal people. The murder of Gonçalo da Silveira—who until two years before his death had served as the Governor of India—was never avenged.

Following the failure of Barreto's expedition, the Portuguese confined themselves mainly to the eastern littoral and left the hinterland well alone.

The next notable incursion would only occur in the 19th century after Mzilikazi, a member of the warlike Zulu nation (now the Matabele), migrated northwards to found a new and independent tribal faction in the western corner of present-day Zimbabwe.

It comes as no surprise, consequently, that until the mid-1800s, Portuguese colonial rule on the African continent tended to concentrate on exploitative economic activities—such as the slave and ivory trade—along the coast. In truth, Lisbon tended to focus minimal effort on establishing a proper colonial government or exploration of the continent's interior as the French have done in West Africa or the British were to do in Kenya and Uganda.

By then Lisbon's empire abroad was organized by the appointment of four military commanders that covered the overseas territories. They headed what was termed the Army of West Africa (Luanda), while Mozambique had another, as did the Indian military attachment on the Indian subcontinent at Goa. The last was in Macau on the eastern fringes of China, and also had responsibility for Portuguese Timor in present-day Indonesia.

Parts of the West African army consisted of five battalions of light riflemen called *Cazadores*, who fielded an artillery battery, two line battalions, as well as 28 mobile units in company strength, the majority based in Angola.

There were two more battalions in Portuguese Guinea (also responsible for security on the tiny tropical islands of São Tomé and Principe, both of which nestle in Africa's Bight of Benin). Mozambique had three battalions of *Cazadores* in addition to a single company of "Veterans."

Local people entered the equation, obviously, because they were readily available as volunteers. Indeed, Lisbon always made good use of indigenous military talent, with many Black troops serving under the command of White Portuguese officers within the colonial army. Structure was flexible and, by the end of that century, included more than 30 indigenous infantry companies—16 of whom served in Angola, and a dozen in Mozambique.

The principle of "effective occupation" required that Portugal pursue the notion of "territorial integrativity" and "effective control" in the Portuguese colonial territory of Mozambique. In theory, this required tighter control over all African inhabitants living in the area; in reality, it was impossible for the

Portuguese government—incapable of even controlling the areas designated as *prazo*—to manage an area a third larger than Spain.

By the 1880s, it was also accepted that Lisbon's armed forces would carry out a "pacification campaign" that would establish total control over the groups not yet ruled by Portugal. These strategies were developed to comply with international pressure for effective occupation and at the same time would enable Portugal to maintain a stronghold over its colonies.[4]

As a result, more than 800,000 square kilometers (nearly 65 percent of the territory designated as Mozambique) was entrusted to the following patent companies: the Niassa Company (*Companhia do Niassa*), which occupied the far north of Mozambique (25 percent of total land); the Zambezia Company (*Companhia da Zambézia*), which together with several other companies, occupied the Zambezi River Basin (15 percent of total land) and the Mozambique Company (*Companhia de Moçambique*) which occupied the middle region of Mozambique (25 percent of total land).

Some researchers agree that while the system worked, it was counter-productive. It was cumbersome and expensive to run. Also, the outcome did not result in the intended economic development of the area, nor in any benefits for the broad spectrum of people in Mozambique; instead, it had disastrous results for local inhabitants. The "Great War" not long afterwards changed all that.

***

The international community has all but forgotten about Europe's 1914–18 worldwide conflict. So too in modern-day Portugal, because there is not one in ten individuals who knows that Imperial German forces twice invaded Portuguese East Africa out of Tanganyika (Tanzania today).

There were 5,533 Portuguese troops killed in the process, another 5,640 soldiers missing or captured, and an unknown (but quite a significant number) wounded. Reading between the lines in the journal kept by General Paul von Lettow-Vorbeck—the only German general in World War I who never took a beating from the Allies—it was a relatively straightforward effort on the part of his forces to come and go across the Rovuma River, almost as they pleased.[5]

When war began, the Germans had 14 colonial companies, each composed of approximately 200 Askaris (the Swahili term for African troops) and 16 to 20 European officers. That totaled 260 European officers and 2,472 Askaris in German East Africa alone (with still more in what is Namibia today and German *Kamerun* and Togo in West Africa). Each company had four machine-guns and 250 porters and normally operated independently, dispersed throughout the colony.

This force, known as the *Schutztruppe*, was expanded sixfold upon wartime mobilization to 3,007 Europeans and 12,100 Askaris.

For a short period in the beginning, Berlin's army was resupplied by sea directly from Europe; however, the British blockade of the Kaiser's colonial ports effectively eliminated this support after April 1915.

In the process, some hefty battles took place. The Portuguese were routed at the Battle of Ngomano, and the German *Generalmajor* then marched through Mozambique in caravans of troops, carriers, wives and children for a solid nine months. Von Lettow-Vorbeck had divided his force into three groups that acted independently of one another in different geographical regions.

In traditional Teutonic form, the illustrious German general who evaded defeat by the Allies for the entire war, kept a detailed account of the time that he commanded in Africa—several years, in fact—battling enormous odds after his links with the *Vaterland* had been severed.

***

With the end of the two world wars, life in Lisbon's African colonies continued as before.

Mozambique was then part of Portugal's *Ultramar*—Lisbon's overseas possessions—and as with everyone who visited the country, whether on business or vacation, thrived.

At the same time, Portugal was still one of Europe's poorest nations, which meant that there was never much ready cash about in the streets of cities like Lisbon or Oporto. But in Mozambique—with its extensive 2,470km coastline stretching all the way north to what was then still the Tanganyika border; azure, tropical seas and forgotten islands that might have been taken out of context from the Pacific—life was good, for the Whites especially.

Those expatriates who chose to make Mozambique their home soon discovered that there was money to be made if one bent one's back. More to the point, nobody starved. Everybody, Black and White, seemed to manage, as long as they "knew their place."

Even after the war started, conditions went on very much as before. As far as the residents of Lourenço Marques and Beira were concerned, hostilities could be on another planet. It was notable that during the entire war in the East African colony, the capital city in the extreme south never once heard a shot fired in anger.

Looking back—I went into all three African territories many times before the 1974 army coup in Lisbon—and, broadly speaking, there is no question that for ordinary folk in Mozambique, things were a lot better in those pre-war days than they are today. Prior to independence in 1975, almost every town and village had a clinic; nothing fancy, but basic medical care was available if you were hurt or sick. You got help, if not from a doctor, then from a medic who had qualified.

Also, there were ample schools, though undoubtedly not as efficient as in the Western World, most managed to impart the basics of the "Three Rs." To achieve that much, there were teachers on call and all instruction—as in Brazil, another of Lisbon's former colonies—was in the Portuguese language. It still is in all of Lisbon's former African colonies, half a century after the colonial wars ended, though most Africans also speak one or two of roughly a dozen tribal dialects.

Politics in Lisbon's African possessions were another issue. Real politics, such as it was—because there were no free elections—was for ethnic Portuguese only, most of whom were White. Once the war started, things began to change, and more Black and *Mestiço* people found themselves in uniform in the perpetual "battle against *comunismo*."

Not all military types subscribed to that dictum, because by the early 1960s, Marxism had made discreet but significant inroads into Lisbon's military establishments. Inexorably, these sentiments eventually came to play a role in the colonial wars that followed, and it was elements from the "radical left" that devised and implemented the 1974 "Young Officers" revolt.

However, that was still some way ahead and, until the government was overthrown in the army putsch back home, conscription was as much a part of life for young men just out of school or university as *bacalhau* might have been on the menu at least once a week in the metropolis.

What soon became apparent was that from fairly early on, there were never enough soldiers available to serve in Portugal's colonial wars. So, Lisbon had to acknowledge that the strategic role of indigenous people might be part of the answer. By doing so, those in the *metrópole* in charge of recruitment started to make a number of concessions, including the ability of suitably qualified Blacks to achieve officer status.

Nevertheless, as critics of the system subsequently conceded (even though there were at this time Black officers in the Portuguese Army), it was, as the well-worn aphorism goes: far too little and far too late...

***

The war in Mozambique took a while to develop. From the first invasions by FRELIMO "Liberators" southwards out of Tanzania, their foreign-trained cadres had difficulty explaining to the various African tribes that conflict with the colonial government would be fought in their interests.

Eduardo Mondlane, the FRELIMO leader when war was declared in 1962 (but only got fully underway more than two years later), had solid support from the Makonde tribe, a belligerent group that had always opposed Portuguese presence in Africa. The Makonde people straddled both sides of a border with Tanzania defined by the great Rovuma River.

However, the problem there was that the Makonde made up less than two percent of the population, and the tribe seemed to have been in a permanent state of hostility with the Macua tribe, who were predominantly Muslim and not blatantly opposed to a colonial presence. In a nutshell, if FRELIMO were going to take its guerrilla struggle southwards, it would have to go through country dominated by the Macuas.

Mondlane did achieve support from the Nyanja people in the expansive Niassa region to Mozambique's north-west, adjoining present-day Lake Malawi, but it was not enough to make any kind of decisive thrust. That said, Lisbon had to contend with a full-scale guerrilla uprising in the north, and her young men were becoming casualties at an alarming rate; landmines taking a steady toll on lives and equipment—vehicles especially.

So, it continued for several years; hostilities escalating markedly after Mondlane had been assassinated and the more aggressive Samora Machel voted into power in Dar es Salaam, with the Portuguese Army backed by the air force hanging on. Things changed radically in favor of the guerrillas after Zambia's President Kaunda allowed FRELIMO to open a second front along the Zambezi that targeted the Tete region along the great Zambezi River.

Yet things were still not right for the aggressors. To their frustration, and contrary to their strident propaganda claims, FRELIMO's supreme command found that the Africans of Mozambique (Makondes and Nyanjas apart), while hardly apolitical, were generally not motivated enough to become totally committed to the armed struggle. Had more African tribes in Mozambique's interior answered the call, the war would certainly have progressed a lot better for the rebels.

However, that did not happen, in part because tribal leaders feared that if the colonial forces were ousted, the country would devolve into a vicious series of tribal wars, which happened after 1974—albeit with a significant amount of devious power play on the part of both Rhodesia and South Africa in supporting RENAMO. This pro-West revolutionary group was essentially anti-communist and thus opposed FRELIMO's Marxist tenets.

During the colonial epoch, the Portuguese administration played heavily on these fears, while at the same time it set out to provide the Africans with security and protection in exchange for loyalty—or simply not opposing the Portuguese rule.

The Portuguese held other strong cards, not least the steady drive towards interdependence and overall unity. The government and the army looked at the situation from the simplest—and the most audacious—standpoint.

Their attitude could be encapsulated along the lines, referring specifically to the war being waged in Vietnam, that the United States would never win because it was generally accepted that sooner or later, Washington would order a withdrawal from Vietnam. Lisbon forcibly declared, and I quote one of many similar news reports: "We will win our wars in our African provinces because unlike the Americans, we are staying."

Dr Caetano frequently underscored that commitment to Portuguese rule in Africa after he assumed power in 1968, following Dr Salazar's incapacitation by a stroke and subsequent death. The problem that ensued was very much *vieux jeu.*

As we all know, Salazar defied the "Winds of Change in Africa" promulgated by British Prime Minister Harold Macmillan in South Africa's Cape Town Parliament in 1961. While wealthy industrialized Western states relinquished their colonies one by one—starting with the British colony of Gold Coast in 1957 (renamed Ghana), Salazar alone decided to back the Lusitanian experience of many centuries in the area—despite the fact that Portugal had invested more in Africa than it had received. With good old-fashioned paternalism, he refused to look at the situation in cost-effective terms, because he believed that history was on his side.

Nor, for that matter, did he care for Western liberal democratic thinking, which steadfastly hoped that independence in African territories could be guided by the "one man, one vote" principle. He was certainly never even prepared to consider a timetable for departure.

Indeed, he was partly correct in his assumption about Africa accepting anything like the European democratic systems. In almost all cases, it became "one man, one vote *once,*" after which a myriad of coups, army mutinies and revolutions followed.

It is also worth mentioning that under the post-Salazar regime, the institutionalized commitment to stay in Africa was firm, and it remained that way until the government was toppled by the "Young Officers" revolt or the "Carnation Revolution." It was of little or no importance to the old or traditional order that Portugal was spending about 40 percent of its budget on defense, or that almost 150,000 men were continually under arms to contain the guerrillas in Angola, Mozambique and Guinea.

Meantime, Dr Caetano had promised major reforms, including giving Mozambique, Angola and Guinea greater autonomy and, more salient, increased responsibilities and accelerated advancement to the Africans. There was no other way.

The most important reforms were free and compulsory primary education, and a large-scale expansion of secondary schools. Introduced cautiously at first, these improvements gained their own momentum. The real "time of testing" followed when major questions and problems of assimilation were pushed to the fore.

As was to be expected, more and more Africans were drawn into the administrative and political structure in Lisbon's African empire. The forecast for the 1980s—had the revolution in Portugal not taken place—was for the vast "Africanization" of the government and countries that would not have been dissimilar to what Brazil is like today. They would have been fully multicultural and multiracial, everybody integrated by a single common language: Portuguese.

As we now know, it never happened, and only the language has remained intact.

CHAPTER 3

The Challenges that Faced Portugal

In his doctoral thesis, completed at Kings College London and titled *"Portuguese Counterinsurgency Campaigning in Africa—1961–1974: A Military Analysis,"* former United States naval aviator[1] Dr John P. Cann—better known to his friends as Jack—takes as his starting point, the fact that Portugal faced the extremely ambitious task of conducting three simultaneous counter-insurgency campaigns in Portuguese Guinea, Angola, and Mozambique.

Jack has written extensively on Portugal's wars in Africa—more than anyone else I know—and offered me access to many of his findings, including those in this chapter.

Lisbon, taking on the world in its bid to retain its African colonial holdings, was something that had never been done before. As he declares in his introduction, Portugal at the time was neither a rich nor a well-developed country. In fact, as a Western European nation, it was the least wealthy among its neighbors by most standards of economic measure.

Thus, for Portugal in 1961 to have mobilized an army, transported it many thousands of kilometers to its African colonies, established large logistical bases at key locations there to support it, equipped it with special weapons and materiel, and trained it for a very specialized type of warfare, was a remarkable achievement. It is made even more noteworthy by the fact that these tasks were accomplished without any previous experience, or doctrine, or demonstrated competence in the field of either power projection or counter-insurgency warfare and thus without the benefit of any instructors who were competent in these specialties. To put this last statement in perspective, other than periodic colonial pacification efforts, Portugal had not fired a shot in anger since World War I, when Germany invaded northern Mozambique and southern Angola.

In following both broad and narrow campaign strategies, Portugal attempted to disrupt the organization of the nationalist movements through the operations of agents and to counter their armed action with appropriate military force and diplomatic pressure. Concurrently, it sought to protect its people from insurgent contact and to win their loyalty by elevating their standard of living and redressing their grievances. These elements; their particular combination, and their style of execution, reflect what may be termed "the Portuguese way of war."

Jack Cann reckons that arguably, the biggest single obstacle to fighting a series of effective wars is distance: the colonies were all a long way from Lisbon. This very serious impediment compounded the problem of logistics and produced an associated strain on transportation resources.

The British were forced to fight in Malaya and Kenya, which from London were about 9,300 and 5,700km distant respectively. French Indochina was 10,600km from Paris, and Vietnam was halfway around the world from America. Only Algeria was a close 800km from southern France. The rest of these insurgencies were far from the home of the defending power.

Regarding multiple fronts, only Britain had to face three separate insurgencies simultaneously: in Malaya (1948–1960), Kenya (1952–1956), and Cyprus (1954–1983), and in the latter instances had severe difficulty mustering adequate troops for the conflicts. France and the United States in their regional conflicts were not faced with multi-fronted campaigns and the associated strain on resources that such situations would impose.

Not only were these colonies distant from Portugal, but they were also distant from one another. This separation added another dimension to the conduct of the African campaigns and exacerbated difficulties in the logistical support of Portuguese forces.

While Bissau (the capital of Portuguese Guinea, today Guiné-Bissau) is 3,400km south of Lisbon, Luanda (Angola) lies an additional 4,000km south of Bissau, and Lourenço Marques (Mozambique) a further 3,000km south-east of Luanda. For the most modem inter-theater transport aircraft in the Portuguese fleet of the time (all propeller-driven, immediate post-World War II planes) these distances represented a hard several days' work for both aircrew and machine.

Also, Angola and Mozambique were vast by any standards, further complicating their defense. Angola covers $1,246,314km^2$, an area which is about 14 times the size of Portugal or as large as the combined areas of Spain, France, and Italy. Its land frontier with its neighbors Zaire (formerly the Belgian Congo), Zambia (Northern Rhodesia), and Namibia (South West Africa) extends 4,837km.

Mozambique, the second largest territory, covers an area of 784,961km² or about nine times the area of Portugal. Its land border of 4,330km is shared with Tanzania (formerly Tanganyika) in the north and towards the east Malawi (Nyasaland), Zambia, Zimbabwe (Southern Rhodesia), the Republic of South Africa and finally Swaziland in the extreme south.

Portuguese Guinea was the smallest of the three colonies, a tiny tropical enclave about the size of Switzerland. It covers an estimated 36,125km², but because of tidal action that affects 20 percent of the country, only about 28,000km² remains perpetually above the mean high tide mark. This tidal delta and its characteristics further complicated its defense while the Portuguese ruled.

Distance was not the only obstacle. One of the biggest problems that faced Portugal for the duration of its colonial wars in all three overseas provinces, was international frontiers that provided the guerrillas with readily accessible sanctuary whenever needed.

FRELIMO forces operating from Tanzania could cross the Rovuma River with comparative ease, strike at a camp or lay their mines in the vicinity and then scoot back to where they came from. Similarly, they could enter Portuguese territory across Lake Malawi, where borders were equally ill-defined and manpower on the ground too sparse to monitor even a fraction of this movement.

The option to strike at cross-border targets in "hot pursuit"—attacking guerrilla camps in neighboring countries—obviously entered the picture from time to time, but apart from a rescue of Portuguese soldiers from prisons in Conakry, the capital of the Republic of Guinea (brilliantly executed under the command of General Antonio de Spínola), it hardly ever happened because of fear of United Nations sanctions.

A few attacks did take place: there were Zambian accusations that the Portuguese Army had crossed the border and attacked targets or laid mines (September 1967; November and December 1969 as well as May 1972 and May 1973), but these were never substantiated. A Portuguese Air Force Harvard T-6 was also shot down over Tanzania in April 1972. The relative paucity of such claims was an indication of Lisbon's reluctance to incur international censure, either at the UN or in other world bodies.

***

Mozambique presented a uniquely challenging topography. Physically, this vast country largely consists of an extremely long coastal belt, rising in the north and north-west to forested areas. Its extensive, open and sparsely populated northern areas always proved difficult to police, particularly in the regions where the wide-ranging, often nomadic, and isolated population was vulnerable to insurgent intimidation and difficult to protect.

It was no different once the war started, but by then Lisbon's military establishment had been taught much about guerrilla modus operandi which was similar for all three African provinces.

Mozambique shares a tropical climate with Angola, though it lacks the agricultural highlands of the west coast colony, but the population diversity was vastly different and that posed yet another obstacle. Angola's population—according to the 1960 census—was 4,830,283, or about four people per square kilometer, which was 95.2 percent Black African, 3.5 percent White, and fractionally over one percent of mixed parentage.

Tribal loyalty was always of prime interest to Lisbon: some chiefs accepted Portuguese patronage while others did not. In Angola alone, there were scores of identifiable tribal groups (100 distinct tribes divided into nine primary ethno-linguistic groups, each of which had its own degree of loyalty to Portugal). Most of this population was concentrated in the coastal west and central plateau of Angola while the eastern semi-desert and steamy northern jungles were only sparsely populated. It was in these remote areas that the guerrillas operated and posed a severe military challenge.

Mozambique's population in 1960 was 6,603,653, or about eight people per square kilometer, 97 percent of which was Black. This segment was fragmented into approximately 86 distinct tribes in 10 ethno-linguistic groupings, again each with its own conviction of loyalty to Portugal.

The north and northwestern regions consisted almost entirely of open, sparsely populated bush country adjoining Tanzania and Zambia, and tended to be the most vulnerable to guerrilla infiltration. Here, isolation and the relatively sparse population were acutely vulnerable to insurgent intimidation from these sanctuary countries. Those who did not answer FRELIMO's revolutionary call were brutally (and often terminally) dealt with, which underscores the maxim that it is often the civilians caught in the middle of any war who suffer the most…

Peculiarly, though, the mosaics represented within these population groups were both a problem and a source of strength to Portugal, largely because of their varying loyalties both to government and to each other. Lisbon was able to exploit these differences to its advantage in that the guerrillas were often from a group that had little in common with other groups. The reverse of this coin was that Portugal found it necessary to adjust its psycho-social program specifically to each group (or tribe) and to tailor its appeal to various and sometimes vastly different cultures.

The people living along the Mozambique coast were largely Swahili-speaking, often with a strong infusion of Arab blood from way back and many of them, as a consequence, followed the tenets of Islam. Obviously, they had very little in common with tribes of different heritages living in the interior, and in some cases regarded them as inferior.

***

The Portuguese armed forces, according to official figures released in Lisbon after the colonial wars ended, numbered 79,000; the army accounted for 58,000, the navy 8,500, and the air force 12,500, with a defense budget of US$93 million.

Compared to other nations which had fought or were then combating counter-insurgencies in various corners of the globe, Portugal's military might was decidedly modest and underfunded. Britain, by way of example, then had almost 600,000 men (and a small number of women) in uniform and a defense budget of US$4.5 billion.

With conscripts, France boasted a very substantial armed force of more than a million, the greater part of which was fighting in Algeria, and a defense budget of US$3.3 billion. Both countries, though, were small fry when compared to what the United States had to offer: an armed force of 2,489,000 and a defense budget of US$41 billion. Alongside these major powers Portugal registered a very faint blip on the radar.

Other statistics are equally illuminating. Britain's manpower, for example, was 7.5 times that of Portugal, and its defense budget 48 times as big. France registered about the same multiples, and the United States was 32 times bigger in manpower and 441 times greater in funding.

In summary, Portugal's armed forces were totally dwarfed by those who had fought or were fighting counter-insurgencies; and in any event, when hostilities in Africa kicked off, Lisbon's commitment was to NATO and the majority of its forces were in Europe. Yet, by the end of 1961, it had moved 40,422 of its European troops to the three colonies, a figure that represented about half of its armed forces.

At the end of the conflict in 1974, Portugal had an armed force of 217,000, of which 149,000 or 69 percent were located in the three African theaters. Its defense budget had grown to US$523 million, almost six times the earlier figure, but it still remained meager in comparison to these three other powers.

Astonishingly, with those paucities, it still managed to battle in Africa for 13 years.

In the process, Portugal faced an intimidating array of insurgent organizations. The rebels, as they were at the start (they only qualified for the "guerrilla" label much later), were always quite fragmented—but, to the extent that they could mend their relationships with one another, they went on to present a solid and quite often a rather formidable front.

Altogether there were roughly 27,000 insurgents spread over three hostile African theaters. This posed a major problem for the Portuguese nation in that it was difficult in the extreme to prevent their entry and, once across the border, equally difficult to locate them.

The ability of large groups of guerrillas to cross the long unpatrolled borders in some of the most remote regions of Africa and to make contact with the population always represented a severely dangerous threat, and it had been that way from the start. In retrospect, one needs to concede, that in no other modern insurgency was there such a multiplicity of national movements spread across such a wide front in three totally separate regions where the wars were being fought.

In contrast to the odds facing Portugal, Britain's security forces at the height of the 1948–60 Malayan Emergency numbered 300,000 British and locally recruited troops as well as police in 1952. They faced approximately 8,000 Chinese communist guerrillas, giving a numerical superiority of almost 40 to one. In Kenya from 1952 to 1960, British security forces numbered 56,000 men and faced 12,000 Mau Mau terrorists, a ratio of 4.6 to one. Similarly, in Cyprus from 1955 to 1959 British security forces totaling almost 25,000 faced a thousand EKOA guerrillas, a ratio of 25 to one, with the British still taking serious casualties.

Then there was Algeria, where nearly 400,000 French troops were up against 8,000 FLN guerrillas by the close of 1956, a ratio something like 50 to one. The biggest test of all in these types of unconventional wars came with Vietnam where the United States held a ratio of four to one prior to 1964. Four years later it had elevated to 8.75 to one.

Portugal's security forces—army, navy, air force and marines (*fuzileiros*) of about 149,000 faced 27,000 guerrillas at the close of the war in 1974, giving a nominal superiority of about six to one, although this ratio was increased somewhat through local militias. That said, it is also a reality that few contemporary insurgencies last long against such odds.

That Lisbon believed it could overcome the numerical shortcoming through its own particular strategies and, in reality, undertook to do so with military success, makes those three African counter-insurgencies unique in the modern period.

***

The fact that Portugal was prepared to initiate and sustain such a comparatively large military campaign was impressive in that it appeared to have few national resources for such a venture. By European standards Portugal did not have a sufficiently strong economic engine that could readily support a large and distant military venture. Compared to its southern European peers—both at the start of its wars and a decade later—Portugal did, by its own standards, present fairly strong economic growth but it failed to displace its neighbors in its peer group rankings. However, none of these countries were involved in major counter-insurgency campaigns. Indeed, serious doubts were raised whether Lisbon would actually be able to mount any such military enterprise.

Portugal's gross domestic product (GDP), its broad measurement of overall economic activity, on the eve of the war in 1960 was US$2.5 billion. Britain's, at US$71 billion, was twenty-eight times Portugal's. France's at US$61 billion was 24-fold greater.

In contrast, the American economy at US$509 billion was 203 times greater than that of Portugal and when these numbers are reduced to per capita GDP (an indicator of the ability of wealth to be generated and taxed to support a war), Portugal's economic weakness was so apparent as to question its capacity to wage any war.

Given the statistical shortfall in resources that Portugal faced in conducting its counter-insurgencies, it would have to adopt different strategies from those of the British, French and Americans. It would have to address these serious limitations by devising ways to work around them and to avoid their full impact on its ability to wage war.

There were two key elements that underpinned Portugal's effort in this sphere. The first was to spread the burden of the war as widely as possible, and the second was to keep the tempo of the conflict low enough so that the expenditure of resources would itself remain affordable. The counter-insurgency practices that Portugal adopted and that reflected these two national policies in conducting the campaigns can be termed the "Portuguese way of war."

In the first instance the burden would be spread to the colonies. Portugal's capacity to support a distant military campaign perforce must include the large and dynamic economies of Angola and Mozambique. These additions, which are not reflected in the figures above, are important in that they supplied a significant share of the military budget and manpower for the wars.

Early in the beginning of Lisbon's colonial wars, European Portugal's GDP was US$2.88 billion. To this figure must be added the US$803.7 million GDP of Angola, a similar US$835.5 million for Mozambique, and US$85.1 million for Portuguese Guinea. This fuller picture reveals a nation with a GDP of US$4.6 billion and alters the equation of wealth significantly. It also reveals why Portugal had such a powerful commitment towards its colonies. With the exception of Rhodesia and South Africa, per capita GDP in Portuguese Africa during the wars exceeded that of all other countries in sub-Saharan Africa.

Roughly four years into Portugal's African wars, the defense budget amounted to 48 percent of metropolitan Portugal's national budget. Comparatively, this allocation was greater than any other European nation, Canada, or the United States. The next highest was the United States at 42 percent, followed by Britain at 34 percent.

However, observers tended to overlook the contribution that the colonies made to their own defense structures. These additional colonial resources enabled Lisbon not only to reach an apparently high level of expenditure but also to sustain it over a lengthy 13 years.

The three colonies contributed approximately 16 percent of the defense budget over the term of the conflict. This contribution, along with the inclusion of the colonial economies in the broader consideration, meant that Portugal was spending, on average, only 28 percent of its national budget on its military, which peaked at 34 percent in 1968.

These figures reflect a more readily sustainable expenditure and place it proportionately equal to similar national defense budgets.

It should also be noted that a great portion of the defense budget was allocated to social programs that benefitted the population in the areas of health, education, and agriculture, and contributed directly to the planned economic expansion in Portuguese Africa. Consequently, while fiscal resources were seemingly modest from a traditional perspective, they were quite adequate for the low-technology campaign that Portugal envisioned.

If the colonies were thought to contribute relatively modestly to the defense budget, they conversely shouldered an increasingly important manpower burden that gradually replaced metropolitan Portugal's soldiers with African ones. The population of continental Portugal in 1960 was almost nine million and that of the three African colonies was aggregately 12 million. The potential of the African population to supply troops therefore was about a third greater than that of European Portugal.

Local recruitment began at modest levels in 1961, where it represented 14.9 percent of the forces in Angola, 26.8 percent in Mozambique, and 21.1 percent in Portuguese Guinea.

By the end of the wars in 1974 and with the expansion of the security forces into militia and other paramilitary organizations, Africans represented fully half of the armed forces in both Angola and Portuguese Guinea and 70 percent in Mozambique.

This shift accelerated following 1968; after seven years Portugal had exhausted its European manpower pool and increasingly sought African recruits from its colonies (as will be seen in Chapter 8).

While there were problems inherent in this shift (such as the low educational level of the majority of the Black soldiers) these were addressed with enough success to ultimately develop a reasonably effective fighting force. Officially the troop level exceeded 149,000 men in the three theaters of operations; however, with the consideration of paramilitary forces, its true level was something like twice that number.

Official records of these forces were difficult to maintain at the time, and following the conflict were largely lost or destroyed. Thus, only approximations can be made. Nevertheless, the impact of using this broader manpower pool for recruiting enabled the Portuguese armed forces to maintain adequate force levels almost indefinitely. This unique capability was critical in extending the conflict for almost a decade and a half.

***

The Portuguese had had the benefit of earlier British, French, and American experiences in the 20th century prior to 1961 and proceeded to develop their military policies accordingly. Despite having no experience in prosecuting this kind of warfare, Portugal's defense establishment eventually evolved an excellent counter-insurgency doctrine, though as with all guerrilla conflicts it had its problems.

This was begun in 1962, soon after the first outbreaks of violence in North Angola. It eventually comprised four huge volumes and drew on the experiences of every modern conflict: the Americans and French in Vietnam, Britain in Malaya, Borneo, Kenya against the Mau Mau, Cyprus as well as the Aden insurrection. France's military role in Algeria also featured, as did other obscure conflicts such as that of the Huk uprising in the Philippines.

The entire principle was brilliantly applied by the staff corps, but in truth they lacked the basic attitude and experience of some of the officers who had already seen a useful amount of active service. Thus, while planning was thorough and technically competent, execution was inferior.

On more than one occasion I heard South African officers who had come into contact with their Portuguese counterparts discussing these aspects and how some very well constructed Portuguese Army operational plans had fallen flat because of poor groundwork.

Portuguese uniqueness in fighting African wars in extremely challenging environments came from their understanding of the struggle and adaptation to it at theater level, as well as in successfully converting national strategy to battlefield tactics. With comparatively few resources and no army trained in this type of fighting initially, Portugal's high command simply had to improvise.

While it anticipated employing standard types of counter-insurgency operational practices, it also sought innovations that were able to play upon the unique terrain and demographic characteristics in each of its three theaters. Some of these concepts might have been borrowed from other wars and modified so extensively as to be almost unique, while much of it was purely Lusitanian.

Some of the broader challenges and solutions characterizing the Portuguese way of counter-insurgency warfare included the complete reorientation of Lisbon's military might from a conventional force to one geared specifically for counter-insurgency. The realignment in recruiting for this force to the indigenous colonial manpower pool, to a degree not seen in modern times, allowed the colonies to shoulder a substantial portion of this burden.

Additionally, the shift to small-unit tactics and associated training based on experience in these conflicts—thus matching Portugal's force with that of the insurgents—kept the tempo of fighting low and cost-effective.

Having been forced to use increasing numbers of its African citizens in the war (and as a consequence, implementing various economic and social development programs which raised living standards for all) these measures went some way towards negating insurgent arguments.

Extensive psychological operations also helped to rationalize the Portuguese presence in Africa to the population: the end result being that—in spite of the retarded state of Portugal's economy, the enormous geographical challenges and an unprepared armed force—Lisbon felt confident that it understood the job at hand and could overcome these difficulties.

Out of this national self-confidence, Portugal eventually developed its own style of counter-insurgency warfare through a synthesis of the experience of similar conflicts and of its own experience in Africa since the 15th century. The application of this systematic thinking to the threat posed by the nationalist movements was made with a view to the national strategy of containing the cost and spreading the burden as well as addressing the battlefield situation.

***

On a totally different tack, as Portugal's African wars progressed, there were few people outside government in Lisbon who were aware of the extent of what was termed "The Propaganda War" in Western circles.

It was an intense campaign, extremely well-orchestrated by a shadowy division within the walls of the Kremlin, achieving most of its aims with the help of radical or Socialist "fellow travelers" in many Western countries. The Nordic states—Sweden in particular—were very well represented within the ranks of some of the organizations involved and the same went for Canada.

Essentially anti-colonial or anti-imperialist in concept, these campaigns were originally well-intended and kicked off on a sound and honorable footing: the world wanted an end to European colonies in the Third World, which was why France and Britain divested themselves of the majority of their colonial liabilities. Then Vietnam changed everything with anti-war protests proliferating. Because of the forceful level of censorship imposed by the Salazar regime, the average Portuguese man or woman only learned much later that their African wars were very much part of the agenda.

Unquestionably, the United States' escalating involvement in the Vietnam War gave blanket cover to many of the groups who were intent on voicing opposition to what was regarded as something akin to gunboat diplomacy. At its core, the sentiments voiced were powerfully anti-colonial and Portugal was soon labeled as a major human rights transgressor for trying to hold onto its African provinces, even if Lisbon viewed issues differently. Eventually the movements also targeted Rhodesia, followed by what was termed South Africa's Border War in present-day Namibia.

Among the anti-Portuguese lobbies operating in the United States—there were dozens—was one calling itself the Africa Committee of Returned Volunteers (one surmises that some of those involved were returnees from the Vietnam War). It had numerous catchphrases, one of the most prominent being that they were opposed to those who "work for forces that maintain the status quo of wealth and privilege for the few and poverty and ignorance for the many."

If that sounds simplistic, their publications were anything but: they were well constructed and presented at venues across the nation, no mention being made that many of the handouts and much of the information came from the Soviet Union. Obviously, the FBI was aware of all that, but in the United States free speech is always paramount, as dictated by the Constitution.

One of the booklets published in 1969 in New York by the Committee of Returned Volunteers, was titled *Mozambique Will Be Free* and ran to 48 pages. It provided background to many of the products that Mozambique produced and which were "bought at cheapest rates from the exploited African peasantry."

No doubt, that was the case in many instances, but it is also true that nobody in the country starved and, indeed, there were many prosperous African farmers until FRELIMO took over and nationalized all industries, making farming communal in accordance with traditional Marxist tenets. It also stated that 83 percent of the country's people still lived on the land and in spite of the war, Whites were still trying to deprive Black people of their farms.

While there was some evidence that this went on (Samora Machel's family lost their land) the statement went unchallenged. But it was simply not true to suggest that the government was offering serving soldiers farms in the war areas, which was patently absurd. The equivalent would be offering American soldiers land in the Mekong Delta after the war in Vietnam ended.

Lourenço Marques' links with Pretoria, in spite of the Mozambican port being a major outlet to the sea for South African industries also came under fire. On page 17, the report quoted Sir de Villiers Graaff, former leader of the opposition in the South African Parliament, stating that Portugal was fighting South Africa's wars and should be supported.

In reality, Graaff's emphasis was on securing his country's trade route to the useful Indian Ocean harbor and had nothing to do with sending in the South African Army. But, of course, that was ignored.

In a bid to swing opinion in the United States, propaganda put out by dissenting organizations both in Europe and in the U.S. offered a good deal of information that could be used to harry the Portuguese presence, its role as a member of NATO as well as goodwill in the West. Numerous contact addresses in all major cities of groups that were ready to offer support, newspapers, magazines and other media that might be sympathetic to the cause in many countries (with those in Britain predominating) were listed, together with publications of "Liberation Movements in Southern and Colonial Africa" and their contact details.

The document prominently featured "Direct Action Projects—Ways and Means," divided into sections. The first dealt with "Selection of a Target," which suggested "clarifying your focus through a discussion of priorities; for example, at universities where the campus Reserve Officers Training Course (ROTC) might be persuaded to become aggressively involved with a Portuguese dignitary who had been invited to a debate." To achieve results, the document provided lists of targets which included individual, corporate, commercial or academic foils.

"Visits" came next. This included the names of companies, industrial plants, distributors and retailers that had economic or trade interests in Portugal or the provinces and could be harangued by groups, pickets or guerrilla theater acts which, the booklet suggested, "all aided in building knowledge of the policies of a corporation" and which it declared, had been effective against American banks investing in South Africa.

Thereafter, "Disengagement," which targeted individuals or organizations who held stock in these companies "and who should be urged to dispose of those assets, write formal letters to the company, contribute their earnings to the liberation cause" and so on.

"Portuguese Representatives" formed the biggest section and it mentioned Lisbon's consulates and embassies, offering the names of senior officials at all these institutions. Similarly, it listed travel agencies and tourist offices which, it declared, "are geographical foci for action." Those pages ended with a suggestion that anything related to the Portuguese national airline TAP should not be neglected, nor any special tours to Portugal. Thereafter it gave the addresses of all TAP offices in North America.

Arguably the most powerful section in one of the booklets dealt with the Portugal's defense links to United States and Western Europe. This is a brief excerpt from *Mozambique Will Be Free:*

> The Portugal/South Africa/Rhodesia alliance is important for strategy; but for military equipment, supplies, training and economic support, Portugal has more powerful partners. The most important are the U.S. and West Germany, but other NATO countries are also involved.
>
> Portugal must have these "partners" in order to support her three colonial wars. Spending 48.7 percent of her entire budget on her military, Portugal does not even build her own airplanes. Instead, the Portuguese Air Force is almost totally equipped with planes made in NATO countries.
>
> Most prominent are: 1) American-made fighters and bombers, such as F-84s, F-86s, PV-2s and B-26s; 2) Transports such as military versions of the DC-3, DC-4 and DC-6 and 3) Trainers such as the T-6, T-33 and T-37s which can easily be converted for combat use. The T-37s were delivered in 1963: 18 were paid for by the American government while 12 were bought by the Portuguese. Almost all would be of little use in a European war such as NATO might be engaged [in] … and were supplemented by German Do-27s and by Fiat G-91s jointly manufactured by Germany and Italy.
>
> Not only are the Portuguese planes made in NATO countries, but the Portuguese Air Force is NATO-trained and Portuguese pilots in Mozambique drop NATO-model bombs and American napalm (made by the Dow Chemical Company in Frankfurt, Germany).

> The American government maintains that no current U.S. aid is used by Portugal in Africa and that such aid is only for NATO purposes. Thus, in theory, the new 1.700-ton destroyer 5-escort delivered to the Portuguese Navy in November 1968 will not be used in Africa. Yet reports from guerrilla movements in Angola, Mozambique and Portuguese Guinea again and again refer to the use of American equipment by the Portuguese.

The same booklet provided far more detail and went on to implicate the Central Intelligence Agency in Lisbon's war efforts. It mentioned (correctly) the smuggling of B-26 bombers (together with bombsights, armaments and technical manuals) from a base in Tucson, Arizona to Portugal for eventual deployment in Africa.

Also detailed were American vehicles that ended up in the African wars. These included those that came from the Kaiser (Willys) Jeep Corporation in Toledo, Ohio, and then went on to display a copy of a full-page Willys advertisement that appeared in the Portuguese Army magazine *Jornal do Exército* in April 1969.

There is no question that the "liberation" booklet was both thorough and well-researched. It obviously served as a guideline, not only to the media and politicians, but to many ordinary folk—the majority with almost no knowledge or understanding of what was going on in Africa at the time.

The depiction of the United States' role in supporting what was portrayed as a rogue country exploiting Black people was little short of masterful. Specific instances of what had come up for debate or submission in Congress were mentioned, like hearings before a Subcommittee of the House Appropriations Committee, 90th Congress, Second Session 1968, where Portugal was labeled fascist and instances quoted of American training of the country's secret police. Here it was declared that "key military personnel" with whom the Americans develop "such good relationships" end up leading Portuguese troops into battle in Africa.

Obviously, Lisbon's Azores base, used by the U.S. navy and air force since 1943 and contributing US$6 million annually to Portuguese coffers featured prominently; former Secretary of State, Dean Acheson, was quoted as calling it "perhaps our most important overseas base." Yet little mention was made of the fact of Washington's often proclaimed support for self-determination for all African countries, including those under Lisbon's distinctive red and green national banner.

The Cahora Bassa hydroelectric project to build Africa's largest freshwater dam was criticized, with suggestions that its links to American companies had malevolent implications. Included in that diatribe was Morrison-Knudson, an Idaho company with wholly-owned subsidiaries in Portugal and the fact that Anglo-American—with whom it had unspecified links—headed the consortium (ZAMCO) which won the construction contract.

The main gripe was that when completed, Cahora Bassa would attract European farmers to settle in the Zambezi Valley. Anybody who has been anywhere near the place would appreciate that that argument is fatuous; the lower reaches of this tropical, triple-tiered valley still remain one of the least developed and unhealthiest places in sub-Saharan Africa, where malaria's Anopheles mosquito has always ruled.

Propaganda, as in any war since time immemorial, has an adverse effect on those doing the fighting. Lisbon's borders were porous and a good deal of subversive literature found its way into military camps in the metropolis; one of the reasons why the Portuguese Communist Party emerged as a powerful political entity within domestic politics after the 1974 army coup.

In fact, during a visit to Lisbon in 2018, I learned that the Portuguese political left still has a good standing in some quarters and continues to influence some Parliamentary issues in the capital. As the age-old homily goes—it is easy enough to start a war or a dissident movement—how to control the outcome is what really matters.

CHAPTER 4

Portugal's Enemies

One of the realities of the "Liberation Wars" in Southern and Central Africa that started in the early 1960s—and only ended 40 years later—was that without substantial support from Tanzania's radical President Julius Nyerere, those conflicts might have been smartly halted very early on.

Mozambique's insurgency, from beginning to end, got all the support it needed from President Nyerere to wage its revolutionary war against the Portuguese. The reality is there would never have been a ten-year war in this East African colony had the Soviets not recruited the Tanzanian president to its cause. The bottom line here—seminal to the entire liberation equation—is that just about everything required to wage war, down to the last AK bullet, came through the port of Dar es Salaam. That applies not only to Mozambique but also to insurgencies in Rhodesia and northern South West Africa, at least during the earlier phase of the latter struggle.

Yet in Europe—and in London, in particular—*Mwalimu* Julius Nyerere was portrayed as one of the leading pacifists of the epoch. This man, more than any other, is regarded by the majority of students of Africa's so-called Wars of Liberation as the architect of events that eventually changed the modern face of Southern Africa from White to Black. He was determined to end "White Rule" in Africa and his efforts ultimately succeeded.

A small man, hardly ostentatious but shrewd, calculating and manipulative—blessed too with a solid tactical appreciation of modern politics—Nyerere was regarded by most as a modest African academic. Throughout Tanzania he was respectfully referred to as *Mwalimu*, the Swahili word for teacher. Having graduated at Kampala's once-prestigious Makerere University, he gained a scholarship to attend the University of Edinburgh in 1949, a remarkable distinction at the time because he was the first Tanganyikan to study at a British university. He then went home to start laying the groundwork for his own revolt.

Much to the chagrin of the British colonial authorities, Nyerere was already very much of a political factor in his East African homeland by the time the "Revolutionary 1960s" arrived. He was abrasive towards the establishment, espoused a new form of African socialism which he called *Ujaama* and had the kind of charisma that could sway large crowds. After numerous confrontations with London's representatives in Dar es Salaam, he led his country to independence to first become Prime Minister, and later President of the Republic of Tanzania (as Tanganyika and Zanzibar came to be called).

Nyerere was also one of many post-war African heads of state with strong academic and emotional links to the radical British left. Others were Kwame Nkrumah of Ghana, Milton Obote of Uganda, and Kenneth Kaunda of Zambia.

With World War II over and a new brand of politics having emerged in Europe, it is pertinent that all four chose the socialist path, usually through the good offices of the London School of Economics.

Outspokenly radical in their political make-up (as with Venezuela today), it has not been lost on anybody interested in what is currently going on in Africa that the economies of all four countries, as a consequence, are in ruins. Certainly, the healthy economic structures left behind when Britain granted their respective *Uhurus* a couple of generations ago, were quickly squandered by collective or governmental ownership and administration, coupled to the rejection of anything resembling or linked to Capitalism.[1]

Political sentiments apart, Nyerere ended up embracing every revolutionary who arrived at his door, including a good few to start with from Mozambique and more thereafter from Angola.

Within a year of Tanganyika's independence in 1961,[2] a dozen Southern African revolutionary movements from Rhodesia, South West Africa (today Namibia) and even a few states that were not yet independent—like Nyasaland and Kenya—had set up shop along "Liberation Row" in Dar es Salaam. This was the ultimate irony, as Dar es Salaam, in Arabic, means "Harbor of Peace," but Tanzania now fostered armed revolution.

It was not long before South African revolutionaries established a secure base for their leaders in the Tanzanian capital. Larger groups of political malcontents that had left South Africa, usually on foot, were housed in camps in the interior.

With time, a revolutionary culture of its own evolved in Tanzania, together with a fairly distinct terminology. Tanzania resolutely called itself a "Frontline State" even though the distance between Pretoria and Dar es Salaam is greater than between London and Athens. Zambia embraced the concept as well, but this was more appropriate because it bordered on Rhodesia, then in a state of war that put Zambia on the receiving end of cross-border raids launched by Rhodesian security forces.

While all this was taking place, there was also communication between East Africa and the two most prominent revolutionary states on the West Coast; Ghana under *Osagyefo* Kwame Nkrumah and Ahmed Sékou Touré's Republic of Guinea—not to be confused with today's Equatorial Guinea (formerly Spanish Guinea) or Guiné-Bissau (Portuguese Guinea under Lisbon's rule).[3]

Much of the military hardware needed by these radical groups—that still had some way to go before they became fully-fledged guerrilla armies—was landed at Dar es Salaam Harbor. This materiel was then moved first by road and then on human backs, often for hundreds of kilometers into the interior. A Soviet TM-46 anti-tank mine, for instance, which weighs about 12kg, might have been hauled 1,000km overland by a minor army of porters by the time it was placed in a hole in the ground in Mozambique to lie waiting for the next convoy out of Tete.

The effort that went into shifting thousands of tons of war supplies into the Mozambique interior each month was not only formidable, it was a supremely commendable logistical effort and forcefully underscored FRELIMO's determination to undermine Lisbon's influence in Mozambique. In this, it shared a good deal of the kind of revolutionary effort put in place by Amilcar Cabral in his guerrilla campaign in Portuguese Guinea.

Dar, as we hacks covering the Africa beat knew it under Nyerere, went on to become a hub of a succession of new African revolutionary organizations and cults that stretched all the way across the continent, their adherents numbering millions. But even in those days, Nyerere was sharp enough to accept that as a consequence of such actions, some of the countries to the south might be tempted to try to destabilize his nation, which indeed is what both Rhodesia and South Africa eventually tried to do.

Security in Tanzania, consequently, was stringent. I went into Dar es Salaam several times while those conflicts were ongoing and was always aware that my movements were carefully watched. It was disconcerting to know that your hotel room was being searched each time you stepped out and that there were security people keeping track of everything you did: where you went, who you met, where you ate, shopped, posted your letters and the rest.

Irrespective of nomenclature, the Tanzanian connection was marginal compared to other problems that Lisbon was forced to counter as her expanded colonial conflicts gathered momentums of their own.

The Vietnam War in Southeast Asia, meanwhile, was providing Europe and America with a huge and fertile anti-war lobby which, when circumstances permitted, was conveniently switched to focus on what was then going on in Africa. These radical movements were opposed not only to the Portuguese war effort but also to a Rhodesia struggling to survive and, a short while later, more forcibly in South Africa which had adopted apartheid as a political dictum.

These were the great years of contemporary liberty, equality and fraternity, and in the eyes of these libertarians, the Portuguese government was badly out of step.

A similar attitude was to be adopted by some of the educated classes in Portugal itself. While popular stereotypes tended to depict Portugal as a stagnant backwater, students, professional people, academics, the military, and government officials—along with politicians in this nation of 10 million people—became increasingly sensitive to the opprobrium that resulted from the reactionary policies of the Prime Minister, António Salazar, who suffered a stroke in 1968.

Optimists on both sides of the Atlantic had hoped that under Caetano, his successor, the country would enter a more liberal phase, but it was not to be: some of the faces in Lisbon's corridors of power did change, but politics in general did not.

Most of the infiltration into Mozambique, as we have seen, came overland from Tanzania, already then regarded by Western nations as powerfully under the influence of both Moscow and Beijing. Insurgents would cross the Rovuma River, which forms the boundary in the extreme north, and wend their way, on foot, southwards towards the Zambezi—a trek that could sometimes take months since they had to carry everything they needed with them, and on their backs. The Mozambique bush and jungle with its endemic tsetse and other insect-borne diseases has never been kind to travelers.

Later, once Kenneth Kaunda's Zambia had entered the fray, logistic lines were somewhat eased but even then, the Portuguese had only marginally developed Mozambique's interior; roads and other communications infrastructures, as we have seen, were sparse.

***

Dr Eduardo Mondlane assumed leadership of FRELIMO in the early 1960s, but he had already absorbed the Angolan lessons of 1961 about going into the country unprepared for what lay ahead.

Soviet support or not—and the fact that this wherewithal had been waiting in the wings from the start—the FRELIMO leader was not prepared to launch a full-scale guerrilla war until some three years later, in September 1964. That was well after his small army had been properly trained and many of its officers received lengthy instruction in the Soviet Union and elsewhere.

What gradually emerged after his death—and was also mentioned by his wife Janet, when we had dinner in Dar es Salaam in later years—is that Mondlane was very much influenced by other colonial wars then taking place. Always the academic, he had made a close study of some of these conflicts that ranged from France's debacle in Indochina, all the way through Algeria as well as British efforts at curbing communist insurgency during the Malayan Emergency. Those who were able to exchange ideas with this vigorous young revolutionary were soon made aware that he certainly knew his oats where the fundamentals of guerrilla warfare were concerned.

Initially, he allowed FRELIMO to develop along similar lines to those employed by Amilcar Cabral's PAIGC on the upper West African coast and, along the way, experienced many of the same sort of problems in subordinating military operations to political leadership. Mondlane, the inveterate Marxist–Leninist, always emphasized strong political indoctrination for his cadres and it was along these lines that he sought to guide his movement into the future.

That said, while the man was a classic communist in the traditional mold, his ideas about equality of man as well as financial exploitation were formed by observing what was going on around him while living in Gaza Province. He was not an extremist like Fidel Castro or President Sékou Touré of Guinea, the West African leader who had come to despise everything linked to European culture, France's especially.

Married to a White American fellow-student and throughout adulthood maintaining strong links with those in the United States who had originally backed him, he saw a way forward in the long term of possibly being able to work together with Washington to uplift both his people and, when the time came, an impoverished Mozambique.

It was possibly these sentiments that eventually earned him the ire of the Soviet Union and could explain why Moscow did nothing to stop more radical political interests taking over after he had been assassinated.

At the same time, he was a committed militant. He declared at one of FRELIMO's council meetings—the movement's equivalent of the Kremlin's Supreme Soviet—that the Mozambican people had exhausted their patience waiting for Lisbon to ameliorate matters in the African colonies. He and his cohorts had tried peaceful means to change the status quo, but that had never worked, he concluded, pointing to what had taken place in 1960 when a reputed 400 demonstrating Africans were gunned down by security forces, even though figures quoted were demonstrably flawed.[4]

Mondlane also stressed that political expression—both in the *Ultramar* and the *metrópole*—was forbidden except in the narrow context of staged elections every four years, "and in that regard, people of color are not considered eligible to vote."

In February 1969, Eduardo Mondlane was assassinated by a parcel bomb delivered to his office by, as it was declared at the time, "unknown foreign agents."

Earlier he had recognized the existence of factionalism and its opportunities for exploitation, particularly by the Portuguese secret police (*Polícia Internacional e de Defesa do Estado* or PIDE), and also maintained that it was essential to be aware of the kind of threats that might by devised by their agents.

The threat, as Mondlane and those under him were only too aware, was real. Portugal's secret police had been active in Lisbon's African conflicts for years—sometimes even within the headquarters of some of the various liberation groups. What was particularly acute during the earlier stages of development, when many of the movement's members knew little about one another, was that it was not too difficult to put your own people in sensitive positions, almost always with promises of money.[5]

Other problems that arose—especially within the FRELIMO hierarchy—included a continual undercurrent of dissent within the organization's leadership which Mondlane, being more of a pragmatist than some of his hard-line associates (like the Marxist Samora Machel and his more militant Makonde backers) regularly attempted to ameliorate, not always successfully.

The complexity of motives behind divisive conduct within FRELIMO made it the more difficult to guard against the kind of factionalism that Mondlane recognized and spoke about. It included individual neuroses, personal ambitions and real ideological differences that were often entangled with the efforts of the enemy secret service to disrupt.

Over the years, several authorities suggested that FRELIMO was split behind the scenes by a succession of political divides often found in the liberation movements. These were attributed to internal or tribal disagreements, Cold War dynamics and in the case of Dar es Salaam at the time, relations with the Tanzanian state, all active within the context of the cosmopolitan public sphere introduced by Julius Nyerere.

***

An authoritative background to Eduardo Mondlane comes from a profile published in 2010 by the *Encyclopedia of World Biography*.[6]

Eduardo Chivambo Mondlane was born in 1920 in the Gaza district of southern Mozambique. The son of a Tsonga chief and the only member of a fairly large family to receive even a primary education, he later attributed his educational drive to the vision of a "very determined and persistent" mother.

Since the colonial school system was almost exclusively for Europeans and there was no hope that he, as an African, would be admitted, he gained entry to a Swiss mission school and from there to an American Methodist agricultural school on the outskirts of Lourenço Marques.

His family, reasonably well connected on the periphery of colonial politics, managed thereafter to have him enrolled at a Presbyterian secondary school in the Transvaal, South Africa. In 1948, the budding student was admitted to the Witwatersrand University of Johannesburg, the first African from Mozambique to enter a South African university. But that did not last long because with a change of government in 1949 and the start of the apartheid racial system, he was declared an unwanted "foreign native" in a White university and his student permit revoked.

Following his return to Lourenço Marques he was arrested and interrogated about his role in the formation of a local African student association. But having already shown leadership capabilities, he was not that easily deterred.

In June 1950, Mondlane entered the University of Lisbon as the only African student from Mozambique pursuing a higher education in Portugal. After a year during which he complained of harassment by the secret police, his Phelps Stokes scholarship was transferred to the United States, where he entered Oberlin College in Ohio at the age of 31. After he attained a bachelor's degree from Oberlin in 1953, he undertook graduate work at Northwestern University in Illinois and received a doctorate in 1960.

By this time Mondlane had become Mozambique's best-known, best-educated, and most consistently "watched" African. The uniqueness of his position can be appreciated when one notes that perhaps a dozen out of nearly six million Africans in Mozambique were attending secondary schools in 1955, while slightly over 200 were enrolled in technical schools or seminaries.

In June 1962 Eduardo Mondlane flew to Dar es Salaam, Tanzania, where he helped to unite several groups of exiled Mozambique nationalists into the Mozambique Liberation Front, or to give it its correct title *Frente de Libertação de Moçambique.* He was confirmed as the movement's first president at a congress held that September in Tanzania, after which he returned to America to complete his academic obligations at Syracuse University.

Early in 1963 he and his wife Janet and their children moved to Dar es Salaam where Mondlane assumed his new role as a revolutionary leader.

***

With Mondlane murdered, his deputy—the Reverend Uriah T. Simango—was expected to step into the breach. A moderate socialist, Simango had been with FRELIMO from its start, but it was also clear to many of his associates that he was not the kind of firebrand needed to continue a sophisticated guerrilla campaign.

Consequently, FRELIMO's Executive Committee appointed a presidential triumvirate consisting of Simango, Samora Machel—already a well-blooded guerrilla—and the poet/revolutionary Marcelino dos Santos who I met several times and once spent an evening over drinks at an Organization of African Unity (African Union today) summit in Addis Ababa. It was accepted early on that the moving force in the war would be Machel, a doctrinaire communist and close to his Soviet advisors.

Unlike Mondlane, Machel's origins were humble. Also born in Gaza Province in the south, to a farmer who for some years battled to keep body and soul together because of restrictive practices that included forbidding Black farmers to brand their livestock and being paid lower than market prices for their produce. Nevertheless, the family, through hard work, became quite successful and by 1940, owned four ploughs and 400 head of cattle.

Young Machel was sent to a Catholic mission school where he was taught the Portuguese language and its culture. With his basic education he was able to apply to become a nurse at one of the Lourenço Marques hospitals—which was just as well because, as we saw earlier, much of his family's property on the Limpopo River was expropriated by the government and handed over to White farmers.

By now staunchly anti-establishment and clearly politically orientated, he first came to the notice of the authorities when he campaigned for better wages for Black medical staff, which were about half of what White Portuguese nurses received.

Machel decided to leave the Mozambique capital when João Ferreira, a White pharmaceutical representative, warned him that he was being watched by PIDE, the Portuguese secret police. He slipped across the border into Swaziland and made his way through South Africa to Botswana. From there, he was flown with other radical recruits to Dar es Salaam.

An interesting aside here—sourced to veteran ANC activist Joe Slovo—is that Machel was not scheduled to board the flight, but J. B. Marks, a senior ANC official, having interviewed and been impressed by Machel, bumped one of his own ANC recruits off the flight so that the young Mozambican could fly instead.[7]

Once in the Tanzanian capital, Machel volunteered for military service, and was in the second group of FRELIMO recruits to be sent for training in Algeria. Back in Tanzania again, he was put in charge of his organization's own guerrilla training camp at Kongwa, about 70km east of Dodoma in the heart of the Great Rift Valley.

After FRELIMO launched the independence war on September 25, 1964, Machel soon became a key commander, having been severely tested in the tough eastern sector of the vast and sparsely populated Niassa Province. He proved both decisive and aggressive as a section leader and rose rapidly through the ranks of FRELIMO's guerrilla army, the *Forças Armadas de Defesa de Moçambique* (FADM), to become its head in October 1966.

Machel's biggest problem on taking over, and later, as head of the Mozambique government, was that he was staunchly Marxist–Leninist. He knew little of free trade, nor would he accept advice on such matters if it did not concur with Soviet policy. The immediate result was that after he had enacted legislation to bring key areas under state control, all land, businesses and industries were nationalized.

In February 1977 at its Third Congress, FRELIMO's Central Committee declared that it was now a Marxist–Leninist party and dedicated to the building of socialism, based on a "worker–peasant alliance."

It took only months for the economy to collapse and has never recovered since.

***

As a leader, Machel—as some of those who were linked to him were to tell me in later years—was not a popular man. He was both demanding and efficient and there were those who claimed he could sometimes be ruthless. That meant that the leader was feared by those with whom he was closely associated, rather than admired.

But where he differed markedly from his fellow revolutionaries—many of whom found themselves in comfortable environments while in exile, usually with good homes and everything paid for by the Party—Machel was a man of action and got things done, the hallmark of an efficient leader. Also, he was known to cross the frontier on occasion and observe the progress of his military struggle from up close.

More importantly, while Mozambique was no less corrupt than any other African country, he was able to keep these excesses more or less in check compared with the kind of rampant criminal activity that emerged within the Maputo government in the 21st century and which all but crippled the country.

Some interesting insights into the final days of Samora Machel's rule emerged when I spent some time diving off Bazaruto Island, a short distance by boat from Vilanculo in the central part of the country. There I met Luis Cardosa, a retired Mozambique bank official who had originally been conscripted to fight Lisbon's guerrilla war in Angola, which he in fact did, for three years.

After the wars ended and on his return to Mozambique, where he was born, Cardosa had several options. He could leave the country and join hundreds of thousands of his fellow countrymen who had left everything behind and fled to Europe after the guerrilla armies had taken over. Alternatively, being an African—and a White one at that—he could settle in the country of his birth, but only as long as he accepted FRELIMO's rigorous quasi-Marxist credo. He chose the latter option.

Luis Cardosa went a lot further. Being financially inclined, he asked to join the recently nationalized state bank and, as a loyal party member, spent decades doing good work for the government, eventually being appointed to a senior position at its headquarters in Maputo. Cardosa had apparently been instrumental in averting several financial crises and was popular with the leadership, so on his retirement when he was asked what he would like to do, he replied that he hoped to find an island off the coast, build a small house and live out his life in the kind of surroundings that most people can only dream about.

FRELIMO went one better. They not only allowed him to settle on a choice piece of palm-fringed waterfront land owned by the state on Bazaruto Island, but also built his lovely little house for him. There he was eventually to host Martha Gellhorn, the famous American war correspondent and erstwhile wife of Ernest Hemingway: she was holidaying at the nearby Bazaruto Lodge.

I spent long hours talking politics with Luis. One of the issues that emerged was how he had managed to fit into a society that was obviously totally alien to him when he returned from Angola and the way he was able to gain the trust of what was clearly a Marxist elite. He had no problem, this quiet-spoken former banker declared: he was not a political animal and anyway, he enjoyed helping to create a new society, literally from the ground up.

He had a single scathing criticism and that centered on the Soviets. They did much damage when they indirectly ran the show in Maputo, he strongly felt and was not afraid to say so. He added that it was "always Moscow's interests first, and that caused the country serious economic damage … in the end, it was the Soviets that actually murdered Samora Machel," he told me, adding that he had proof.

That statement floored me, if only because it came from a loyal party functionary whose commitment to the Party was unquestionable.

Cardosa continued: "Moscow always told Machel and other FRELIMO leaders that their true enemy was not capitalism, but South Africa, Mozambique's nearest neighbor. They were right, of course, because Pretoria was intent on destabilizing our government, but at the same time, the apartheid government there was constantly putting out feelers to try to establish better relations with us." It was also no secret in South Africa because the newspapers were full of it.

But, as Luis Cardosa told me, the Soviets throughout worked feverishly against any of this, until a point came when Machel declared at an open meeting that it was not the Kremlin's place to dictate to his people who could or could not be their friends. He said something about facing the reality of economic relations: South Africa was wealthy and had much to offer. Machel's reaction, according to Cardosa was:

> "He made a statement that shocked us all. The Russian ambassador was there and he turned to him, stating that when FRELIMO had taken power so many years before, Moscow promised that in a decade every single child in Mozambique would have a pair of shoes and every child would be able to go to school.
>
> "But that has never happened … far from it," Machel said, turning towards Moscow's representative. "Moreover," he declared, "we might be able to choose our friends, but we cannot choose our neighbors."

Not long afterwards, Samora Machel was killed in an air crash, the circumstances around which have never been fully explained.

A Tupolev Tu-134 jetliner was involved, with a Russian crew and 43 passengers onboard, nine of whom survived. Samora Machel died hours later and there are many people in Mozambique who still blame Pretoria, maintaining that the president's plane had been sabotaged.

"But I know differently," Cardosa candidly elucidated. He explained that he was still close to government when the disaster happened and what emerged shortly afterwards was that the aircraft was headed from Mbala in Zambia's north-east to Maputo, having first landed at Lusaka to refuel. The airstrip lies only a short distance from the Tanzanian frontier.

"But what had never been made public was something that took place immediately prior to take-off from Mbala, when one of the Zambian security guards spotted a man emerging from the aircraft, somebody who was not supposed to be there…"

The man accosted was a Russian. He explained to the security man that he was part of the Moscow delegation, producing a diplomatic passport to prove it.

"Obviously, it all appeared to be quite above board and that person was released without further questioning … Machel was on board when the aircraft took off and we all know the rest of the story."

The event involving the Russian on the airstrip at Mbala emerged within hours of the accident and Zambian security officials called the head of that delegation the following morning to speak to the individual who had had his passport checked.

He had already left the country for Tanzania, the Zambians were told.

CHAPTER 5

Mozambique's Military Contradictions

"Why the hell doesn't anyone talk about [our war]? I'm beginning to think that the one and a half million men who were sent to Africa to fight never existed and I'm just giving you some spiel."

ANTÓNIO LOBO ANTUNES:
A PORTUGUESE SOLDIER IN LISBON'S COLONIAL WAR

There were several anomalies with regard to Portugal's three wars in Africa; the first being that Lisbon, with meager resources, managed to hold on for as long as it did, fighting three wars far from home.

In many quarters Portugal's African conflicts ended up being viewed with unqualified disdain. There were others who reckoned that Lisbon's three wars in Africa might have been regarded as a hopeless rearguard action: almost 13 tough years in Angola and more than a decade in Mozambique or, as it was listed on earlier maps, *África Oriental Portuguesa*.

With the benefit of hindsight, we are today aware that what went on militarily in Africa almost half a century ago can hardly be rated as "rearguard" because the odds of a tiny European nation countering Soviet might were disproportionately poor. In this regard one needs to bear in mind that Moscow, following the defeat of Nazi Germany, became one of the world's great powers, second only to the United States.

Somehow though, using every resource in the book including all the help it could cadge from its NATO partners (coupled with huge dollops of guile and intrigue), Lisbon surprised everybody and for quite a few years it managed, if not adequately, then better than anybody anticipated.

Nor can one ignore the reality of what was taking place in the international arena. By the time the "Carnation Revolution" came along in April 1974, a new generation of libertarian international politics had evolved and that had a lot to do with countering anything that smacked of colonialism and the kind of "gunboat" actions which had become abhorrent to the new world order.

Had Prime Minister António de Salazar not clung to power for as long as he did, things might have been very different. But it was not to be, though one needs to accept that there was undoubtedly a genuine belief in what he termed a "civilizing mission" on the African continent. For all this, there was an unquestionable realization in Lisbon that while the world frowned at Lisbon clinging to its colonial outposts, the continued possession of its African provinces conferred on Portugal an international standing that it could not otherwise have attained.

Another incongruity that came with the African wars was that there existed within the upper echelons of Portugal's military command structure frequent dissension. This could be seen within the country's air force, its navy and the army especially, yet these differences were rarely commented upon either then, or even today.

As one observer opined about that period, the structure of the Portuguese armed forces was ill-designed, its staff corps was an anachronism and brigadiers were two-a-penny, with more generals and admirals in the Portuguese Army and Navy than in any other comparable defense force. More pertinent, by the time hostilities kicked off, few of these senior officers had ever heard a shot fired in anger or had exercised active command: the result was that they never really learned to understand some of the crucial problems at middle-command level.

Most salient of all, especially for those who were there, is that it took decades after the war was filed away in some obscure historical recesses for the nation to accept that there had actually been a war, never mind that it was fought in "distant Africa" and that many brave young men had given their lives for their beloved country…

In fact, João Ribeiro, a Portuguese journalist, in his book *Marcas da Guerra Colonial* ("Marks of the Colonial War") declared that by 1974 "the shame reached such an extent that the colonial war was cautiously swept away from the collective memory."[1] There are others who talk about a form of "national amnesia."

He went on to suggest that in terms of official indifference, there was an absence of this topic from the history curricula of state schools. He went on to urge that the colonial conflict be thoroughly studied and revealed in order to overcome this "open wound of Portuguese society."

There was good reason for Ribeiro to make his stand. By the time the so-called "Carnation Revolution" of April 25, 1974 had taken place—the army mutiny in Lisbon that ousted the government—there were 149,000 European Portuguese regular troops on active service in the African dominions; 65,000 in Angola, 32,000 in Portuguese Guinea and 51,000 in Mozambique. The total number of guerrillas in all three wars totaled well over 100,000.

Ribeiro went on: "History exists so that all of humanity can see it, study it, rethink it so that later one can do better, differently, or even to do justice. But, not here [...] here people try to forget, bury everything that happened in the colonial war, everything..."

Which does not contrast with what another veteran from those wars reckoned: "I was just one more [soldier] among many, one more to add to those thousands who have been there, one more—who went there—among so many, from so many villages, mountains, cities—I was just one more who went to the *Ultramar*... [Now] I am part of this group. I too got drafted."

It was those running the war in Lisbon that were the most culpable, brutally unkind to the men who served in Africa, followed in short shrift by a bunch of radical officers who plotted the overthrow of government and with the help of extraneous influences, believed they were actually saving the world. They certainly did not save anybody on the African continent.

Few today are aware that their actions resulted in a civil war in Angola that cost about a million lives, give or take a couple of hundred thousand. The same disaster followed in independent Mozambique where a civil war followed and tens of thousands of people died. In former Portuguese Guinea, those who served the Portuguese while they still ruled in any role whatever were slaughtered to the last man, woman and child.

Bruno Sena Martins of the *Centro de Estudos Sociais da Universidade de Coimbra* wrote a brilliant assessment of what was taking place at the time under the title "Imperial Memory—The Home of Silences in the Portuguese Colonial War." I quote a few of his more striking excerpts:

> In fact, for decades the Colonial War has been a taboo that only now—fifty years from its inception—starts to be broken. During the war the dictatorial regime never recognized the existence of a war and it always tried to hide the negative consequences of the conflict (ADFA, 1999).
>
> A telling example of this attitude is the way in which the bodies of the soldiers were removed from the boats throughout the night or the way in which the wounded soldiers had to remain out of sight during recovery and rehabilitation (Maurício, 1994; Antunes, 1996).
>
> The period after the [army putsch] created a socio-political moment in which the war was seen as an unjust and useless conflict, an appalling stubbornness—against the winds of history and the self-determination of African populations—which everybody wished to forget.
>
> Moreover, the silencing of [this] Colonial War was also the product of the conviction that raising the issue would lead to the confrontation of a whole range of acts of extreme violence (including the massacre of entire populations) which ought to involve complex processes of attribution and assumption of guilt.

> Therefore, a new political and ideological order was founded, which was anchored to an identity narrative of Portugal which actively led to the silencing of the Colonial War.

It is important to recall that during his regime, the "eternal" Portuguese Prime Minister Salazar (working in senior government since 1926) liked to affirm that his country, as he put it, was "pluri-continental and multiracial." This kind of sentiment was being passed onto his people for decades.

A man from Leiria told one commentator that in the 1940s it was normal in schools to show students a map of Europe, where it was admitted that Portugal was a small nation on that continent. "But the teachers made a point of overlaying on the same map, drawings with the outlines of the three Portuguese colonies in Africa: using this contrivance effectively, Portugal would then indeed be *the greatest nation of Western Europe.*"

***

To get an idea of how things progressed during the war (referred to as *Guerra Colonial Portuguesa* and also as the "Overseas War" or *Guerra do Ultramar*), the Portuguese military establishment in Angola—when hostilities began, and three years before Mozambican guerrillas began to pursue their own revolutionary aims—was limited to three regiments. It comprised two battalions of Hunters (infantry), a reconnaissance group and an engineering battalion, with a total of 6,500 soldiers, of which 1,500 were from the metropolis.

A year later this number had increased to 33,000 soldiers, and the tally kept mounting until 1971 when the force reached 65,000 Portuguese fighters in Angola. In Mozambique, Lisbon's fighting components were reinforced in 1961 when 11,000 more troops were added. By 1973, a year before hostilities ended, this figure touched 51,000. Similarly, in Portuguese Guinea it went from about 5,000 men to 32,000 serving soldiers, sailors and aviators 10 years later. It has been estimated that by 1974, more than 800,000 combatants, all told, would have spent time in one or other of the African wars.

Interestingly, Salazar's *Estado Novo* regime never recognized the existence of an actual war.[2] Instead, it regarded those challenging Lisbon's hegemony as terrorists, very much as the Rhodesians and South Africans had reacted when faced with similar uprisings, a kind of "communist under every other bed" philosophy.

On the broader canvas of the epoch, these were extremely difficult times, underscored by one officer who suggested that the African fighters they faced, being profound connoisseurs of the terrain, "liked to employ a variety of guerrilla tactics … and they were able to do so with remarkable aplomb … in the process they caused the opposition a great number of casualties…"

He was right of course, because it was the men who were killed, wounded or maimed in action—a large proportion as a consequence of landmines set in roads daily in use by the Portuguese Army—that did it for Lisbon in the end. During 13 years of Portugal's African wars, a total of 8,290 serving military personnel of all races died on all three fronts, the highest number registered in Mozambique (1,481), followed by Angola (1,306) and Guinea (1,240).

These figures are modest when compared to the 57,000 Americans who were killed in Vietnam in about half the time that Portugal was militarily active in Africa, though to be fair, Vietnam was a major conflagration that involved millions and the kind of budgets that no European nation would have countenanced should they have been faced with similar issues.

That situation also held for the Korean War of the 1950s where there were military personnel (ground, air and sea) from 16 nations involved. American casualties were 36,574 killed, while wounded in action totaled more than 100,000.

In relation to Portuguese wounded, figures are difficult to calculate, but estimates point to a total of something like 30,000 wounded. Without question, there is still a large body of former soldiers who continue to suffer serious psychological consequences as a result of actions in which they were involved on the African continent. Some prefer to call it "war stress," others post-traumatic stress disorder or PTSD.

In this regard Britain and France—obviously having taken careful note of what had taken place militarily in French Indochina, Malaya and Algeria in the aftermath of World War II—were prescient in handing self-government to their African colonies when they did, the majority in the early 1960s. Gold Coast jumped the gun under Kwame Nkrumah in 1957, who renamed his fledgling West African state Ghana.

But, as we have seen, Salazar stood fast and refused to budge on the critical issue of any kind of power sharing with the indigenous peoples, and one of the consequences was that Portugal's East African territory was the last of Lisbon's colonial possessions to launch what the guerrillas liked to refer to as their "glorious war of liberation."

∗∗∗

The nationalist movement in Mozambique, led by the Marxist–Leninist Liberation Front of Mozambique, carried out its first attacks against the

Portuguese Army on September 25, 1964 in an obscure village called Chai, situated about halfway between Porto Amélia (Pemba today) and the Tanzanian border in Cabo Delgado Province.

Fighting was soon to spread to Niassa, Mozambique's largest province in the north, which fringes on both Tanzania and erstwhile Nyasaland (Malawi today), a good part of the western frontier bordering on Lake Malawi.

Early communiqués of engagements are fragmentary. A report from Portuguese Army Battalion No. 558 makes a reference to the first violent action, in Cabo Delgado Province on August 21, 1964 (with no casualties).

It was a gradual process; only three months later did the Portuguese Army take its first losses while fighting in the Xilama region well into the north of the country. By then the guerrilla movement had substantially increased its number of combatants with squads of trainee guerrillas being shipped abroad for advanced military training. It meant too that the level of fighting had escalated markedly.

For the first few years, fighting remained centered in the north and it was not until 1967 that the guerrillas showed any real interest in Mozambique's Tete region, centered around the country's rugged and largely inhospitable Zambezi Valley. The difficulties encountered in this remote, mostly isolated and difficult terrain cannot be overstressed because in places the transport of weapons on any large scale was almost impossible. But everything changed after Zambia allowed the insurgent army to operate from its soil.

By then too, landmines had become the most favored means of damaging Lisbon's war effort as well as fracturing the morale of those involved. In fact, it went a lot further: the deployment of mines by FRELIMO resulted in this war becoming the living nightmare of the average Portuguese grunt.

Once the rebels had become active in Tete Province, things moved up several notches with the war now also experiencing Rhodesian Army and Air Force involvement, though almost nothing of this ever reached the media. Ostensibly, Rhodesian military involvement was in support of Portuguese ground and air operations, but with the Salisbury regime quite often conducting their operations independently. This issue is dealt with at some length in Chapter 12.

Those of us who went in to report on how these wars were progressing usually came up with conflicting assessments, a good deal depending on the measure of trust extended to us, which dictated who we were able to talk to and to what extent we were allowed access to the conflict zones. The *Daily Telegraph's* John Miller, an old friend from Cape Town, went into Angola in 1973 with excellent bona fides and was able to travel quite freely about the north of the country. His published report shows that he felt quite optimistic about Lisbon being able to hold out, if not indefinitely, then for some time longer.[3] As it turned out, he was wrong: the army mutiny in Lisbon less than a year later ended everything.

John Grimmond, another colleague who covered similar issues (he reported for the *New York Times*, which was hardly sympathetic to Lisbon's "Colonial Wars"), had his own take on these matters. Among his initial comments in an article published on November 4, 1973 (shortly before the war ended) was probably linked to his first visit to Lourenço Marques:

> There is a statue outside the cathedral in Lourenço Marques, the capital of Mozambique that depicts a Portuguese woman standing over a small African boy and cupping his head in her hand. To supporters of Portugal's role in Africa, the statue symbolizes the maternal role that this European country plays in protecting the simple African. To the authorities' critics, she is measuring the child for a job in the gold mines of neighboring South Africa.

It was an old joke, said Grimmond:

> …but both the joke and the statue have something to say about Portugal's involvement in three far-flung territories of a hostile continent. Portugal has been in Africa since the 15th century, longer than any other colonial power, and had no intention of giving up any time soon.
>
> Her determination was born of a strange combination of economic exploitation—exemplified, if you like, by the traffic in laborers to the South African mines—and the rigidly held belief that the Portuguese are fulfilling a civilizing mission in Africa. Together, these make Portugal look very like an immovable object. But, in the best traditions of immovable objects, she is now confronted by a seemingly irresistible force.

He went on to declare that as in Portuguese Guinea, the guerrillas in Mozambique were fighting not only a guerrilla war, but the more familiar African battle against poverty, disease and ignorance. As he suggested, schools and clinics, usually rudimentary affairs that can be quickly abandoned or packed up and reassembled, go hand in hand with military advances.

> And, slowly, the Portuguese are responding with improved facilities for Africans. The main feature of the Portuguese program is the resettlement of Africans in fortified villages called *aldeamentos*. Thus corralled, Africans are thought to be less susceptible to the advances of the guerrillas. In Mozambique more than 1.25 million people will be placed in *aldeamentos* by the end of the year.
>
> There is good reason to believe that this forcible resettlement is often unpopular and antagonizes the local population. It sets the scene for such actions as the alleged killing of about 400 villagers of Wiriyamu in Tete by Portuguese troops last December.
>
> Atrocities no doubt occur on both sides and seldom come to light, which is one reason why casualty figures are so suspect. It is probably safe to assume that 5,000 people die each year in Portugal's African wars. Many of them are killed in skirmishes, in attacks on military posts or army convoys. Others die from mines or mortars, and some are burned in their huts.

The war in Mozambique was no ordinary conflict, and barely resembled most other regional insurgencies of the period. It was certainly like nothing we have seen in Afghanistan, or more recently against Islamic State in either Iraq or Syria.

For instance, what made it different from Kenya's Mau Mau Rebellion (that conflagration lasted years but Whitehall never allowed it to be called a war)—or even what was going on in Rhodesia at the time—was that the interior of that vast East African landmass had always been wilderness, to the extent that it was only properly settled by Bantu peoples moving down the east coast of Africa during the course of the last millennia. Also, economic and commercial development beyond the easy reach of the two biggest cities did not really take off in Mozambique until after the Kaiser's War.

Early history has always indicated that as with the rest of Southern Africa, this was "Bushman" country, inhabited by people better known today as the San, members of various Khoisan-speaking indigenous hunter-gatherer groups that are the first nations of the entire subcontinent, including Mozambique. Evidence of their ancient culture which dates back 70,000 years is found throughout the region.

Additionally, Mozambique (apart from its river valleys) was nowhere near as verdant as many places in tropical Africa further towards the north; countries like the Central African Republic, Gabon or the Congo. As the American writer Robert Ruark once described it, Mozambique is truly "Africa Wild", though one needs to accept that that he was talking about wild animals, or rather, a proliferation of them.

Nobody will ever be able to say how many Portuguese soldiers were taken by lion, leopard or crocodile, but one can be fairly certain that there were quite a few. Nor will we ever know how many people were trampled by elephant, which happens when some males are in musk, a periodic and temperamental condition of high aggression linked to testosterone levels.

The African bush can sometimes be horrifically unforgiving, especially to the unsuspecting. On many of my safaris in Zambia, Zimbabwe, Kenya and elsewhere, there were always fireside chats about somebody having been killed by a charging elephant or mauled by a hippo. Sad to relate, these incidents sometimes take place for no apparent reason.

Cape buffalo, for example, normally passive until angered or wounded, have probably killed more professional hunters than have lions.

The same conditions held for Portuguese troops deployed in the African bush, and naturally to their African adversaries as well.

All the necessary precautions would have been taken but it is commonplace to "bump into" something wild and aggressive in the African bush. Occasionally poisonous snakes were found in the toilet, scorpions by the bucketful in the shower cubicle, and small spiders that have the potential to kill.

Obviously, unit medics must have had their hands full tending to soldiers with these sorts of "hits" and while most survived, some didn't. Malaria, in particular, proved to be lethal. Indeed, the loss of servicemen under such conditions would almost certainly have been classified as operational and the family would probably not have been told the actual cause of death: though they might hear the truth afterwards from a fellow soldier.

Hannes Wessels, a Southern African author who started his career as a professional hunter, ended it quite abruptly while on safari in northern Tanzania after he had been gored by a Cape buffalo that can move at astonishing speed when disturbed.

In his article titled "The Man-eating Lions of Mozambique," Wessels gives us an interesting insight into the kind of wildlife threats Portuguese troops might have encountered in parts of Mozambique, the Zambezi Valley and northern regions especially—an area that until recently was divided into safari concessions, or *coutadas*. The insurgent war now being waged in the north of the country has put an end to much of this activity.

This fascinating read includes vignettes about the Makonde people who preferred to have their women have two-inch nails blatantly sticking through their upper lips. While this might originally have been ornamentation, it also had the happy result of making them unappealing to Arab slavers that trolled through Makonde villages seeking to stock Sultans' harems in faraway Zanzibar and Oman.

He deals with the Lugenda River in the extreme north of Mozambique where I spent a while a long time after the colonial war ended. While it raged, that region of Niassa, adjoining the Mueda Plateau, was consistently active militarily and it stayed that way until hostilities ended—the guerrillas laying their mines on every possible access route, none of which had been professionally surfaced.

It was also part of an Africa that had always been regarded as "lion country." Wessels explains that while poaching had always been a problem, there were times when there was a dearth of antelope and the lions would end up preferring human flesh. One report spoke of a lion along the Rovuma River that was thought to have killed something like 40 humans: when it was eventually shot, it was found to be only four years old.

These big cats are not only physically powerful, extremely fast when on the chase and surprising smart, borne out more recently by Derek Littleton who ran a wildlife operation in the area when I last visited in 2017. By way of example, he explained how he had been tracking one of these big cats for more than a year:

> He's a cunning fellow, operates alone, moves into an area and is not shy about announcing his arrival by roaring into the night.
>
> The villagers light fires, some sleep in tree platforms or barricade their homes, but the animal bides his time until things settle down. On one occasion, a large male lion broke through the door of a hut and attacked a child, but the predator couldn't bite through a heavy straw mat that shielded the youngster. Failing to breach the door of another hut, the cat leapt onto the thatch and went through the roof to snatch a young girl inside.
>
> The lion kills, then moves on a fair distance and it is tough work following and staying on its tracks in the kind of bush country we have in this part of Africa.
>
> A lot of the ground is rocky and hard, making tracking extremely difficult, but I'm going to get him in the end.

Anticipating an attack one night, Littleton waited outside a village but heard nothing. When he gathered his kit in the morning, he found a human shoulder bone of someone taken by the lion that same night a short distance away. "He's a capable killer…"

Such is the confidence of some lions that they have moved close to the coastal town of Mocimboa de Praia. One victim, a disgruntled gambler, emerged from the local casino to take stock of his losses under a mango tree. Unbeknown to him, there was a lioness in the branches above and just when he thought his evening could get no worse, she attacked.

Luckily people heard the commotion and their arrival scared the animal away. In the process he not only lost his money but also a big chunk out of his butt.

For all those diversions, what was significant about Lisbon's colonial wars is that Mozambique was the last of the three African territories to become embroiled in a war of liberation.

The harnessing of the Zambezi River—with its enormous diversity of animal life—would eventually play a major economic role in the future of the East African territory, with the construction of the Cahora Bassa Dam utilizing large numbers of Portuguese troops (a fair proportion of all the troops in Mozambique according to one estimate).

Opening a new subversive front in Tete had other consequences for the guerrillas because for the first time they were able to move their forces further south. Indeed, by 1974, the revolutionary movement was able to launch a few mortar attacks against Vila Pery (now Chimoio) an important city in the region adjacent to Beira and the first and only heavy populated area to be hit by FRELIMO.

For the rest, the Portuguese Army went about its business in Mozambique on a largely piecemeal basis: a thrust here, an attack there. But unlike Angola, when General Bettencourt Rodrigues took over, very little evolved into anything substantive.

In the north, there was the *Gordian Knot* Operation, conducted in 1970 and commanded by Portuguese General Kaúlza de Arriaga—a conventional-style operation to destroy the guerrilla bases in the north—but actually the only major military operation of that territory.

A hotly disputed issue, the *Gordian Knot* Operation was considered by several historians and military strategists as a failure that even worsened the situation for Lisbon. According to others however, including its main architect, troops, and officials who had participated on both sides of the operation—including highly ranked elements among the guerrillas—it was globally described as a tremendous success of the Portuguese armed forces.

But as many of us were aware, the vacuous General de Arriaga could be quite verbose and, at times, an accomplished self-publicist. Not everybody was fooled, and not long thereafter somebody within Lisbon's defense hierarchy removed the man from his powerful military post, an event that tended to hasten the end of the war.

There were several reasons for de Arriaga's rather abrupt departure from Mozambique, one being a penchant for recklessness, a la *Gordian Knot*.

Also averred was an alleged incident involving the indigenous civilian White Mozambicans who might have been planning a unilateral declaration of independence from the motherland (as Ian Smith's Rhodesia had done a short while before from Britain). And finally, suspicions (never proved), that the general might have been planning a military coup against Marcello Caetano's administration.

***

The decade-long war along the fringes of the Indian Ocean littoral did end up producing some good results for Lisbon's military establishment in the country and it did not take long for Lourenço Marques command to emulate Luanda's military efforts by forming a variety of Special Force units. These included (among others):

- *Grupos Especiais* (GE) (Special Groups): Locally raised counter-insurgency troops similar to those used in Angola—Units of volunteer Black soldiers that had commando training
- *Grupos Especiais Pára-Quedistas* (GEP) (Paratrooper Special Groups): Units of volunteer Black soldiers that were given airborne training
- *Grupos Especiais de Pisteiros de Combate* (Combat Tracking Special Groups): Special units trained in tracking and locating guerrilla forces
- *Flechas* (Arrows): Unit similar to the one employed in Angola—a very successful body of fighters, controlled by PIDE. In Angola they involved mainly members of the Bushman community and specialized in tracking, reconnaissance and pseudo-terror operations, similar to what was being carried out in Rhodesia by Lieutenant-Colonel Ron Reid-Daly's Selous Scouts

Oscar Cardosa, another old friend who was active militarily for many years with the *Flechas* in Angola, a unit that he helped to create, commented on its particular effectiveness. Part of its inherent strength, he suggested, was its self-sufficiency.

When conflict erupted in 1961, Portugal was hardly ready to cope with the demands of an extensive counter-insurgency conflict. It was standard procedure, up to that point, to send the oldest and most obsolete materiel to the colonies.

Thus, initial military operations were conducted using World War II radios, the old m/937 Mauser rifle in 7.92mm caliber, and the equally dated German m/938 7.92mm (MG-13) Dreyse as well as Italian 8mm × 59RB m/938 (Breda M37) machine-guns.

Much of Portugal's older small arms derived from Germany in various deliveries which were made mostly before World War II. Later, Portugal would purchase arms and military equipment from France, West Germany, South Africa, and to a lesser extent, from Belgium, Israel and the United States.

Within a short time, the Portuguese Army saw the need for a modern selective-fire combat rifle, and in 1961 adopted the 7.62mm *Espingarda m/961* (Heckler & Koch G3) as the standard infantry weapon for most of its forces.

Weapons of the Enemy

The armaments of all African nationalist groups came mainly from the Soviet Union, which included Eastern Europe and (especially in Mozambique) Communist China.

However, the guerrillas also fielded small arms of American manufacture in the early days (such as the .45 M1 Thompson submachine-gun) along with British, French, and German weapons derived from neighboring states sympathetic to the rebellion.

Later in the war, apart from the ubiquitous AK, most guerrillas would use roughly the same Soviet-origin infantry rifles: the Mosin-Nagant bolt-action and others. SKS semi-automatic rifles were also found within guerrilla ranks but only because nothing else was available and would be discarded when more AKs came along.

Rebel forces made extensive use of light machine-guns (LMGs) for ambush and positional defense. The Degtyarev was the most widely used LMG, together with the DShK and SG-43 Goryunov heavy machine-guns. Support weapons included mortars and recoilless rifles.

Anti-aircraft weapons also came into their own, especially by the African Party for the Independence of Guinea and Cape Verde (PAIGC) as well as those rebels fighting in Angola and FRELIMO. The ZPU-4 AAA cannon was the most widely used, but by far the most effective was the Strela-2 missile (MANPAD in NATO terminology), first introduced to guerrilla forces in Guinea in 1973 and in Mozambique the following year.

While Lisbon had a hard time at the start of its colonial wars to adequately supply its forces in Africa, the Soviets ended up providing almost all of the wherewithal needed by active guerrilla forces in Africa. Indeed, towards the end there was a plethora of modern and sophisticated weapons, each one of them handed over free of charge to all the "Liberation Armies" active from the early 1960s onwards.

The much-cherished Kalashnikov AK-47 needs no introduction: it still remains the ultimate "weapon of choice" in almost all developing world wars, including those ongoing in the Yemen, the Congo and with Jihadist groups like Nigeria's Boko Haram as well as al-Shabaab in Somalia.

Portuguese troops in Angola, Portuguese Guinea and Mozambique were up against it from the first day of each of these conflicts.

Complementing this remarkable weapon throughout was the Soviet rocket-propelled grenade; first the RPG-2 and thereafter its successor, the RPG-7, and here we deal with the latter which became the indisputable "ground force weapon of its time." Anyone who has been to war in recent decades will bear that much out. In truth, the RPG-2 and the RPG-7—both veteran fin-stabilized, rocket-propelled anti-tank launchers—changed the face of warfare in the modern period not only in Africa but also in Asia, the Middle East, Central America and elsewhere.

The RPG-7 went on to capture the imagination of film studios and became a go-to Hollywood prop. The classic 1980s film *Red Dawn* portrayed ordinary American high school students blowing up Soviet tanks with captured RPGs, and you can hardly make it through most video games these days without tripping over the weapon. In the real world though, it is one of the deadliest weapons on the planet because of its sheer destructive power for its size.

Lester Grau, another associate as well as an analyst with the U.S. Army's Foreign Military Studies Office at Fort Leavenworth and author of *The Bear Went Over the Mountain: Soviet Combat Tactics in Afghanistan* reckons that the RPG-7 anti-tank grenade launcher is one of the most common and most effective infantry weapons in contemporary conflicts. He comments:

> Whether downing Black Hawk helicopters in Somalia, blasting Russian tanks in Chechnya, or attacking government strong points in Angola, the RPG-7 is the weapon of choice for many infantrymen and guerrillas around the world.
>
> For American soldiers, the weapon is responsible for their single deadliest day in Afghanistan. On August 6, 2011, Taliban insurgents fired up to three RPG rounds at a CH-47 Chinook heavy-lift helicopter.
>
> Part of its secret for success lies in that the RPG-7 is a remarkably simple weapon to handle. Without much practice, a user can hardly miss a vehicle-sized target at a range of 100 meters and most times double that. More practice enables the engagement of targets by unschooled, barely-trained fighters at even longer ranges, which, as a consequence, also tended to provide relatively better safety to the user.
>
> At its maximum range of 920 meters, RPGs self-detonate (4.5 seconds from firing) and that is why the weapon is sometimes used as a form of air-burst "artillery," spraying shrapnel over troops huddled together, military installations, or slow, low-flying or hovering helicopters. Anti-personnel grenades also have good destructive power.
>
> I have fired this rocket launcher quite a few times and was astonished how easy it was to handle, sitting comfortably on the shoulder and with the weapon's iron sights directly in sight. As a squad weapon, it is slightly larger than average, so there can be no mistake who or what you might be aiming at. Once you've checked that there is nobody standing behind you (during the firing process a mighty sheet of flame is emitted that can stretch back ten or 15 meters) you aim and pull the trigger.
>
> It is actually the launch detonation that intimidates most of those who haven't handled RPG-7s before because the blast is enough to burst an eardrum; hearing protection is essential.
>
> A moment after firing, you are able to very briefly track your grenade as it heads in towards the target at close to the speed of sound.

Other armaments in guerrilla arsenals included many Chinese as well as Yugoslav weapons, with Belgrade specializing in anti-personnel landmines and bombs.

In is interesting that the AK-47 along with the AKM rifle were both highly thought of by many Portuguese soldiers as they were shorter, slightly lighter, and more mobile than the G3. Also, the AK-47s ammunition load was lighter. A fairly common misconception is that many Portuguese soldiers used captured AK-47 type weapons, but this only held for a few elite units for special missions.

Like American forces in Vietnam and, later, South African troops operating behind enemy lines in Angola, ammunition resupply difficulties and the danger of being mistaken for a guerrilla when firing an enemy weapon generally precluded their use.

The average Mozambican rebel would haul five 30-round magazines loaded with 150 7.62mm x 39 cartridges as a combat load during bush operations, compared to five 20-round magazines with 100 7.62mm x 51 rounds for the Portuguese infantryman on patrol.

***

Almost every single shipment of military equipment intended for guerrilla forces operating in Mozambique was channeled through Dar es Salaam in Tanzania. Ships would arrive at the port with nothing but weapons on board, though obviously some of it went westwards towards Zambia and Angola.

Among a lot else, the Kremlin financed the full range of mortars (light and heavy), rockets and their launchers, as well as tons of POM-Z stake-mounted, anti-personnel fragmentation grenades, much favored by the guerrillas.

Also taken in were Soviet BM-21 multiple rocket launchers, good for mass attacks but which to my mind made more noise than caused real damage, as well as the B-10 recoilless rifle, a Soviet 82mm smoothbore recoilless gun which could be mounted on the rear of BTR-50 armored personnel carriers.

There were quite a few variations of military vehicles then manufactured in the Soviet Union and Eastern Europe and many went to Africa, including the all-popular GAZ truck or troop carrier which included models such as the GAZ-52, GAZ-53A and GAZ-66. Fortunately, the majority were inferior to anything similar produced in the West and they torched quite easily when captured and set alight with a bit of accelerant, which happened quite often, particularly in South Africa's Border War.

Landmines supplied by Moscow and its associates in these wars were seminal to the overall conduct of these African wars and are dealt with at length in Chapter 13.

There were two other weapons used by guerrilla forces which were generally a lot more lethal than mines, both Soviet heavy machine-guns and which I have seen in action in many wars, several times finding myself at the receiving end.

The first is DShK 1938 ("*Degtyaryov-Shpagin* Large-Caliber") with a V-shaped "butterfly" trigger that fires a 12.7mm cartridge. It is sometimes nicknamed *Dushka* (a dear or beloved person) in Russian-speaking countries.

Seen in action in many wars up to the present day, its wrath has been experienced by British forces in Al-Almarah, Iraq and in Syria where rebels liked to mount the gun on pick-ups and claimed to have destroyed 40 armored vehicles on a highway in Aleppo on the same day.

In Mozambique the *Dushka* was a favorite with the guerrillas because it was both handy and easily transportable. In the field it comes with a tripod, can fire 600 rounds a minute and is said to be the smallest anti-aircraft gun by caliber on the open market.

The second, far more lethal heavy machine-gun the Soviets supplied to the PAIGC was the KPV 14.5mm with a range of 3,000 meters horizontally and which could penetrate most armored cars.

How Others Viewed Mozambique's War

An interesting assessment made by some British officers who served in Britain's Malayan Emergency—one of the first post-World War II guerrilla wars—was that troops on the ground took roughly ten hours to trudge the same distance that a helicopter could cover in nine or ten minutes.

In theory, at least—according to Lieutenant-Colonel Ron Reid-Daly who saw action in both Malaya with the SAS as well as in Mozambique—that analysis also held true for Lisbon's war, though because the terrain in this East African territory is less severe than anything like the heavily foliaged Malayan Peninsula, the time factor on foot could probably be halved.

In other words, troops on the ground would probably march twice the distance covered by those in that southern Asian theater of military activity.

What quickly became clear in Africa however, is that the French-built Alouette and Puma helicopters gave Lisbon's colonial forces a significant advantage over the guerrillas, the majority of whom would never have viewed any aircraft from up close.

Though Portugal's African campaigns ended almost two generations ago, there are several long-standing misapprehensions relating to what went on in Mozambique, Angola and Portuguese Guinea, many of which still need to be clarified. The first involves the guerrillas who managed to keep what many regard as a minor or low-intensity conflict on the boil for ten or more long years.

For decades the consensus—and especially among some cognoscenti, senior officers and politicians back home—was that the average enemy fighter in the region was little more than an ill-trained, modestly equipped subversive acting almost solely on the whims of his Soviet-trained commissars.

In reality, these rugged combatants were anything but. For a start, the political concept of Marxism, while embraced by the FRELIMO leadership, was as alien to the majority of these fighters as *pâté de foie gras*. In fact, the average FRELIMO combatant was probably the same kind of soldier you would find today, with variations of course, in any developing world army.

For a start, most of the men on the ground were illiterate. Many came to don footwear for the first time when they were issued with their distinctive Soviet Chevron-soled combat boots. Indeed, few had previously owned anything but the clothes they stood up in. But that did not prevent them from being powerfully motivated to fight for what they rightfully believed was theirs: a plot of land that they could call their own in a fairly remote corner of Africa that they could till unimpeded, a small clinic in the nearest town and schools where their children could be educated.

They were not asking for much, but then this was Africa and many of those people viewed the average European as being both exploitative and the intruder. At least, that was the message—powerful and compelling—routinely propagated among Africa's masses by the Soviets and their cohorts.

These modest guerrilla strike forces would enter from Tanzania (and later Zambia) largely without hindrance because their bases and civilian assistance on Portuguese soil were relatively secure. Also, as Lisbon discovered early on, it was almost impossible to flush them out. And if things really did become tough for the insurgents they could just as easily scoot back across the border from whence they originally came.

Despite a general lack of literacy or education, there were specialist Black combatants who managed to give the Portuguese Army a right runabout and, now and again, a bloodied proboscis. All that in spite of them having no air cover, very little logistical back-up, having to carry most things they needed—including ammunition and heavier stuff like landmines and rocket grenades on their backs—almost no medical facilities for their wounded and an adversary that started badly, but gradually developed many of the skills linked to effective counter-insurgency warfare.

Unlike forest-clad Vietnam with its jungles and guerrilla tunnel links, the region in which the fighting was taking place in Mozambique was not generally heavily overgrown. There were jungles and heavy bush terrain in places, particularly in the Zambezi Valley, but for the rest the terrain was rarely difficult to penetrate in depth if you put your mind to it.

With all the disadvantages facing FRELIMO, its cadres went on to become celebrated masters of some of the most arcane disciplines of landmine warfare, and it was that which was eventually Lisbon's undoing.

As in any war, there are prisoners, as I was reminded by Janet Mondlane when I first met her in Dar es Salaam after her husband Eduardo, first leader of FRELIMO, had been murdered. More interesting, this American national who had originally studied with her husband in the United States mentioned that some Portuguese soldiers within FRELIMO's ranks played a useful role as the war progressed. They had intimate knowledge of their own forces, which was used to good advantage in some of the extensive propaganda programs that the rebels disseminated abroad. Quite a few had lectured in Europe and North America about what she termed "Lisbon's evil colonial regime in Africa."

Conversely, guerrilla prisoners of war taken by the Portuguese were not so easily dealt with. While early captives (in Angola in particular) were usually summarily dealt with, it did not take Lisbon's High Command very long to accept that some of these seasoned enemy troops could become a useful adjunct to their own efforts at countering insurgency.

Consequently, almost all former guerrillas captured were given the option of switching sides and joining a Portuguese unit like the *Flechas* or even—depending on the man's previous role within FRELIMO, PIDE—the country's secret police. The alternative, of course, was unspoken, or as one officer phrased it when we discussed this matter at Lourenço Marques' ultra-smart Polana Hotel, "they are appropriately dealt with." The implications were clear.

The Portuguese were not unique in using captured enemy troops to their own advantage. Britain did it in both Malaya and with Mau Mau regulars in Kenya and so did the French in Algeria. In all three of Lisbon's African colonies, it did not take the colonial army long to accept that many of those guerrillas who had taken what they liked to call "the sensible option" most times provided valuable service.

As Oscar Cardosa, that seasoned old veteran from the Angolan War can still testify, almost to a man these former guerrillas distinguished themselves, even though they were battling their old comrades. I was to see this for myself when I visited him at his base in southern Angola on my return from N'Requina.

Over the years, they divulged a lot else to do with their former comrades. In addition, they stood up well to the kinds of privations that soldiers on both sides of the front were likely to encounter while deployed in harsh tropical terrains. Indeed, they were usually able to do so much better than their new-found compadres in the Portuguese Army.

The majority were tough, physically superior to their European counterparts (with exceptions, of course), very well trained, had few basic needs apart from essentials and could handle the most rigorous routines, often a lot better than the majority of Portuguese soldiers. When wounded, they tended to suffer in silence.

As I was to see for myself while covering Nigeria's civil war in Biafra in the late 1960s, African soldiers who had no recourse to modern medicine would often resort to home-grown measures. A rebel with a bullet wound that had passed through a limb (or through his body) would be happy to have the unit medic apply a white-hot strip of metal out of the fire to cauterize the damage.

In Biafra, the forerunners to *Médicins sans Frontières* would use a rifle cleaning rod, to which was attached a small strip of cloth dipped in an antiseptic liquid, and run it through the wound. I saw that many times, the rod thrust into the chest and emerging out the man's back. The same would be done with flesh wounds in other parts of the body, though obviously it did not work if vitals had taken a hit. It was all done in total silence and few of the wounded would utter a sound, even when there was no anesthetic available. Two or three days later the man would be ready for action again.

I was actually witness to the amputation of the lower part of an arm that had been crushed, probably by a vehicle. The man was not sedated because supplies had run out, so a fresh sliver of wood from a tree outside was shoved between his teeth; with two orderlies holding him down, the limb was removed. The only sound in the room—lit by oil lamps—was of the surgeon's strained breathing as he tackled this grisly task and of the hand saw as it sawed through bone.

I spoke to the French doctors several times afterwards and they would always admit that the majority of their patients were incredibly brave. Very few ever cried out or complained, they told me, and from what I gathered afterwards in Mozambique, rebels faced with these problems were equally uncomplaining.

The hospitals that the guerrillas established behind Portuguese lines more often than not were underground bunkers or improvised bush shelters. There would very rarely be any running water and hygiene, of necessity, was almost always a make-do affair. While there were a few doctors on active service with FRELIMO—almost all of them foreigners and among them quite a few European volunteers—the majority of medical personnel active in the war zones were what would be termed "barefoot doctors" (and quite a number actually just that). Not many had progressed beyond rudimentary instruction in modern medicine and while the majority had been taught the basics and some had drugs and medicines, the vagaries of conflict in the distant interior allowed for few indulgences.

Generally, it was discovered as the war progressed, many Africans were somewhat wary of Western medical procedures. Tribal culture dictated that they would much rather have the local traditional healer handle the problem, which was understandable when you consider that Tanzania—the country from where the war was launched—currently has more than 75,000 registered witchdoctors in the country. Known as *Babu*, they were as readily accepted for their arcane traditions and skills in Mozambique and Zambia as in former Tanganyika.

More often than not these healers would apply their own concoctions, which might consist of a primitive poultice suffused with cattle or goat dung and placed over the open wound. There was some debate among Portuguese doctors whether this had the required effect, but while sepsis was commonplace, the majority of patients did survive and that says a lot, though there were never any records kept.

Those that did not probably died within a day or two, usually of septicemia; similarly, tetanus was fairly common and usually fatal.

***

Much else emerges in a fairly modest chapter on Portugal's last African military campaigns written by Professor Ian F. W. Beckett, in his day a leading light at Britain's Royal Military Academy Sandhurst.[1]

The book in question, titled *Armed Forces and Modern Counter-Insurgency* is well worth a read because, as always, this well-published author has been thorough in his research and comes up trumps.

The professor highlights the fact that through the late 1960s, Portugal's military strategy slowly started to change. Back in 1968, General Antonio de Spínola began pursuing the policy of concentration of population in strategic hamlets or defended villages. He initiated a coordinated "hearts and minds" campaign, named the "*Aldeamentos* Program," based on building new villages and improving farms, establishing medical centers, cattle dips and a road-building effort that achieved a rate of 1,400km per annum by 1972—more than the USA had built in six years in Vietnam or Britain in a dozen years in Malaya.

Clearly though, the main reason for surfacing the roads was to limit mine attacks: much more difficult on a tarred road than on laterite.

Contrary to General de Arriaga's efforts in Mozambique, Spínola actually believed the war to be winnable, but as he was to confide when I spent time with him in Portuguese Guinea, he had doubts as to whether a purely military solution was feasible. The fact was, however, that although a million people—some 15 percent of the Mozambican populace at the time—was resettled, Spínola's campaign of civil development not only suffered a setback, but eventually failed. For example, according to contemporary assessments, up to a third of all food crops grown in the *aldeamentos* went straight to the guerrillas.

Professor Beckett details NATO support for Lisbon's war efforts and I quote selectively:

> Although the United States refused to allow the Portuguese to deploy the F-86 Sabres in the colonies from 1967 onwards, all Portugal's military equipment was supplied by NATO allies, such as the standard G3 German carbine with which the infantry was armed, the French Panhard and British Daimler armored cars, French Alouette helicopters and the Italian Fiat G-92 fighter that was the mainstay of Portuguese aerial operations in Africa.
>
> It can be noted, however, that most of the aircraft were elderly by NATO standards; 17 aircraft types being in use in 1973. The Portuguese argued that they were essentially fighting the West's battle against communism and that the continued possession of the Cape Verde Islands in particular was of great strategic importance to the West's control of the Atlantic Sea routes.
>
> Within Africa itself, the Portuguese could also count on the support of other White powers. It was frequently [correctly] alleged that South African forces were active in Angola, particularly in defense of the important Cunene Hydroelectric Project in the south and Portuguese forces in Mozambique did in fact intercept a joint COREMO/PAC (Pan Africanist Congress) guerrilla force en route for South Africa in June 1968.
>
> Similarly, although nominally complying with international sanctions against Rhodesia, the Portuguese had contacts with the Rhodesian Security Forces from at least 1969.

He goes on to explain that by 1970, a command system had evolved for military operations by which each of the three overseas colonies was divided into a number of territorial or theater commands. There were five such commands in Angola and three in Mozambique—with joint military headquarters in each theater.

At theater level, elite units were made available for an intervention role in "reduction" operations such as clearing areas or protecting urban centers from sabotage. Below theater level, tactical responsibility was subordinated into sector commands further subdivided into battalion and company areas, although intervention forces were also available at local level for immediate reinforcement, convoy escort or similar mobile roles.

As Lieutenant-Colonel Ron Reid-Daly avers in Chapter 12, and echoed by Professor Beckett, there was a regrettable tendency for incoming commanders-in-chief to mount large-scale operations at the beginning of their tenure. For most of the period of the wars, however, the Portuguese had relatively little contact with insurgents whose main and most effective retaliatory weapon was the landmine. That, in turn, resulted in Lisbon's response of road tarring throughout the territory.

Similarly, defoliants were widely used from 1970 onwards to clear roadsides of vegetation which might conceal ambushes as well as the lobbing of grenades

Chopper and ground ops attack in bush country in Mozambique's Mueda Plateau region adjacent to Tanzania. Some of the heaviest fighting of the war took place here.

Portuguese Air Force Harvard ground support aircraft returning to base following a strike.

Shocking war casualty images such as this one were never circulated in Portugal while the wars lasted, but they were regular occurrences in all three African fighting regions.

All three Portuguese colonies were targeted by insurgents who laid landmines to good advantage: anti-tank and anti-personnel mines became the primary insurgent weapon.

Mozambique was largely undeveloped in the interior, which meant that the Portuguese most times were forced to cope with extremely difficult bush or jungle conditions that perfectly suited the guerrillas.

Army patrol in the north: in the later stages of the war discipline in the bush was poor, soldiers talking or smoking while out on patrol in the bush.

A shot of Dar es Salaam Harbour taken clandestinely by the author during the war from the roof of the Kilimanjaro Hotel.

A panoramic view of the great Zambezi downstream from Cahora Bassa.

Armed civilian irregulars addressed by a Portuguese officer at a muster in the interior. Many of these people were killed after FRELIMO came to power.

Southern start point of the Tete convoy headed north to Malawi and Zambia. Once we had crossed the bridge over the Zambezi, we were in "Injun Country" (Author's photo).

Portuguese Navy patrol craft brought overland from the coast to Lake Malawi. South Africa loaned Lisbon one of their tank carriers for the job which took weeks to cover difficult African terrain.

Alouette helicopter gunship over the jungle in the northern Cabo Delgado Province, the same region where a Jihadist guerrilla war is being fought today.

As insurgent attacks increased, the authorities were forced to expand protective measures to the railways.

Both insurgent and government forces would encounter wildlife in the bush—elephants were everywhere. Many detonated landmines, and were killed.

Insurgent attacks gradually moved towards the south and eventually most roads north of Tete needed convoy protection.

Harvard T-6 flight crew back at one of the Portuguese Air Force bases in the north.

A Portuguese Air Force helicopter touches down next to a road convoy after a landmine blast (Author's photo).

Portuguese naval craft on Lake Malawi during an interdiction patrol. They were on the lookout for insurgents entering from Tanzania by boat.

Guerrilla fighter in Mozambique with his Soviet RPG-2 rocket launcher: it was a classic pose and much used by the media.

No words are needed to register distress (Photo Bernardes Neves).

Parts of Mozambique's northern interior—as well as the Zambezi Valley—were extremely difficult terrain in which to fight a guerrilla war.

Italy sold Portugal a number of their advanced Fiat G-91 jets which were soon put to use in both Portuguese Guinea and Mozambique in ground support roles.

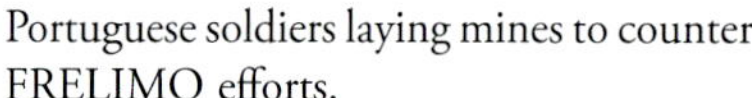

Portuguese soldiers laying mines to counter FRELIMO efforts.

In all three war zones in Africa—Angola, Mozambique and Portuguese Guinea—combat conditions were mostly primitive in the extreme. Troops battled the harsh bush terrain as much as they did the enemy.

FRELIMO guerrillas in training in an unnamed Tanzanian military base.

Eduardo Mondlane—FRELIMO's founding leader and commander—together with his American-born wife, Janet. The couple was on a European visit at the time.

Checking a suspected guerrilla holding base in the interior.

Colonel Ron Reid-Daly, who founded the Selous Scouts, spent long periods with the Portuguese Army in Mozambique. His role there was instructive and advisory rather than combative.

A Dakota DC-3 hit by a SAM-7 Strela missile in Mozambique towards the end of the war—the plane crash-landed.

Mozambique's war would never have succeeded but for Tanzania's President Julius Nyerere taking a powerful anti-colonial initiative and allowing a war to be launched from his soil.

Black Rhodesian troops off to war. Some of these men provided solid backup for operational Portuguese units.

Destroying a cluster of Soviet anti-tank landmines in situ after they were discovered by a patrol.

French Puma trooping helicopters arrived too late in Mozambique's war to affect the outcome. To most Portuguese, Africa was already a cause that had been lost.

FRELIMO's leader Samora Machel added a new and more aggressive dimension to the war after Eduardo Mondlane had been assassinated.

FRELIMO would often attack while mines were being cleared.

Patrol clearing landmines along a stretch of bush roads.

Portuguese Air Force bush base in Africa. Many such installations were makeshift.

This Portuguese Army truck became a write-off after having been mined. Unlike the South Africans, Lisbon never found an answer to enemy landmine techniques.

Samora Machel exhorts his troops at one of the forward FRELIMO operational bases in northern Mozambique. He often took an active part in hostilities, which gained him much support from his men.

Too few, too late—Puma helicopter on ops in Africa with the Portuguese Air Force.

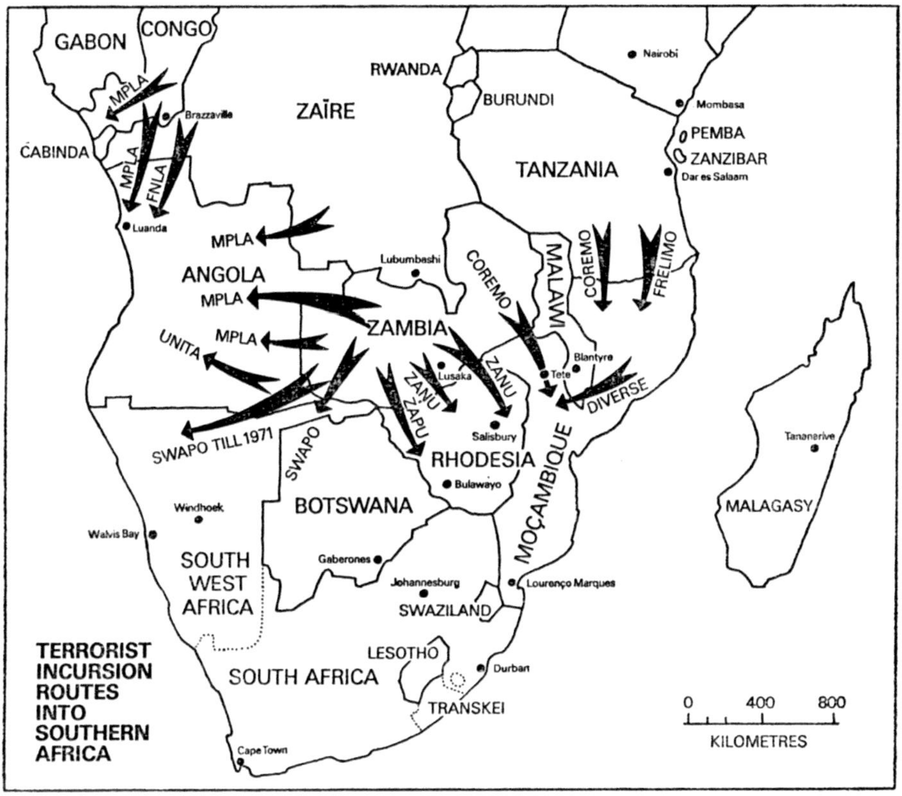

Early sketch of the extent of hostilities in Southern Africa: the insurgent thrust from the north, and particularly out of Tanzania remained constant for the duration.

Fidel Castro and Julius Nyerere came out in powerful support for the guerrillas.

Uncovering an anti-tank mine along a track in the Mozambique's northern bush country adjacent to Tanzania.

Prime Minister Antonio de Salazar refused to follow in the footsteps of the British and French in granting independence to his African possessions. In the end the indigenes fought for freedom and though it took more than a decade, they won it.

Portugal went into her African rebellions with few resources. Within a few years the country had developed a significant weapons industry.

into the verges ahead of troops evacuating vehicles, which was actually quite effective.

On the "hearts and minds" issue, Professor Beckett is specific. He reckons that while it can be argued that the Portuguese successfully adapted to the military requirements of counter-insurgency, they were less able to develop a convincing psychological policy to win support from the indigenous population as a whole.

By 1973–74, he tells us (the period immediately before the military putsch in Lisbon), the Portuguese had a significant force deployed in the colony and the air force had grown to comprise 12 Fiat G-92s, 15 Harvard T-6 converted trainers, 14 Alouette and two Puma helicopters. Transporters included five Nord-Atlas and seven DC-3 transport aircraft.

Apart from this build-up of might and materiel, the Portuguese also derived advantage from the natural barrier provided by the Rovuma River separating Tanzania from Mozambique, as well as the problems of tribal demography placed in the way of FRELIMO's attempt to penetrate beyond the Mueda Plateau—heartland of the Makonde. In a population of over seven million Africans, the Makonde were but one of at least 19 tribes from nine major ethnic groups speaking 17 different languages.

Although guerrilla activity was extended to the Niassa region in 1967, where the Nyanja tribe proved more cooperative towards FRELIMO, this was again offset by the willingness of the Moslem Yao to back the authorities. Guerrilla activity in the north consisted thereafter mostly of minelaying or hit-and-run attacks, known to the Portuguese as *flagelaçao* ("whipping burst").

***

Beckett goes into some detail about the many claims and counter-claims made by both sides, the guerrillas especially. Between June 1970 and July 1971, for example, and overlapping *Gordian Knot*, FRELIMO claimed to have killed 1,507 Portuguese troops, to have destroyed 261 vehicles, two aircraft and one helicopter and to have attacked 59 Portuguese posts, 17 bridges and four trains.

FRELIMO figures rarely bore much relation to reality, while those of the Portuguese can at least be used to indicate the scale and nature of the fighting. In 1971, for example, the Portuguese undertook 3,657 ground operations in the colony, 14,398 air missions, 28,060 air sorties and 675 naval missions and claimed 319 guerrillas taken and 1,041 killed. In 1972 they undertook 6,038 ground operations, 15,461 air missions and 627 naval missions and took 274 prisoners and captured 964 weapons.

Linked to de Arriaga's drives in the northern regions was a more ambitious scheme to completely neutralize infiltration by constructing a "human" barrier along the Rovuma line.

Indeed, General de Arriaga's definition of "winning" the war was of being able immediately to detect and destroy any infiltrations into the colony. It was planned that the human element of Operation *Frontier* would be provided both by new White settlers and resettlement of the native population, the settlements being linked by all-weather roads which would widen every 10km (six miles) to form an airstrip.

As in Angola, the idea of White kibbutzim or military colonists proved unsuccessful, but 150 *aldeamentos* were constructed in the Cabo Delgado and Niassa regions with a population of some 250,000 people, one model *aldeamento* at Nangade housing 2,500 alone. The program was behind schedule in the north by 1974, rains having eroded many of the newly-laid road surfaces and the troops by then available being too few to prevent all infiltration.

As already indicated, *aldeamentos* in Mozambique were generally unsuccessful in providing their inhabitants with the desired amenities—one in Niassa was actually sited in a swamp. But the eventual construction of 980 *aldeamentos* in the colony, with a population of around a million people, made nonsense of FRELIMO claims to be controlling over a million in the same areas.

Although mostly associated with military rather than social or political solutions to insurgency, de Arriaga's social promotion program was just as extensive as elsewhere in the colonies.

Interestingly, there were a number of important rebel defections to the Portuguese, including Lazaro Kavandame in March 1969 and Dr Miguel Murrupa in 1970.

The number of Black or local troops in the army was increased from approximately 40 percent of the total to over 60 percent between 1968 and 1974, including some 10,000 to 12,000 Blacks serving in the elite GE, GEP or *Flechas*. Alone among Portuguese commanders, de Arriaga also instituted political instruction for his own troops. Known as *mentalização* ("mentalization"), the program was conducted through unit officers, slogans and leaflets. In the case of Black elite troops instruction of at least an hour a day was devoted to it.

By July 1974 guerrillas had penetrated the Zambezia region for the first time while and, as already related, SAM missiles made their appearance in the colony in March 1974. There had clearly been a steadily escalating level of violence.

FRELIMO had always conducted terrorism against the native population, although the party disputes this today. We know from official records which can be inspected in Lisbon that at least 689 deliberate assassinations had taken place between 1964 and February 1973, together with over 2,000 people of all races wounded over and above 6,500 abductions. In Tete alone 55 tribal chiefs were murdered during 1971.

Similarly, Mozambique accounted for twice as many Portuguese casualties between November 1973 and January 1974 than either Angola or Guinea, and it is perhaps significant that most allegations and counter-allegations of atrocities came from Mozambique.

Nevertheless, it is important to stress that the Portuguese were still far from losing the campaign in the colony by 1974. Indeed, there is no reason to suppose that insurgency would have succeeded in the immediate future. As it was, politics intervened and the coup in Portugal brought about Portugal's abrupt withdrawal of all its forces from Africa, transfer of power to FRELIMO being agreed in September 1974 for independence in June 1975.

Daniel Roxo—Legend of a Guerrilla Fighter

During the course of the war in Mozambique, one man, Daniel—Danny to his friends—Roxo was the undisputed counter-insurgency specialist in the north of the country. In achieving this distinction, he stood out above all others because the man knew and understood the African environment almost as well as his trackers, and certainly a lot better than the enemy.

In the latter stages of his irregular Mozambique operations, said one American magazine, he created a personal army and ended up with a price of US$100,000 on his head. The report went on:[1] "That man became a warrior, at the head of his 100-strong squad that was said to have killed more FRELIMO combatants than Lisbon's entire colonial army…"

While the stats are certainly exaggerated, there is no question that Roxo was a remarkable man: quiet, soft-spoken, not very big in stature and, as his old colleagues still tell you, proud of his humble origins. Somebody once quoted his personal maxim: "Soldiers are made, but warriors are born: a premise that holds even today."

Originally from Portugal's north, he was born in 1933 in the village of Mogadouro, a name that suggests the original Arab occupation of that region in the Bragança district, situated in the historical province of Trás-os-Montes e Alto Douro.

He was the youngest of four brothers, the oldest being Alípio who emigrated to Mozambique in 1947. Two other brothers, Silvano and Alfredo, moved to Brazil. It took young Daniel four years to join Alípio in Mozambique and once he had put Europe behind him, he never returned.

But moving to Africa in those days, even for a Portuguese national shifting permanently to one of its possessions, was not quite that simple. The prospective "emigrant" (for that is how he was categorized by the over-bureaucratized Lisbon establishment) had to obtain a *Carta de Chamada*, a document that was a prerequisite if you wanted to settle in the colonies. The restriction was eliminated after Salazar had died and Caetano took over as Portugal's prime minister in 1968.

Alípio had himself been sponsored by an uncle, "a navy officer" who arranged a job for him in Nampula with the railways, where he worked from 1951 to 1956. In 1957 he would be posted to Lourenço Marques Harbor. Since Alípio was working as an official with the railroad company *Caminhos de Ferro de Moçambique,* he was able to arrange a job for his young brother as a "boss boy" of the African workers involved in the construction of the Nampula-Malawi line.

The move suited Daniel perfectly because he was going into the bush. And because he had always been an enthusiastic hunter as a boy, chasing up wild birds and small animals like hares back home, he had already developed into a fairly crack shot with a rifle. For this reason, he was promoted to "official" hunter for the railways working in that area, with the job of supplying meat for the railway employees.

His first task was to put a team of skilled locals together that would assist him in tracking game, many of whom would stay with him and remain loyal for many years in addition to forming the core of the militia he created once the war began.

Paid a normal salary and provided with the requisite equipment—hunting gear, rifles and ammunition—he took advantage of his position to befriend the locals, get to know the terrain and learn native dialects, something that was to be of great assistance in the future. He could eventually speak many of the local dialects fluently.

According to Stephen Dunkley who has made a study of the man and provided many of the quotes used here, it wasn't long before Daniel met Orlando Cristina in 1953 at the office of the administrator Manuel Belchior at Nova Freixo (today Kuamba), the final station on the rail link between Lumbo and Nampula-Freixo. At the time Orlando was a 2nd Lieutenant of the infantry company based in Vila Cabral and had himself been hunting in the area since 1951.

The area that Orlando and his army unit patrolled was about a third the size of metropolitan Portugal and in 1953 perhaps only a dozen Whites lived there: in fact, in the entire northern Niassa Province—about 110,000km^2 in size—only had about 500 Whites who called it home. The area also hosted the nine recognized so-called "Big Game Hunters" in Mozambique and was one of the most isolated regions in the *Ultramar.*

In 1955, after three years with the railways, Daniel was becoming bored and restless. He resigned his job and set out on foot into the interior with only a small bag and his hunting rifle and for the next three years made the bush his home, with only fleeting contact with the outside world. His only associates were those Africans with whom he made contact and obviously, that helped immeasurably to perfect his language skills. Meantime, he hunted, sold some of the ivory and skins that he acquired in the process but had little contact with his fellow countrymen.

Information is vague regarding Daniel's activities from 1955 to the early 1960s. His brother Alípio heard from Daniel briefly in 1956, just as the older man was about to be promoted and relocated to Lourenço Marques. His brother emerged from the bush only when he had enough money to buy an old truck.

His brother, Alipio, recalls that from 1957 to 1969 he only received a few letters from Daniel. Most times he got news about what he was doing or where he was from other hunters who had been working in the Niassa Province. What became evident was that the enterprising Roxo had got to know the region adjacent to the Tanganyika frontier better than any other White man alive and that perfectly suited his purposes. Obviously, the government also became interested in what he was doing in regions about which very little was known in Mozambique's "Deep South."

What did emerge in the interim was that he met his future wife Cecília in 1956. The couple got married and made a home for themselves in the bush where Roxo went on doing what he always did. But by now it had become evident to Lisbon that war was threatening from Tanzania, to the immediate north.

An interesting little aside came from Cecília concerning this period. She explained to her family: at one stage Daniel had to shoot a crocodile as she and two of their children were crossing a river. Daniel had gone across first and as Cecília and the kids started to ford the river, a crocodile that had been submerged made a lunge at them. Her husband reacted swiftly and killed the beast before it could harm his family.

Another story that emerged years later was his fight to the death with a leopard. The American magazine *Soldier of Fortune* described it thus in their issue of October 1979:

> The big game hunter was preoccupied with making a head count in an area near a remote village when the leopard attacked. Who would expect an early morning attack? His rifle was not close by, so man and beast struggled for over an hour. The hunter bit the leopard until the animal's body was covered with wounds … the man did not even have a hunting knife and soon all his protective clothing was stripped away by the leopard's desperate clawing.

> Finally, naked and covered with blood, the hunter succeeded in getting a death grip on the animal. He felt the lithe, muscular body weaken, relax and fall to the ground; neck broken.

Then, a few years later came the war and Daniel Roxo was involved from the start, most times clandestinely in northern bush and jungle country, vast reaches of it adjoining the great Rovuma River that he had come to know so well. This was the same river used by the insurgents to infiltrate out of Tanzania.

News about his activities constantly filtered southwards to both Beira and Lourenço Marques. The word was that there was a guerrilla fighter called Daniel Roxo who was making the lives of the invading guerrilla army difficult. Obviously, and of necessity, he would be in contact with regular Portuguese Army elements operational in those regions and as the tales spread, the legend grew.

By 1962 Daniel had the nickname "the Red Beard Hunter" very appropriately given to him by the locals.

What did emerge soon enough was that the man was both fearless and extremely successful at striking at the enemy. His exploits, brought back to civilization by national servicemen, only added to this mystique. He was regarded by some as "invincible," though as he would be the first to admit, that might be stretching it…

According to Dunkley, Roxo's brother Alípio mentioned that their relatives found it difficult to imagine that their beloved "Chico"—Daniel's family name—as "a killing machine." He'd always been kind-hearted "and was still a rather gentle boy of only 20 when I last saw him."

It is notable that a lot of this activity took place under Major Carlos Augusto da Costa Matos who, before the war, based himself at Vila Cabral after he had replaced the civilian governor for the Niassa Province in 1962. Costa Matos had held a senior position from 1959 to 1962 in the military intelligence section at the army headquarters in Lourenço Marques. Trained by French intelligence personnel in Algeria, he perfectly understood the importance of military intelligence in fighting a guerrilla war and Daniel Roxo would have perfectly fitted the mold of a competent undercover agent. The fact that he was working in the shadowy world of transients between Mozambique and Tanzania (and later, Mozambique and Zambia) fitted the requirements of the major very well indeed.

While still at army headquarters and prior to the invasion (the first guerrilla onslaught was only launched in September 1964) the new governor Costa Matos had set up three hunter-intelligence gathering teams, each under the control of one of three European first lieutenants (Orlando Cristina, Gomes dos Santos and a Lieutenant Pestaquinni). All three teams—with Roxo still working independently—had about a dozen volunteers from various army units serving in their ranks, in addition to 20 local men who had been in uniform prior to 1962.

The officers and their men all wore civilian clothes and posed as hunters in the Cabo Delgado as well as the Niassa Province. It was a perfect set-up for the kind of subterfuge in which they were involved.

The three intelligence groups were each provided with a truck and four jeeps; their business was to hunt and make money so that, in theory, they could finance what they were up to. White members of this improvised intelligence-gathering unit were paid from a secret army slush fund and initial start-up funds were used to set the hunting ventures in motion, while Black group members would receive a share from hunting profits, which included ivory.

Part of their cover was to make their presence known to the local population and let them think their job was actually that of professional hunters, when in fact, they were covertly gathering intelligence. There were times when, to avoid being compromised by overly suspicious potential enemies, they would do what was needed to eliminate them, something at which Roxo was particularly adept.

As mentioned, it was during these years in the bush that Daniel honed his hunting skills and according to some he also became a master tracker, learned the moods of the bush and experienced its meanness. In the process he assimilated many of the finer points of bush tradition, using those skills to become an expert tracker and hunter.

Once the war kicked off, he would employ those same skills to kill enemy insurgents and with time, became astonishingly good at it. That was the main reason why Dar es Salaam put a price on his head.

Daniel, during his years in the bush, also learned several local African dialects such as Chi Nyanja and Chi Yao, both of which enabled him to communicate with and be accepted by the locals of Niassa Province. In turn, this allowed him to become aware of many things that might have been going on there. In the process, Daniel Roxo was never called up to do his military service by the Portuguese government, because only after 1962 did military service become compulsory for the White population of Mozambique and by then he was over the age limit.

In 1963 Governor Costa Matos offered Daniel a job to officially assist with a census of the population of Niassa. This he gladly accepted, says Dunkley, because by then he had stopped hunting and all his men but nine had gone on to seek employment elsewhere. Essentially, he needed something solid to back him up and pay the bills.

The governor was obviously aware of Daniel's experience, as well as his contacts in the province. At this time his intelligence background was fully developed, and he was obviously looking to harness this expertise in the areas in which he operated. The ex-hunter accepted the job and was given both transport and a contingent of five Black policemen, referred to as *cipaios* by the local military, or what would have been labeled Askaris in the Tanganyika of old.

In the process, Daniel and his men would visit each village in the province and do head counts. After the census had been completed, he was employed by the government at the births and deaths office in Vila Cabral, many believing that this was a shrewd move by Costa Matos to have Daniel around from 1964 onwards to defend Vila Cabral.

There is no question that while Roxo was working in the outlying villages, he was also assiduously collecting intelligence and recording the movement of people from Niassa to Tanzania and Likoma Island situated on Lake Malawi. There was quite a bit of that activity then, with FRELIMO agents and political commissars making regular recruitment forays into Mozambique for new recruits. Roxo would deal with these insurgents quietly and efficiently whenever they were encountered and nobody would breathe a word…

After the hunting teams were disbanded in 1963, Governor Costa Matos was solidly behind this former professional hunter, well aware, according to Dunkley again, that he had in hand what he referred to as "an extremely valuable diamond in the rough."

By the end of 1963 Daniel Roxo was asked to take a squad of about a dozen armed *cipaios* and visit the far-north villages of the Niassa Province to gather as much intelligence as he could, especially with regard to the numbers of locals leaving Niassa to join the rebel movement across the ill-marked frontier. He and his men—who at this stage numbered about 17 (and some with no military training)—became the first group that the government used to try and stop the local population from leaving, their role at that stage to be "soldiers in the shadows."

There was good reason for this action. Portuguese intelligence had already established that large numbers of young guerrilla recruits were being sent abroad from Dar es Salaam for advanced military training. Some went to Russia, others to Communist China and quite a few to insurgent training establishments in African countries sympathetic to the revolutionary cause. Here Algeria was a favorite, as was Sékou Touré's Marxist Guinea Republic on the West Coast of Africa and also Ethiopia.

Late in 1964, Governor Costa Matos—still only 38 years old and the youngest governor of the Portuguese empire—requested that Roxo assist him in promoting an advanced anti-communist propaganda campaign. That meant addressing rural populations about the danger of socialism and what it would mean to fight an anti-government war. These men were also tasked to detect subversive elements and to try to rehabilitate any of the local population that had come under the influence of FRELIMO, one of the reasons why some said that Roxo had started to work for PIDE, the Portuguese secret police.

Whether he ever did or not we will never know, though obviously any intelligence organization would have had more than a passing interest in the kind of work Daniel Roxo was doing. However, Governor Costa Matos was hardly likely to give way to other government organizations—including PIDE—when he needed him for his own clandestine intelligence purposes. Obviously, the secret services would have received some of the military intelligence the former hunter generated, but the maverick outsider also knew on which side his bread was buttered. PIDE was already regarded with distinct disdain—and in some instances distrust—by most government departments by the time the war started.

Roxo's role, therefore, working for the governor's office was pretty basic. For instance, Costa Matos would call him to his office, close the door and tell him in confidence that he needed to know strength and plans of the guerrilla movement for a specific region in the Lake Niassa region. Or it might be an area along the Rovuma.

As someone said, Roxo would take a few men and head off into the bush and return a week or so later with the information. Most times he would provide a verbal report during a routine debrief and then either leave on another mission or wait until Costa Matos called him again on another project, the set routine prior to war actually getting properly underway.

In March 1964, the man was instructed by Costa Matos to recruit up to 20 men, and it was then that the former hunter put the word out on the mysterious "bush telegraph" and called together the hard core of his old tracking group. He never had to wait long for them to respond: one and all these African people adored their old leader and they needed nothing more than a nudge to join forces with him once more. More importantly, most were without work and they would be paid for doing what they loved.

As the war progressed, still more men were recruited, almost all with connections that went way back, until eventually Roxo had mobilized a force of roughly 100 men. Those who had not received military and weapons training in the past were put through their paces in a training base by Roxo himself, assisted by several NCOs provided by the army. The new men then rejoined the unit, almost none of them working in the field in any kind of uniform. As far as the rest of the world was concerned, the team was a bunch of civilians gathered together for a common purpose: hunt animals.

Daniel Roxo, by then, had achieved his objective. He had a fairly large body of men under his command and every one personally answerable to him alone. One of his conditions—accepted by the authorities in Lourenço Marques because they could hardly argue with his remarkable success rate—was that he was not required to recruit more men and enhance his unit strength. He always felt that it was essential, in doing what he did in the back and beyond of the Mozambique jungle, to be totally "hands-on." Anyway, his sentiments about the regular army were well known: he wanted none of it.

For those who never met Daniel Roxo while he was still alive and had heard of him from reputation alone, the usual impression put out by some were visions of a fairly large man with broad shoulders and muscular arms, coupled to a bushy beard and some severe battle-scarred features. In reality he was just over 1.76m (almost 5 feet 8 inches) tall and weighed in at about 75kg (165 pounds). His hair was of a tawny color and customarily he wore a neatly trimmed beard.

It was his eyes, arguably, that were his most impressive attribute: sky blue and disturbingly penetrating. Many of those who met him for the first time reckoned that that was probably his most distinguishing feature.

In his thesis, Stephen Dunkley explains that his voice—according to those who knew or worked with him (including his wife Cecília)—was quiet and controlled: soft, but clear. Others that had made contact with him said there seemed to be a shroud of invincibility about his persona, all of which became part of the legend.

His relationship with the press was strained. In fact, he passionately avoided the media because few articles written about this reserved and generally uncommunicative man were well received. He told one of his confidants that any kind of publicity wrongly interpreted might end up putting himself and his men in danger.

However, he did make use of one interview with Chris Vermaak, a South African journalist and good friend of mine, to his own advantage. Published in the Afrikaans newspaper *Rapport* on October 31, 1976 (soon after the failed White-backed counter-coup in Lourenço Marques and in a bid to put the country's new revolutionary government off his tracks) the interview made it clear that Roxo was going to leave Mozambique and retire in Portugal.

Meantime, he had already made plans to continue his fight elsewhere in Southern Africa.

***

FRELIMO's war came to Mozambique's Niassa Province in late 1964. A group of seven insurgents attacked a small northern town on Lake Malawi about two days' march from Mbamba Bay in southern Tanzania.

The following day another rebel group, led by a cadre named Mateus Malopa, fired on the Portuguese navy patrol boat *Castor* while it navigated on Lake Niassa. Both targets lay close to Likoma Island, where the guerrillas had established a base and to which they returned.

The next attack in Niassa came three months later in December when the guerrillas attacked Olivença, a town roughly 30km from the Tanzanian border.

Probably the first effective counter-action by Lisbon against the rebels came on January 5, 1965, when a *fuzileiro* (marine) force attacked Ngomba Island where the guerrillas had set up camp with 50 to 60 men. That onslaught lasted over three hours and the results are inconclusive, except that some regard it as the real start of the war in Niassa.

While it is doubtful that Roxo's people were involved, it is feasible that the *fuzileiros* used intelligence gathered by his squads in its planning. Likoma and Ngomba islands are both in Malawian territorial waters and while the Portuguese did attack Ngomba, they would never have launched an attack on Likoma due to it being the heart of the Anglican Church in that area (Malawi, Tanganyika and Mozambique). It is also relevant that Father John Paul of the church was very well connected in Vila Cabral and in London, being a distant relative of the British royal family.

While 1964 saw the start of the war against Portuguese rule in Mozambique it was the period 1965 and 1969 that saw a marked increase in FRELIMO activity in the Niassa Province. By October 1966 they were active in Nipepe, Metarica and only a few kilometers north of the Portuguese Army barracks town Nova Freixo. From then on hostilities escalated exponentially in northern Mozambique and the army was obliged to send in 3,000 new conscripts to help stem the insurgency.

Naturally tales about Roxo and his prowess in the bush had already become something of a legend, and those few who met him in the field would proudly relate their experiences. There was always a story or six about this unconventional combatant doing the rounds, even a photo perhaps, which the troops would pass around among friends and say they actually knew the "White Devil" or, as some preferred, "the Red Beard Hunter."

In strong contrast, many of the upper-class officers in the Portuguese Army were largely disdainful of Daniel Roxo: he was regarded by them as either a vagabond, or as a few phrased it, the ultimate "barbarian,"—something that I was told by several serving officers after his name had been mentioned, usually in the mess. One source referred to him as an unruly, undisciplined civilian who "used unorthodox methods to get the job done."

There was no question that the majority of adversaries on the government side resented his hard-won success, based first on good organization and only second on his exceptionally detailed counter-guerrilla methodology, which he'd managed to inculcate into his men. In retrospect, they could not have been more wrong because his single most important forte in the bush among his men was discipline.

I was told by an ex-officer after the war had ended that the *povo*, "the peasants" [Portuguese conscripts sent to Africa to fight the war] "knew absolutely nothing about Daniel and invented the most fantastic stories about his abilities and exploits, thus falsely creating his legendary status."

It was all rubbish, coming from officers who preferred life in the comparative safety of the barracks and very rarely put themselves in the firing line. Some of these youngsters—fresh out of university in Portugal and commissioned in the Portuguese Army—never saw any real action, even though the war lasted more than a decade.

Undeterred, and with the increase in guerrilla activity, Governor Costa Matos made the decision to use Daniel and his men as a "Search and Destroy" unit in his Niassa Province. Initial instructions were clear: Roxo and his men should not venture further than 100km from Vila Cabral. He stressed that should the squad find itself in serious trouble, they would have no helicopter support. The unit was renamed *Milícia de Intervenção* or "intervention militia."

Daniel's fighting group, in effect, was a kind of "private army" of the government of Niassa whose prime function was to track down guerrillas by spending a few days or longer out in the bush and then return to camp in Vila Cabral. During that rest period, they would also be tasked to protect the area. Daniel's men would patrol around Vila Cabral in small groups of between three or four men and in the process mix with the local population and gather information.

Other local militias in Mozambique were there to protect and intervene around a specific area of responsibility. They had a variety of names such as *Milícia de Protecção* (defense militia under command of a Portuguese police official), also commonly known as *Milícias de Aldeamento*. There was also a militia set up to protect the railways that was called *Milícia dos Caminhos de Ferro*.

Ultimately, a militia was established in Tete on the Zambezi in 1972 which people also mention when Daniel Roxo is discussed. But that was only used for local defense and was not an intervention force like Roxo's.

After General de Arriaga started the GEs in Cabo Delgado, new groups of "militia" were set up between 1971 and 1974 to act like intervention militias, but the GEs were part of the army and not civilians like Daniel and his men. Only army personnel or ex-soldiers would be used for these units and no turned terrorists were allowed to join the GEs.

It was also during this period that Daniel realized the only way to fight and beat the terrorists was to engage them on their own terms. To achieve this, he had to ensure that both he and his men were better armed, a good deal better trained and motivated than the enemy they were facing.

Essentially, Daniel Roxo—though crucially involved in the war—was a civilian. His title was "*Comandante das Milícias*" and not "*Chefe do Posto*" as some have suggested. His rank was the equivalent of a sergeant or at best, lieutenant in the army, or possibly a sub-*Chefe de Polícia da PSP* (who also had command of militia or GE groups). If the Portuguese authorities had ever declared a state of emergency (and they came close in March 1974), he and his men would have been integrated into the defense force: Daniel probably with the rank of sergeant, and some of his men becoming corporals.

It has been said, but never confirmed that Daniel was asked by the military in 1965–66 to assist with the training of the new Portuguese conscripts that were being sent to Mozambique in his somewhat esoteric arts of bush warfare. These conscripts, mainly from metropolitan areas of Portugal, knew nothing of the tactics or skills that would be needed to survive in the African bush, never mind fight seasoned FRELIMO guerrillas.

That was simply not true, maintains Dunkley. He would assist with military operations and act as a guide, but the military authorities never asked for formal bush training with Roxo and his squad of irregulars.

Over the period October 1966 to November 1967, it was estimated that the army in Niassa Province killed 221 FRELIMO fighters and captured six, so it would seem that a combination of Daniel's intelligence-gathering and his assistance with the Portuguese troops in the field was paying dividends. But these were limited because one would have expected a bigger tally considering the substantial force that the guerrillas had deployed.

In 1966, Colonel Nuno Viriato Tavares Melo Egídio replaced Governor Costa Matos as governor of Vila Cabral. Governor Egídio's brother was a civil administrator in Vila Cabral and he was to become his secretary as soon as he took over the governorship. Informed sources believe that it was Governor Costa Matos who had championed Daniel's career but that Governor Egídio's brother also knew the value of Daniel and told his brother that he should keep the services of Daniel and his men.

It was at this point that Daniel's team was increased and given additional duties to undertake pseudo-operations against FRELIMO; this meant that Daniel and his men were to become a fully-fledged fighting unit that would attack areas under FRELIMO control. It was also due to the influence of Governor Egídio that the army was not to have any control over Daniel or his men: the army could request the assistance of Daniel, but not make any plans for this so-called private *milícia*.

Governor Egídio on the other hand would often request the assistance of the air force to assist Daniel if he needed it and, as can be imagined, this kind of demand, due to no fault of Daniel, sometimes led to strained relations between the regular military and himself.

In 1966, Mário Tomé, who joined the Armed Forces Movement that eventually toppled the government in Lisbon—and went on to become a member of Portugal's parliament for the Communist Party from 1980–1993—conducted missions in the Niassa Province with Daniel and for his actions in one of these operations he was recommended for and awarded his *Cruz de Guerra*. Tomé was later heard to comment to colleagues that Daniel had always been a very fair person and at one stage indicated that on a number of operations if Daniel and his men captured ammunition, mines or other equipment, he would give them to the troops so they could use this materiel to show their superiors the results of their efforts in the operation.

On one operation in 1967 Daniel himself needed the help of the air force after having been shot in the legs while on an operation in the Malapisia district of Niassa, and had to be evacuated to hospital by helicopter.

By early 1968 Daniel's unit included a number of former guerrillas, the majority "turned" FRELIMO fighters and shortly afterwards he and his men were involved in an operation that was conducted north of Vila Cabral in April 1968. The Portuguese High Command named it *Operação Marte* (Operation *Mars*).

Daniel was there with 26 of his men and supported by 90 men from 4 Commando Company of the Special Forces based in Vila Cabral.

During that operation he and his men were responsible for killing eight terrorists and the commandos 14. Six FRELIMO insurgents were captured and over a ton of arms, ammunition as well as documentation seized. In contrast, Roxo lost one man, not during the operation itself, but in a mishap on the way in. Some of the arms seized that day were:

- 3× 12.7mm anti-aircraft guns
- 15× Simonov rifles
- 7× Kalashnikovs
- 8× various pistols
- 1× G3 rifle
- 86× anti-personnel mines

Daniel's name and those of 13 men from 4 Commando were mentioned in dispatches as having distinguished themselves during the operation.

Another event that emerged in 1968 is that when a bunch of FRELIMO guerrillas attacked the local village of Ngoo on the shores of Lake Malawi with RPGs and machine-gun fire, a number of villagers were killed and wounded. Daniel was requested to track down the attackers.

By Day Two, he had managed to get very close to the fleeing group because they were moving slowly because of their wounded. Also, the insurgents had dispersed over a wide area.

Roxo decided to hold back and see where they were headed. On the third day he and his men were compromised and he was forced to attack, killing and wounding quite a few and capturing another large supply of arms and ammunition.

It is worth mentioning that Daniel was regarded by the majority of the Whites living in the areas where he operated as having some kind of divine protection. Local Africans—and FRELIMO cadres in particular—saw the man as either a demi-god or having magic powers like a witchdoctor. It was possibly stories like this that led them to believe that he possessed the ability to actually bewitch people. Cases in point:

> A FRELIMO cadre that had been captured by Daniel and his men was showing Daniel a secret track back to a FRELIMO camp. The man had been placed third in line with one of Daniel's men and Daniel himself in front of him. Daniel and his man walked over a landmine; the FRELIMO cadre was not that lucky and lost his leg when the landmine went off.
>
> Another time three FRELIMO were laying in ambush as Daniel and a few of his men made their way to a river, just before the men opened fire, a swarm of angry bees attacked the ambushers. They dropped their AK-47s and ran for the safety of the water, where they were captured by Daniel's men and not a shot was fired.
>
> One time when Daniel was ambushed by FRELIMO, one of the cadres with an RPG who was tracking Daniel's moves got very nervous and prematurely fired the rocket towards Daniel, but it hit a tree close to them and killed not only the RPG gunner but two others who were unfortunate to be in the vicinity.

On July 12, 1969, General Kaúlza de Arriaga landed in Mozambique and was made commander of the army (July 15, 1969–March 31, 1970).

Rumors persist that de Arriaga had taken a fierce dislike towards Roxo, regarding him as something of a renegade. In fact, there are several unconfirmed reports that he did all that he could to hamstring the man and his militia during the course of his regular duties in the bush.

Dunkley in turn, reckons that this might not be entirely correct. While General de Arriaga did not have a negative influence on Roxo and his men as well as their role in the war and did little to assist him, this was due in part because they came from such very different environments: the general was a conceited aristocrat linked to an important family in the European mainland; Roxo in contrast was decidedly less privileged. In American terms, he was born on the wrong side of the tracks.

For all that, the irregular Roxo was awarded the first of his *Cruz de Guerras* in Lourenço Marques on June 10, 1968. Alípio and his family were on hand to see him later receive the *Cruz de Guerra* (4th Class), the first and only civilian in Mozambique to be awarded that decoration for valor in the face of the enemy. This was to be repeated when he was awarded another in 1973, this time, much more appropriately, 1st Class.

That he received any decorations at all was surprising since Daniel Roxo neither liked nor trusted the majority of the Portuguese officers with whom he came into contact. He felt strongly, and is on record as having stated that their hearts and minds were just not with the Mozambican people. He was also outspoken about the fact, which cannot be denied today, that most were just marking time before they got better positions—perhaps back home or in Lisbon's far-flung colonial holdings in the East.

Part of the resentment that emerged in the regular armed forces stemmed from money made by Roxo and his men. Arms and ammunition captured by Portuguese forces had a bounty attached and the men were working "Freelance" (in effect as mercenaries). It was no secret that Roxo's squad, due to their regular contacts with FRELIMO, brought in a lot of both. It also makes sense that he would have kept some of this hardware for his own militia to use.

And while it is true that Daniel, as a civilian, did not take control over regular troops in the field, in a dangerous situation, any real soldier or officer for that matter, would be willing to take a tip or two under fire from a man with Daniel's pedigree. He normally operated independently, but on occasion did assist regular Portuguese units in operations. Nevertheless, he would not have allowed his command over his own men to be meddled with.

In 1971 the DGS (the *Direção-Geral da Segurança Social*, Mozambique's secret police force which replaced PIDE) wanted to meet with Governor Egídio in a bid to persuade him to have Roxo and his men join the DGS. This was about the same time that Oscar Cardosa was transferred from Angola to Mozambique to set up "*Flecha*" style operations under the auspices of DGS.

This never happened, and for several reasons. Both Governor Egídio and Daniel had no interest in becoming involved with DGS. For his part, General de Arriaga had other plans for the military in Mozambique.

Daniel Roxo's "weapon of choice" throughout the war was always the AK-47. He always maintained that it was a much better firearm than the G3 issue weapon of the Portuguese Army. On operations he always carried a bush knife and a Walther PPK sidearm. Out in the bush, he tended to wear camouflage and is reputed to have slept in his clothes, which is not unusual when you're on a mission in the interior.

He always left a "calling card" on the bodies of the men he or his men killed. That had a black cross on a white background: the message, always written in very plain Portuguese was: "This man died. Why? Because he was armed and doing malice in Mozambique, on behalf of the leaders of FRELIMO, who want to sell this land over to the foreign communists, the Russians and Chinese."

He would sometimes add a rider to the effect that the dead man was making ordinary people suffer so that his leaders could live the good life abroad.

This unconventional combatant was closely involved with the *Flechas* and their only operation in Mozambique was in September 1973, roughly a month after General Basto Machado became commander-in-chief of Mozambique. His unit comprised 50 men, all from the Niassa Province and the unit was billeted in Vila Cabral and subjected to weeks of physical training prior to what was termed an "exercise." The role of Roxo and his men was essential: they knew the area of operations intimately and were also regarded as an additional form of insurance should the *Flechas* come into contact with FRELIMO.

***

Once FRELIMO had taken over Mozambique after the army mutiny in Lisbon—the country became fully independent on June 25, 1975—Daniel Roxo did not see himself staying after the war. He had made his share of enemies and like many of his associates, was aware that the majority of those who had opposed the revolutionaries in the past, either in the field or politically, simply disappeared.

Aware of his record and his capabilities, Lisbon's military authorities, by now faced with their own insurgency on the opposite side of the continent, wasted little time in persuading this veteran bush fighter that they had a place for him in the developing war on the southern fringes of Angola, at that time also independent and under the auspices of the Soviet Union. He was to join the ranks of an elite Special Forces unit in the South African Army, the Reconnaissance Regiment, or more familiarly, the Recces.

He was killed while doing what he did best in a clandestine operation against FAPLA (People's Armed Forces for the Liberation of Angola), deep inside Angola early in 1976.

Though the exact circumstances surrounding his death have never been released, we know that Daniel Roxo, part of South Africa's Battle Group Foxbat, was sent as part of a small group to engage an Angolan force of more than a thousand men, many of them Cuban.

There were losses on both sides in that brief, bitter exchange, and Angola's dead included Commandant Raul Diaz Argüelles, commander of Fidel Castro's Expeditionary Force.

That engagement, known as the "Battle for Bridge 14" left more than 400 FAPLA troops dead. South African losses in contrast were four men killed in action; including SADF Sergeant Danny Roxo who, on his own, was responsible for taking out 11 of the enemy, including four Cubans.

The Role of African Troops in Lisbon's Wars

By João Paulo Borges Coelho of the Eduardo Mondlane University, Maputo, Mozambique.[1]

It has never been disputed by the Portuguese that without locally recruited forces, Lisbon would have been forced out of Africa much sooner than was the case. Though recruitment of *indigenes* started slowly—in large part because white settler communities regarded armed black people in their societies as a potential threat—a good deal of study went into how the French and British developed a sustainable counter-insurgency doctrine that included African troops.

Indeed, part of its success was due to the ability of the Portuguese army to recruit and train a substantial array of specialized forces that proved to be excellent fighters. Their numbers included enemy guerrillas, having been captured, were forced to "cooperate." Many of these "turncoats" served with distinction within units composed largely of fighters that had switched sides—among them the *Flechas*. It is notable that Britain did exactly the same during the Malayan Emergency as well as the Mau Mau Rebellion in Kenya. The French too, in the Algerian war of independence. João Paulo Borges Coelho explains:

On April 25, 1974, a military coup in Lisbon paved the way to an abrupt end of the long Portuguese colonial adventure and, more narrowly, of a decade of fighting in Mozambique and 13 years collectively in the three African provinces of Angola, Portuguese Guinea and Mozambique. These wars left profound marks on the shape of the economies and societies of all three countries, none of which have fully recovered from the civil wars that followed independence.

One of these marks was a legacy of thousands of Africans with a past of fighting side by side with the Portuguese defense forces against independence.

This study seeks to discuss the historical rationale for such participation, besides shedding some light on the post-independence impacts it produced, which are still far from fully understood.

It is almost a truism to say that the colonization of the African continent would have been impossible without local collaboration. The stereotyped picture of immensely superior European forces defeating small, fragile and unarticulated African resistances rarely corresponds to the historical truth. Much closer to reality is the picture of European officials able to foster and manage internal contradictions, attracting African forces into their orbit to make them fight other African forces in order to install and preserve the colonial order.

One of the more interesting observations provided by João Paulo Borges Coelho, author of this dissertation, was published almost a century before and came from Joaquim Mouzinho de Albuquerque. In a document titled: *A reorganização dos exércitos ultramarinos*, he declared "…if it isn't to be a poor character with little utility, the European soldier will cost us too much. It is therefore natural that to the African, more adapted to the climate and much cheaper, the role will be reserved of *chair à canon*…"[2]

In the two world wars of the last century, African troops fought in defense of the colonial powers' interests both in the African theater and elsewhere. Particularly after the 1950s, when nationalist movements began to fight for their independence throughout the African continent, African participation in the struggle to preserve the old colonial order acquired considerable importance.

In the face of the decreasing resistance of locals to military service, the 1914 regulation prescribed the creation of a military reserve, which permitted the engagement of 25,000 Africans, or 44 percent of the total force, in the struggle against the German invasion of Northern Mozambique during World War I.

Indeed, former U.S. Navy Captain John P. Cann makes the point that the German experience with locally recruited forces, particularly the Askaris, was considered in Mozambique as highly positive. In 1915, he tells us, the German force in Tanganyika was composed of 2,200 European troops, 11,100 regular African troops and 3,200 irregulars, in 24 companies, each one roughly with a dozen Europeans and 300 Africans.[3]

From this point on, service in the armed forces began to be perceived as an important way of "nationalizing" the African population of the colonies. The regulation of June 1933 stipulated distinct service branches for "common blacks" and for "non-indigenous blacks," the latter being enrolled in the same service branches as Europeans born in the colonies. Africans were to be registered in the ranks under a Portuguese Christian name, and it was expected that military service would act as a powerful "civilizing" mechanism or, in the words of General Norton de Matos, as "one of the most effective mechanisms for opening a breach in the tenebrous primitive civilizations."

Local collaboration was fundamental to guaranteeing the colonial project. In this respect Portugal was no exception, and often resorted to the recruitment of Africans in her war effort, particularly since the so-called "Pacification Campaigns" of the late 19th century.

The present study looks at this collaboration in the context of the wars for independence in the former Portuguese colonies—a collaboration that has to be perceived at various levels, since its nature, importance and intensity varied throughout the period in which the wars were fought. Wars tend evidently to involve everybody within the area they cover. Here it will be useful, however, to narrow the focus and look at the involvement which directly derived from the colonial strategy—the "African involvement as strategy" or, as it was called in those days, the *Africanization* of the war effort.

This approach requires an historical perspective. Participation by African troops was uneven throughout the 13 years of the Portuguese colonial military campaigns. It began on the margins, limited to secondary roles or, at the war fronts, to population control, intelligence gathering and reconnaissance by informers and scouts. African troops became increasingly important, however, and on the eve of the military coup in April 1974, Africans accounted for more than 50 percent of the contingent fighting the war.

***

After World War II, the Portuguese Army, as part of the entire colonial system, began to be forced to change as a result of international pressures and as the nationalist wars were anticipated and approaching.

The *Estado Novo* was forced to repeal the *Estatuto dos Indígenas* which had assured for so long that the vast majority of the population remained without access to the status of citizens, and this required the army to deal with a new and unexpected problem: that of having a growing African contingent in its ranks. Until then the infantry recognized the categories of commissioned soldiers (white soldiers born in Portugal or in her overseas provinces), overseas soldiers (African *assimilados*), and native soldiers (Africans under the *indigenato* regime).

Forced to change this system, the regime, through the Decree 43.267 of October 24, 1960, introduced the new categories of 1st, 2nd and 3rd class soldier, in practice corresponding to the previous ones. A little later, this too had to be changed, and although the color of the soldiers' skin ceased to be a criterion, two classes were established on the basis of formal education and, in particular, of the ability to speak Portuguese correctly.

In practical terms, this again meant a perpetuation of the old distinctions. Even so, however, the door was opening ever so slightly for the Africans.

Faced with the threat represented by the Africanization of its army, a certain segment of the regime's establishment had every motive to resist. Firstly, ideological reasons played a role—paradigmatic in this respect is the strong position taken by Kaúlza de Arriaga, who in 1960, as Subsecretary of State for Aeronautics, wrote to Salazar that "a defense concept based on black troops is impossible, independently of the kind of white control … It is therefore necessary to reduce the strength and size of our black troops."

This view, undoubtedly common among the upper echelons, is very well conveyed by Felgas who, commenting on the consequences of a weak metropolitan contribution to the army, wrote that "it is not difficult to foresee that disorder would prevail, as well as insecurity, as happened in the first months of independence of the ex-Belgian Congo. Of course, we could adopt the same solution for Angola, to promote soldiers to colonels and corporals to generals. But the results would be identical: an army deprived of strength, cohesion, prestige and discipline."

Associated with this view was one that, despite all the integrationist propaganda of the Nation in Arms, considered the Africans as little less than potential terrorists, in the international context of the Cold War. This led the Chief-of-Staff to write, as late as 1962, that engaging the native masses in a military effort posed great risks, since they were all heavily exposed to the "propaganda of the enemy."

As a result, and despite the strong effort to prepare the army for the African campaigns, undertaken from the late 1950s onward, the old "philosophy" that had formed the defense and security system in the colonial territories remained basically unchanged, with "expeditionary forces" from Portugal coming to fight the colonial wars and the locally recruited ones playing a limited and secondary role as second-line troops.

That this was indeed so is clear from the constant increase in metropolitan contingents as the wars started; first in Angola in March 1961, and then in Guinea in January 1963 and in Mozambique in September 1964.

Table 8.1 documents a 100% increase in the total metropolitan contingent during the first half of the period of conflict (until 1967). Figures in Table 8.2 show a correspondingly modest increase in the numbers of locally recruited forces during the same period (from 18% in 1961 to 25% in 1967).

Table 8.1 Metropolitan Troops in Portugal's Three African Wars (1961–1973)

Date	Angola	Mozambique	Guinea	Total
1961	28,477	8,209	3,736	40,422
1962	33,760	8,852	4,070	46,682
1963	34,530	9,243	8,336	52,109
1964	37,418	10,132	12,874	60,424
1965	41,625	13,155	14,640	69,420
1966	38,519	19,550	18,868	76,937
1967	43,051	23,164	18,421	84,636
1968	37,547	22,717	19,559	78,823
1969	36,911	23,286	22,866	83,063
1970	36,174	22,633	22,487	81,294
1971	36,127	21,795	23,402	81,324
1972	34,676	22,657	24,036	81,369
1973	37,773	23,891	25,610	87,274

Source: Estado-Maior do Exército, 1988 I: 260.

Table 8.2 Locally Recruited Troops in the Wars (and percentages of total deployment)

Date	Angola	Mozambique	Guinea	Total
1961	5,000 (14.9)	3,000 (26.8)	1,000 (21.1)	9,000 (18.2)
1962	11,165 (24.9)	3,000 (25.3)	1,000 (19.7)	15,165 (24.5)
1963	12,870 (27.2)	5,003 (35.1)	1,314 (13.6)	19,187 (26.9)
1964	15,075 (28.7)	7,917 (43.9)	2,321 (15.3)	25,313 (29.5)
1965	15,448 (27.1)	9,701 (42.4)	2,612 (15.1)	27,761 (28.5)
1966	17,297 (31.0)	11,038 (36.1)	1,933 (09.3)	30,268 (28.2)
1967	14,369 (25.0)	11,557 (33.3)	3,229 (14.9)	29,155 (25.6)
1968	20,683 (35.5)	13,898 (38.0)	3,280 (14.4)	37,861 (32.7)
1969	18,663 (33.6)	15,810 (40.4)	3,715 (14.4)	38,188 (31.4)
1970	19,059 (34.5)	16,079 (41.5)	4,268 (16.0)	39,406 (32.6)
1971	25,933 (41.8)	22,710 (51.0)	5,808 (19.9)	54,451 (40.1)
1972	25,461 (42.2)	24,066 (51.5)	5,921 (19.8)	55,448 (40.5)
1973	27,819 (42.4)	27,572 (53.6)	6,425 (20.1)	61,816 (41.4)

Source: *Estado-Maior do Exército, 1988 I: 261.*

Table 8.1 reveals more modest increases in metropolitan troops during the second half of the war, while Table 8.2 shows correspondingly a much more pronounced increase in locally recruited troops, whose numbers reached nearly half of the total contingent in 1973.

Around 1968 there clearly occurred a certain break in the balance between metropolitan and local forces, with more marked increases in the latter.

This raises the question why, despite all the entrenched resistance discussed above, did the *Estado Novo* and its military apparatus change their attitude so dramatically?

Obviously, the fact that this change occurred when Marcello Caetano replaced Salazar as President of the Cabinet was not purely coincidental. However, there are many other factors that also help to explain it.

The main argument for this Africanization of the Portuguese colonial army has been based on Portugal's recruiting problems. In the late 1960s, according to Henriksen, Portugal, after Israel, had the highest percentage of people in arms in the world, with an annual increase of 11 percent between the 49,422 documented in 1961, and the 149,090 documented in 1973. In parallel, the percentage of deserters also doubled, from 11.6 to 20.9, for reasons linked both with avoidance of military service and with the fact that Portugal was a chronic provider of migrant labor to Europe and the Americas, through a process that gradually drained a population of potential recruits already small from the start.

To these quantitative difficulties, qualitative ones also have to be added, in the sense that the expeditionary contingents had serious problems of adaptation to the African war theaters and that, as the years passed, the Portuguese army faced an acute shortage of commanding officers, with obvious consequences for its military efficiency.

The number of officers graduating from the military academy rose sharply from 68 in 1962 to 146 in 1967, but from then on started to suffer an abrupt decline to only 40 in 1973, as a result of lack of volunteers. In consequence, the military authorities were forced to mobilize conscripts to fill the huge gaps in the professional cadres.[4]

Besides the issue of sheer human numbers, the financial difficulties that Portugal experienced in coping with the three wars also shed some explanation on Africanization. According to this argument, the burden became so unbearable that the progressive sharing of the war effort with the colonies, through increasing local recruitment and financial participation, was a way to minimize the weight. Moreover, this would seem to be quite well in line with the old Salazar principle of involving each colony in the resolution of its own problems.

Notwithstanding these valid explanations, the shortage of metropolitan men and the high costs of war were not the only reasons behind the Africanization process. Despite such difficulties and the fact that they were almost insurmountable, Portugal was indeed capable of sustaining some level of increase in the numbers of her metropolitan troops, and the costs involved were basically covered, even if at the price of going to the brink of economic and financial exhaustion.

Further factors have then to be brought in to explain the process of Africanization. The first, which reveals one of the several internal contradictions of the *Estado Novo*, is of a historical and ideological nature. It was based on the appeal of the integrationist ideology of the Empire and its principle of race miscegenation, which translated into the revival of white settlement plans and into the "promotion" of the African populations, particularly under the short but decisive mandate of Adriano Moreira as overseas minister.

In a sense, it bore elements of continuity with the early days of Salazar's regime, when important steps were made to include an African layer at the foundation of the colonial state and administration, with the involvement of local African authorities in population censuses, tax collection, and labor recruitment in their areas of jurisdiction.

As mentioned above, this "attitude" also had led to the establishment of defense forces based on the inclusion of local troops in secondary roles. The overwhelming majority of these local troops were Africans, who served mostly as auxiliaries, servants in the barracks, and, given their knowledge of the terrain, as informers and scouts.

However, the nationalist wars also introduced a new phenomenon in the sense that a much broader African involvement became required, well beyond such targeted recruitment: early on in the process the colonial authorities understood that the war was also about conquering the population. The "philosophy" of the *Estado Novo*, mixed with the first counter-insurgency techniques to "win" the population, provided the core of a colonial psycho-social doctrine based on the two fundamental concepts of *comandamento* (command) and *accionamento* (driving, setting in motion).[5]

These served as a framework for the creation, in the early 1960s, of local militias of several kinds in the rural areas of the three colonies, as second-line troops under the authority of the civil administration and based on the principle of self-defense against subversive attacks. In 1961, Adriano Moreira, as Overseas Minister, issued legislative diplomas, which created the Militia Corps as second-line forces in the African colonies.

The militia took a wide range of organizational shapes, from very informal schemes of village forces acting under the authority of village chiefs, as happened in Angola, to more institutionally militarized groups assuring the defense of the *aldeamentos*, the protected villages formed along the lines of what the British had practiced in their counter-insurgency war in Malaysia, or the North Americans in Vietnam.[6]

As the war situation aggravated, and with the corresponding difficulties experienced by the armed forces, the militia contingents were brought into more active roles exceeding the traditional defensive ones.

Paradigmatic in this respect was the case of Guinea, where, besides the normal militias, special ones were created for offensive operations in their home areas. This new concept, which led to the emergence of very efficient troops, mixed the old colonial tradition with new counter-insurgency theories. General Carlos Fabião, the so-called "father" of these new militias, would say with respect to their creation: "I studied, I read ancient documents about the pacification campaigns of the end of last century [19th], and concluded that past wars in Africa had been fought more or less with the locals, particularly in Guinea."

These theories, to which the Portuguese high military commanders were systematically exposed from the second half of the 1950s onward, had as one of their core concepts the so-called "same element theory," according to which the guerrillas could be fought more efficiently by troops mirroring their organization, weaponry, knowledge of the terrain, and even race, i.e. by African combat units.

These theories became more extensively absorbed at a time when the need to adapt and to reinforce the Portuguese troops became more pressing.

The changes that started to occur at this point brought a new meaning to the concept of Africanization. From now on, this would not imply merely a growing percentage of locally recruited or black individuals incorporated in the regular forces fighting the nationalists, in the same sense as the French *jeunissement* in Indochina, for example.

More than that, it now meant a process of creating and fostering combat units of Africans operating more or less irregularly and autonomously, and with high levels of operational efficiency. It must be said that this change in attitude, which implied increased trust in the Africans, even if forced, was not sudden, nor was it just due to theoretical considerations.

In fact, in the second half of the 1960s, the military were facing serious problems related not only to a shortage of troops but also to the question of what to do with the Africans demobilized from the regular army. Old suspicions that Africans demobilized from the regular force, already capable of handling weaponry, might simply join the nationalist guerrillas, lay behind new efforts to create auxiliary troops where those men would be kept under the control of military or civil authorities.

Moreover, these troops were much cheaper than the regular ones and their eventual casualties were much "less repercussion-rich" than those of metropolitan forces.

This Africanization was carried out differently in the three territories of Angola, Guinea and Mozambique, not just because of different local and regional contexts, but also owing to the different attitudes and views of the respective commanders.

The period when Marcello Caetano was in power roughly corresponds to an important decentralization in the conduct of the wars. If formerly these were conducted in a relatively centralized manner from Lisbon, now three generals with strong views were appointed to run them from the provinces. Spínola took charge of Guinea as Governor and Commander-in-Chief in May 1968; Kaúlza de Arriaga went to Mozambique as Commander-in-Chief in March 1970; and Costa Gomes was appointed as Commander-in-Chief of Angola in April 1970.

The results likewise varied: while in Guinea, General Spínola planned and fought for the creation of a regular, entirely coherent African army mirroring the metropolitan one, having perhaps in mind a future federation of Portuguese-speaking states; in Angola the African irregular units were much more informal and diverse in nature. Mozambique somehow combined aspects of the two.

The first unit entirely consisting of Africans was probably the *Tropas Especiais* (Special Troops, commonly known by the acronym TEs), which emerged in 1966 in Cabinda, when Alexandre Taty, a former UPA/FNLA cadre, deserted to the Portuguese side with 1,200 men. Organized and controlled by PIDE, the Portuguese secret police, they started to be used in action against the MPLA, which after having initiated operations in the *Dembos* in Northern Angola, had spread its guerrilla activities to Cabinda in late 1964. The TEs operated in Cabinda, their home area, as well as in Zaire and Uíge, in Northern Angola.

Also in 1966, the war epicenter in Angola moved to the East, with the start of UNITA activities in that area and with the opening of MPLA's Eastern Front, which became a threat to the Moxico and Cuando Cubango areas in the Southeast. Besides dispatching a TE unit to the area, PIDE also began to create what would become its private ethnic army.

The first experiment was conducted by Inspector Oscar Cardosa, who worked in Cuando Cubango with Bushmen (San) groups serving as scouts and information gatherers, and soon as true combat units, exploiting the cultural distance between these small men of San origin and the Bantu populations of the remaining areas.

Cardosa's subsequent comments on the *Flechas* are interesting: He mentioned, in particular: "they didn't need logistical support. They could live [on] nothing, with special ability to find food and water and we really some had good operational results with them. We never had a desertion from the *Flechas'* ranks."

The experiment was so successful in operational terms that the concept soon spread to other areas, particularly Luso (Luena) and Luanda-Caxito, where the *Flechas* unit was almost entirely composed of ex-MPLA guerrillas. Towards the end of the war almost all PIDE sub-delegations in Angola's war zones had their own private units of *Flechas*.

A little later, in 1968, the military also favored the creation of their own irregular troops, the *Grupos Especiais* (or GEs, Special Groups), formed of local volunteers who were submitted to the same training as the regular military forces.

Organized in combat groups of about 30 men each, they were controlled by the military, usually one Portuguese battalion having one or two of these groups nearby. Besides the fact that they were cheaper than the regular troops, one of the advantages gained from the creation of this force, which operated in the North, East and South of Angola, was their knowledge of local languages, culture, and terrain.

The sharp increase in the number of GE groups also had to do, however, with problems in furnishing replacements for regular troops that had concluded their operational commission.

Meantime, the infiltration into South West Africa by SWAPO guerrillas southwards very much concerned the South Africans, who were ready to meet the costs of Portuguese reinforcements at battalion level in the area. However, the Portuguese could do little more than reinforce the area with some extra GE groups. Significantly, Lisbon was already getting some support in South Angola from SAAF (South African Air Force) Alouette helicopter gunships.

Also, in the Eastern area of Angola, groups of Katangese gendarmes formerly supporting Moise Tshombé crossed the border into Angola during the second semester of 1967, and were received as political refugees by the Portuguese authorities.

In February 1969 they formed the Front for National Liberation of Congo, with the objective of overthrowing the Mobutu regime. At this time, facing an acute shortage of forces in the Eastern part of the territory, the Portuguese authorities launched the project *Fidelidade* (Fidelity), based on the promise to support the "liberation" of Zaire in exchange for the participation of this force in counter-insurgency operations in Angola, particularly against the MPLA.

Code-named *Fiéis*, they received military supplies and training from the Portuguese armed forces, along with political supervision from the PIDE. This became one of the most effective forces in counter-insurgency operations, despite chronic problems with discipline that translated into frequent riots and desertions and that stemmed from complaints about low pay and from the fact that these men did not feel they were receiving enough support from the Portuguese government in their struggle against Mobutu's Zaire.

At the same time and a little further to the South, a similar project, codenamed Operation Colt was implemented by the Portuguese to receive a smaller group of Zambian ANC dissidents who arrived in Angola in 1967. It says a lot that both the Rhodesians and South Africans expressed their reservations towards Operation Colt mounted by the Portuguese, on the grounds that they did not believe the Zambian ANC had enough credibility to destabilize Zambia at the time.

In 1968, PIDE organized them into a combat group of 45 elements code-named *Leais*, under the same kind of agreement as the one established with the *Fiéis*, namely to fight against the Angolan liberation movements in exchange for support in their struggle to overthrow Kenneth Kaunda's Zambian regime.

The wide, flexible, and diverse utilization of African irregular troops that was practiced in Angola did not have any parallel in the other war theaters. It was the result of several specific factors. The first one was, of course, the vast area to be covered in counter-insurgency activities, together with the great difficulties the Portuguese had in replacing, let alone increasing, the number of their troops, and together with the inevitable financial aspects.

The second factor was the competition among the three nationalist movements, which gave rise to desertions by trained guerrillas who went to join counter-insurgency operations.

Thirdly and very importantly, it is necessary to take into account the attitude of General Costa Gomes, who managed to establish a good relationship between the military and PIDE, one that undoubtedly allowed the spread of this kind of irregular warfare, so that unlike many of his fellow generals he was able to shift a significant operational burden onto the autonomous activity of the African units.

Interviewed in 2001, General Costa Gomes said that "the reason why I got along with PIDE was the following: When I arrived in Angola already as Commander-in-Chief, I heard from the Department of Operations of a conflict which had occurred involving PIDE's *Flechas* and a Commando company of the army that resulted in casualties. I asked myself, how could PIDE be waging a war without the Commander-in-Chief knowing about it? I asked the governor to convene a meeting with the people that mattered and told them: PIDE can do whatever wars but not on behalf of the Governor or PIDE itself. It has to be on my behalf."

Interviewed by the *Washington Post* a decade before, in March 1971, he'd made the point that "the African troops combating against subversion are increasing in number. Their training and experience rendered them outstanding professionals." And in another interview with *Época* magazine, on December 21,1979, he declared: "TEs are a very cohesive group (…) GEs are growing from year to year … as do the *Flechas*. All the irregular troops have proven their merit. That is why we will make efforts to increase their numbers."

Finally, besides the previously discussed advantages inherent in the employment of foreign irregular troops, the colonial authorities in Angola also had in mind interfering at a broader regional level, keeping Zaire and Zambia in particular under pressure.

***

In Guinea, developments were quite different in this regard. When the war started, locally recruited militia groups were created to assure the "self-defense" of the populations, freeing the expeditionary army for offensive operations.

By 1966, Guinea already had 18 militia companies, and the authorities were requesting funds to create more, although still acknowledging the risks involved in having to deal with a "considerable volume of people armed, equipped and trained."

The substitution of General Schulz, a quite conventional and conservative commander, by General António de Spínola brought profound changes. Through selective recruitment among normal militias, he fostered the creation of Special Militias organized in combat groups and operating fairly autonomously.

Spínola structured these militias along the structural lines of the Portuguese army, in companies subdivided into platoons. He faced a tough battle with the upper echelons to end the distinction between metropolitan and locally recruited soldiers, arguing that discrimination against the latter involved serious risks for the Portuguese African campaign, and threatening that its perpetuation "would force us to redefine our counter-insurgency policy based on African forces."

This conflict continued when Spínola pressed to increase the number of special militias. Of the five requested in 1968 only two had been authorized by 1970. Lisbon's resistance clearly had to do with financial constraints, and also with fears that "the informality brought on by the Africanization of the war is spreading to an informality of procedures."

It was perhaps because of this, and in an attempt to counteract the tendency of provincial commanders to keep creating new African forces that, at the end of 1971, the Minister of Defense ordered the centralization in Lisbon of all expenses relating to the irregular troops.

In 1970, Spínola again engaged in a struggle with the upper echelons in order to create—using elite African combatants from the militias and the organizational pattern of the Portuguese army—companies of African Commandos.

These were structured very much like normal commando companies that had been created in the other theaters, but were manned entirely by Africans and carrying out very special combat operations both within Guinea and in Guinea-Conakry and Senegal. The discussion of the project took two years, an inordinately long time, but not unusual for the Portuguese command structure. Only in 1972 did they become operational, which was not long before Lisbon's military putsch.

The Centers for Commando Instruction (CICs) were created in Guinea in 1964, Angola in 1965, and Mozambique in 1969, for training these elite troops. Many of the Guinea African commando combatants were trained in Angola.

***

In Mozambique, this process occurred a little later and, in a manner that combined features of the other two cases, as well as some that were specific to the area.

The first stages of the war unfolded under the command of General Augusto dos Santos, an admirer of the new counter-insurgency theories. It says a lot that this commander took it upon himself to translate Sir Robert Thompson's seminal book on unconventional warfare, *Defeating Communist Insurgency*.

In the mid-1960s, with Costa Gomes as second-in-command, Dos Santos sponsored important "experiments" involving local militias. One of these led to successful collaboration with the Rhodesian authorities to form units of African scouts, something Al Venter deals with, in collaboration with his old friend Colonel Ron Reid-Daly in his own work *War Stories by Al Venter and Friends.*[7]

However, by 1969 Kaúlza de Arriaga had replaced General Dos Santos. The new Commander-in-Chief had an entirely different way of conducting the war. For a long time, the operational involvement of Africans was limited to local recruitment in the regular army or in commando companies, irregular African units being entirely out of the picture, with the exception of limited paramilitary experiments.

In Mozambique, the first four commando companies were created in Montepuez in 1969, and experienced limited growth, despite their relative operational success, to five in 1970, and eight by the end of the war in 1974. There was also the creation of paramilitary groups linked to PIDE, acting as hunters of wild game and, in fact, gathering intelligence on nationalist guerrilla movements and contacts.

Only in 1973 were the first solutions involving African units implemented on the ground, with the creation of Special Groups of Parachutists and other Special Groups, formed in the central regions of the country on an ethnic basis, recruiting volunteers, and operating in particular in their home areas, in coordination with and under the control of the military.

In contrast with the Angolan case, Kaúlza de Arriaga's reservations with regard to African forces operating outside the military's sphere of control, besides his conflicts with PIDE, probably help to explain why the implementation of a *Flecha*-type project took so long in Mozambique.

The introduction of *Flechas* was being discussed between PIDE and the Rhodesian authorities since 1972. The latter were very much interested in the unfolding events in Mozambique and favored "lighter" and more local alternatives to the way the war was being conducted by Kaúlza de Arriaga.

It is therefore probable that discreet and low profile "experiments" with *Flechas* under the aegis of PIDE were in fact taking place since 1972, despite the difficulties. As late as July 1973, the army refused to supply automatic weapons to the *Flechas*, on grounds that all the lots were already consigned. PIDE approached the South Africans who expressed a willingness to finance the supply. Only in 1974, when Kaúlza de Arriaga had already been dismissed by Marcello Caetano, and on the eve of the military coup that ended the war, did they start to operate on the ground.

***

The comparative analysis of how Africans were used as soldiers by the Portuguese on all three fronts of the colonial wars indicates that, beyond very broad strategic guidelines, the factors that mattered were local context and local commanders. Costa Gomes, perhaps the most successful general, sought good relations with the civilians and employed African units within the framework of a counter-insurgency technique.

Spínola, by contrast, appealed for a more political and psycho-social use of African soldiers. De Arriaga, in contrast, the most conservative of the three (and the most ineffectual) feared African forces beyond his strict and immediate control. He never seemed to have progressed beyond his initial racist perception of Africans as inferior beings and terrorists.

Whatever the approaches and their degree of success in terms of furthering colonial interests, the fact is that on the eve of the war's end, Africanization had been accepted as the only way of maintaining the colonial project, in circles as high as that of the Portuguese Chief-of-Staff.

According to him, African troops were more efficient, more cost-effective, cheaper and susceptible of delivering better results not only in military terms, but also politically. Moreover, if properly organized in militarized villages, "they could fight forever."

In 1974, he therefore proposed a substantial reduction in the number of metropolitan troops and a decentralization of the financial resources thus spared, so that the local commands could create further African units. Clearly, the plan was to promote preconditions for civil war in the African territories, if not politically, at least militarily.

The Portuguese Air Force in Mozambique

By 1960, the Portuguese Air Force (*Força Aérea Portuguesa*, most often referred to by the acronym FAP) had deployed more than 20,000 men and 150 aircraft in Africa: obviously there was somebody in Lisbon aware that there was trouble brewing in the colonies.

These included North American T-6 Harvards, Lockheed PV-2 Harpoons, and Lockheed Neptunes. There were also more modern Republic F-84 Thunderjets and North American F-86G Sabres, as well as G-91 trainer/ground support jets acquired from Italy. Also, the FAP transport air arm operated some 66 Nord-1505 Nord Noratlases, Douglas C-47s in addition to C-54/DC-6s, and Boeing 707 transports.

The Portuguese Air Force had been able to acquire 30 Noratlases from various sources (including 18 from West German squadrons), the elephant symbol of their LTG.62 not only retained but applied to those transporters acquired from other sources. Included too were small numbers of Austers and German-built Dornier Do-27s. Tom Cooper reports:

> Although it has frequently been suggested that that some 85 Aerospatiale Alouette III and Sud Aviation 330 Puma helicopters were under army control during the course of Lisbon's colonial wars, that is not quite correct. The Portuguese Air Force did operate in close cooperation with the army during all the African campaigns—functioning much like the Luftwaffe did during World War II—but each was dominant over its own interests.
>
> Apart from aircraft and helicopters, the FAP included paratroopers in their structure, much to the displeasure of the army. The *Caçadores-Paraquedistas* (literally "Hunter-Paratroops") were an élite force used as the ground arm of the air force and deployed in detachments on those front-line air force bases from where they went into action.
>
> When hostilities started in Angola, airborne troops were dropped from transports such as the Douglas C-54 Skymaster or the Nord Noratlas, but as Alouette III helicopters became available in larger numbers they began to work as heli-borne troops.
>
> With the Alouette III having five seats, the standard routine with companies of *Caçadores-Paraquedistas* was based on squads of 25 men customarily deployed in five helicopters. In

contrast, heli-drops involving paratroopers were made in close coordination with other FAP units, quite often with jet and propeller-driven aircraft as back-up. These were invariably complex operations but those involved soon became remarkably adept at providing what was required.

Another form of air support came from specially equipped "Gunship" helicopters known as "heli-cannons" or, in the lingo, *Lobo Mau*: Alouette IIIs equipped with a single 20mm cannon mounted on the port side of the fuselage, the doors on the left side having been removed. These choppers soon became remarkably effective in providing close cover—or more commonly, top cover—for ground forces either going into the attack or countering ground fire from the enemy.

It was not always so. Despite warnings about a possible insurgency in Mozambique following the 1961 uprising in Angola, the initial government reaction in Lisbon towards a likely FRELIMO invasion from Tanzania was hesitant. For a start, there was a serious lack of military resources after hostilities had kicked off in Angola and Portuguese Guinea. Also, troop levels in Mozambique were limited, but it was felt within top command that any increase in numbers could wait until the threat became a reality. That did not take long.

FRELIMO began its infiltration of northern Mozambique shortly after the movement formally declared that a state of war with Mozambique existed in 1961, but early efforts were largely to establish a presence and recruit (and also shanghai future combatants from remote tribal areas) to the guerrilla movement.

When the first attacks did eventually take place towards the end of 1964, those modest Portuguese military and police elements already in position in the Cabo Delgado and Niassa regions withdrew into their reinforced outposts and were forced to rely on air attack (bombs, air-to-ground rockets as well as napalm) and the occasional land-based foray against known enemy camps. The emphasis until the situation could be remedied was centered strictly on containment.

Indeed, much of what took place defensively was improvised because the air force had very few assets in Mozambique to start with.

By late 1961 there was only a handful of North American T-6G Texans and Douglas C-47s deployed at Beira. These heavily taxed planes flew their first operational sorties early in 1963, targeting some of the first hostile encampments that had been established in the north. Thereafter, things moved quickly.

By 1964, the Portuguese Army had increased its strength in the country to 16,000 troops, and working with the air force, had developed operational airfields at Nampula and Vila Cabral. The FAP followed by increasing the number of deployed aircraft to around a dozen T-6Gs Harvards, eight Lockheed PV-2 Harpoons, a dozen Dornier Do-27s and handful of Alouette III helicopters. At the time it was generally recognized that even if there were double the number of aircraft, the counter-insurgency situation in Mozambique would still be tentative.

Between 1964 and 1966, when the rebels began operating in company-sized units, the war appeared to continue at a pedestrian pace. By 1966, FRELIMO had established a central command to better coordinate activities in the different regions in which the guerrillas operated and had grown in size from a few hundred trained combatants in 1962 to 8,000 five years later

Most of the latter were being trained in Tanzania, where the main instruction camp was located at Kongwa. There were more camps run by Chinese military specialists in Zanzibar, where some of these activities were captured by local freelance cameraman, my old *Rafiki* Mohamed Amin, later to establish his major news agency, Camera Press in Nairobi.

Amin (also known as Mo by his British media pals) was briefly jailed after his Zanzibar exploits, having been charged with sedition. But what mattered was that the news was out. By then too, Soviet aid had become manifest throughout the war zones: apart from AKs and a range of Soviet machine-guns like the RPK-74M and the RPD (as well as their variants) a few heavier weapons like the NSV (also known as the *Utyos*) a 12.7mm caliber heavy machine-gun were also being brought into the fray.

Soviet 82mm medium mortars were routinely deployed by FRELIMO in many of the combat regions, and later, 75mm cannons and RPG-7s (or, more usually, Type 69, their Chinese version). The most effective weapon unquestionably preferred by the guerrillas, was the landmine.

From the start, the rebels concentrated on mine warfare, against which the Portuguese Army remained almost culpably ill-equipped for the duration of the war. In fact, landmines—both anti-tank and anti-personnel—became the single most effective guerrilla weapon of choice in all three African wars in which Lisbon was involved at the time—a prevalence which also became dominant in other Southern African wars that followed, Rhodesia especially.

Throughout, air power was used to seal off guerrilla supply routes across the frontiers and as an immediate reaction to guerrilla attacks, but deployed assets increasingly proved insufficient. When the FAP became involved in the crisis surrounding Rhodesia's Unilateral Declaration of Independence in 1966 and its PV-2s of *Esquadrão* 101 began operating out of Beira to prevent British intervention in Mozambique, they had to be reinforced by eight Republic F-84Gs of 93 Squadron.

In 1968, FRELIMO was reorganized with the division between civilian and military sectors abolished and the militia deployed in sectors, each of which had its own "battalion," consisting of three 150-man companies with their own bases.

The "regular" fighters were backed up by the local People's Militia. This reorganization was foremost possible—but also needed—because Zambia became independent and the new nation began providing bases for FRELIMO as well. The rebels were then able to infiltrate Tete Province, posing a threat to the important Cahora Bassa Dam project, which was intended to provide extensive irrigation, navigation and power once brought on stream.

Meanwhile, Lisbon needed 15,000 soldiers to effectively guard the giant construction site which included the construction of what was to become one of Africa's largest man-made lakes. The intention was that once completed, the dam would partially form a barrier against possible rebel penetrations from Zambia.

About then the rebels began receiving Soviet-made 122mm rockets, and these were frequently used to attack the dam, usually fired from the maximum range of 16 kilometers. However, the rebels never managed to effectively interrupt the work.

***

Because of the ongoing war, the rebel campaign in the Tete region during 1968 was noticeably inhibited by the migration of a large proportion of the native population into Malawi.

There were also factional groups—hard-liners opposed to moderates who were involved in power jockeying within the FRELIMO hierarchy. These efforts resulted in the death of at least one of the movement's senior commanders. In spite of these problems the movement was officially recognized by the Organization of African States, today African Union or AU, which significantly increased both its visibility and its prestige nationally and abroad.

Then, early in 1969 the so-called "Inner Struggle" within the rebel organization reached its apogee.

After the traditionalists had been expelled during the much-heralded Second Congress and their leader Kavandame went over to the Portuguese, the most prominent FRELIMO leader, American-educated Eduardo Mondlane—an outspoken moderate—was murdered by persons unknown. Initially it was believed to be the work of one of his field commanders because he died when a book bomb was hand-delivered to his office in Dar es Salaam. That premise changed when the movement's headquarters in Dar es Salaam fingered Portuguese agents for Mondlane's death, but it remained the subject for much discussion within FRELIMO's command circles for years.

One of the reasons put forward was that the dead man was married to Janet, a White American whom he had met while studying in the United States, but those in the know regarded this as something of a red herring in a bid to deflect attention from the true culprit.

A short while later, Eduardo Mondlane was succeeded by someone who was then regarded as much less moderate than his predecessor—a successful field commander by the name of Samora Machel—and it was under his leadership that the rebels became more vigorous. The guerrillas became more efficient, better organized and a good deal bolder in their attacks.

Using Zambia as a base—President Kenneth Kaunda finally succumbed to Moscow's urging that the guerrilla movement be allowed to break out of the confines of Mozambique's remote northern provinces and open a new front in the Tete region—at roughly 600 kilometers across a well-surfaced road and a hard day's drive from Beira, the country's second city. I did the trip by Land Rover several times and never once traveled in convoy.

Initially, the Portuguese reacted forcefully with air strikes to an invigorated guerrilla onslaught and, for a while, the guerrilla situation deteriorated further when General Kaúlza de Arriaga was appointed force commander in the East African province in May 1969.

Mainstay of Portuguese air operations in 1968—and for most of 1969—were still the venerable T-6 Texans and Dornier Do-27s. Until then, FAP tactics were largely centered on spotting and liaison roles—tasks for which the Dorniers were ideal. The T-6Gs, armed with under-wing machine-gun- and rocket pods predominated, while napalm was increasingly used to disrupt identified enemy positions, as had been the case during earlier phases of the war.

There were several operations where paratroopers were taken into action and dropped by Noratlases, but generally, troops were transported into battle in Rhodesian Fire Force fashion by Alouette III helicopters, a number of which were based at Nacala, still one of the largest cities along the coast in the north.

With FRELIMO extending its areas of operations and obtaining heavier weapons—including some with anti-aircraft capability like the Soviet-supplied 14.5mm caliber weapon (that formed the basis of the ZPU series anti-aircraft guns), more advanced aircraft were required to counter the threat.

***

On December 25, 1968, the first eight Fiat G-91R-4 jet aircraft arrived at Beira Harbor in containers. Despite Christmas and New Year festivities, all were assembled in less than a week and transferred to AB.5, entering service with the newly established 502 *Os Jaguares*, commanded by a Captain Fernandes.

This unit joined *Esquadrão* 501—also known as *Tigres*—equipped with the air force's omnipresent T-6s and Do-27s in order to constitute what came to be termed the *Grupo Operacional* 5001.

Fiats were soon active, flying a high number of combat sorties and dropping napalm extensively: given the size of territory they were required to cover, their pilots had a massive task at hand.

Initially, on their arrival in East Africa, the Portuguese Air Force G-9s were painted in tropical light grey overall in an effort to limit the effects of the tropical sun. Each aircraft also had a large national insignia emblazoned on its fuselage, while several Fiats of 702 *Esquadrão* (including examples 5425 and 5429) were seen with the unit's large unit insignia—a black scorpion—on mid-fuselage as well.

For attack operations in Mozambique where longer distances needed to be covered, the Fiats were usually armed with four 12.7mm machine-guns, four 50kg bombs (carried on outboard under-wing pylons), and if necessary, the planes could carry two drop tanks on inboard pylons).

Things were different in Portuguese Guinea and this insight is essential because what took place in Lisbon's West African war invariably affected developments in the colony lying at the other end of Africa, seven or eight thousand kilometers away.

On the deployment of the newly added Fiat G-91 jet fighter/bombers in Portuguese Guinea some time before they became active much further afield, it is necessary to detail roughly how they operated since those same tactics and modifications were later applied to Lisbon's identical jets when they were deployed to the Mozambique theater of military operations.

Although compatible virtually with all weapons in the Portuguese Air Force arsenal, these agile Italian-built jets were armed mainly with unguided 70mm caliber ground-to-air rockets as well as a number of different bomb configurations. These included 45kg, 50kg, 200kg, and 227kg bombs along with the hefty 340kg heavyweights, the latter American M-117s, which arrived courtesy of Lisbon's links with NATO.

Napalm containers with a capacity of 300 liters were eventually added and used to exceptional advantage against guerrilla forces.

The priority weapon configuration in both countries consisted of a pair of 200kg bombs on the inner hard-points and four 50kg bombs or unguided rockets on the outer.

Thus, when Major Moreira's *Tigres* squadron in Guinea intensified its operations, the PAIGC liberation group responded, especially in the southern half of the enclave with the introduction of heavy Soviet ZPU-1 machine-guns in 12.7mm caliber as well as 14.5mm ZPU-4s. These anti-aircraft weapons, mostly operated by Cuban "instructors," proved highly mobile and it constantly astonished Portuguese aviators how often they seemed to "pop up from nowhere," sometimes in positions where they were least expected.

Clearly, tracking and destroying these often-deadly Soviet heavy machine-guns—still popular in many small wars in Africa, the Middle East and Asia—became a challenge for Lisbon's ground forces.

The Fiats operating on the west coast first encountered them during Operation *Estoque*. This deployment—in more than company strength—was to start with a night-time attack by some bomber-refurbished Douglas C-47 Dakotas on August 9, 1966. Fifty-kilogram bombs along with napalm were used in a bid to destroy the enemy's anti-aircraft positions. But things did not always work out that way.

When the Fiats subsequently appeared over the designated combat zone, their pilots discovered that most PAIGC's flak positions were not only still intact, but that their firepower was just as intense. Two of the fighter bombers were damaged by ground fusillades and one had to make an emergency landing on a makeshift landing strip at Cufar.

In November 1966, another Fiat-supported strike, named Operation *Samurai* took place on Como Island (always heavily disputed for the duration of the Guinea war), this time in a series of ground battles between the guerrillas and the Portuguese Army and backed by its naval forces. First, the jets did a number of reconnaissance flights in efforts to provide fire support to a paratroop company supported from the air by several C-47s, a squadron of T-6G Harvard ground support aircraft as well as Alouette III helicopter gunships.

A month later, starting on December 19 and lasting two days, the G-91s participated in Operation *Valquiria*, the intention being to supply a Portuguese Army base that had been isolated on the Cantanhez Peninsula. The object was to provide support for a variety of supply boats loaded with fresh troops, food and ammunition supplies along the Cumbija River. There too, the aircraft took ground fire in quantity.

The Fiat G-91 was soon to become one of the most important FAP assets in the colonies. The type was dependable, easy to maintain, designed to take-off and land on short or ill-prepared runways and had a good strike capability.

Apart from armaments, the plane could also carry three cameras in a specially designed nose, which offered a much-needed photo-reconnaissance capability.

***

It was not until early 1973 that the PAIGC were handed supplies of the vaunted Soviet infrared-guided hand-held air Strela-2 (SA-7 Grail) ground-to-air supersonic missiles with the first Soviet shipment delivered to Conakry in the new year.

At the time, the guerrilla leader Amilcar Cabral was still hoping to resolve his PAIGC conflict through negotiations with General Antonio de Spínola, but this brilliant unconventional tactician was assassinated in January 1973 and a new leadership of the PAIGC involving his brother Luis emerged.

The supersonic ground-to-air missiles soon took effect. Three months after the SAMs had reached the guerrillas that year, two Fiat jet pilots had their first brush with Strela missiles: the planes came under ground fire but were not aware of what weapons were actually being used against them. Lieutenant-Colonel José Fernando Brito and Lieutenant Cardosa Pessoa later spoke of a passing "shock wave" but were unable to detect any damage to their machines. The presence of supersonic missiles was consequently still unresolved and no warning issued to the other pilots.

But three days later, on March 25, the first Strela missile hit home and the pilot did not even see it coming. Nor did his wing man.

A Fiat G-91, number 5413, flown by Lieutenant Pessoa in the skies above Guilege was the target. When the warhead detonated, the aviator flung himself out at very low altitude and broke a leg on landing as his parachute had failed to open fully. Assuming that he had perished in the blast, the insurgents did not launch a search and one of the Portuguese helicopters eventually brought the lieutenant back to his own lines.

But Pessoa still had no idea what it was that led to his aircraft being destroyed. He spoke of an "unknown weapon" in his subsequent debriefing but was unable to be specific. Unaware that a totally new weapon was being deployed by the enemy, the Fiat pilots went about their business as before.

It took another three days for things to change when another jet was hit. This time, the pilot had a better grasp of what has happening, which resulted in the squadron being made aware that the PAIGC was in possession of a new heat-sensitive weapon that was not only destructive but also possessed astonishing speed. They were yet to discover that the missile, with a range of 1,500 meters, was particularly effective against fixed-wing planes operating within that range.

Obviously, the Portuguese referred the matter to NATO for clarification and their experts were able to fill some of the gaps, all of which was passed on to air force headquarters in Bissau. Immediately, a massive reorganization was begun.

For a start, all operational pilots in Africa were made aware that they faced an extremely efficient new weapon and while there was much initial confusion—both on the flight line and at all the bases from which these aircraft operated—every option had to be evaluated.

What soon emerged was that while the Strela ground-to-air missile in the right hands was deadly, but at the same time, it had not proved invincible in other wars.

Also, the weapon had its limitations: hand-held SAMs proved not to be effective against aircraft that hugged the ground and flew almost at tree-top level. This was one of the reasons why the South African Air Force in its 23-year Border War always flew low-level and not a single helicopter was taken out by Strelas. Obviously, Lisbon quickly became aware that certain precautions needed to be observed.

For a start, all slower aircraft then operational on the African west coast—T-6s, Dorniers and helicopters and the occasional Dakota—were prohibited from flying anywhere near the battle zone. G-91s were similarly affected and could only temporarily operate, but only at low altitude and high speed.

As a consequence, the Portuguese Air Force in Guinea was all but paralyzed and for a while it was left to the navy to supply essential back-up and firepower when needed. Additionally, the sudden lack of air support became a heavy burden for Lisbon's men in the field: it stayed that way until effective anti-missile counter-measures were put in place. But even that took time.

Notably, SAMs were also supplied not long afterwards to FRELIMO. Though not as widely deployed as in Portuguese Guinea, Mozambique (at 800,000km^2) is 22 times the size of this West African colony, so its role was limited to specific areas close to hostile frontiers.

In contrast, the PAIGC could use their SAMs just about anywhere in the tiny Portuguese enclave. That done, they could then slip back across the border into friendly sanctuary, while FRELIMO had to cover vast distances in order to strike at Lisbon's aircraft, with some chance of the missiles being captured by marauding Portuguese units.

In a bid to stymie the spread of FRELIMO's influence, General de Arriaga decided that one possible solution might be a major operation, which he called "*Gordian Knot.*"

This was launched on June 10, 1970 in the remotest parts of the north of the country. It took some doing but he was able to marshal roughly 10,000 troops, but most of the serious main fighting was restricted to elite Special Forces units that included paratroops, commandos, marines and naval fusiliers—in some cases consisting mainly of Black troops.

Extensive use was also made of units of captured guerrillas or other enemy soldiers who had defected to government ranks, largely to penetrate their former bases. Cavalry was also deployed to cover the flanks of patrols and where terrain became too difficult for motor transport.

Established rebel bases—by now identified—were subjected to heavy air and artillery bombardment, after which heli-borne troops were flown in to do the necessary. It was a messy business but Portuguese Special Forces, some of whom had seen hard service in either Angola or Guinea had become proficient in what they did best.

That large-scale operation saw excellent coordination between light bombers, helicopters and reinforced ground patrols. The Fiat jets and T-6 Harvards would be on hand, operating with ground forces deployed as stopper groups, but no strikes were undertaken against FRELIMO bases in either of the two hostile neighboring countries. Though planned to last for eight or ten weeks, it eventually stretched out over seven months, mostly during the dry season, and extended into the Moxico Province.

The Portuguese eventually reported 651 enemy killed (a figure of some 440 was most likely more realistic), and 1,840 guerrillas captured, for the loss of 132 Portuguese. General de Arriaga also claimed that his forces had destroyed 61 guerrilla bases as well 165 camps which included numerous recruiting centers. Altogether 40 tons of ammunition was captured in the first two months.

During *Gordian Knot*, the FAP was reinforced by eight additional Fiat G-91s, delivered directly to the Tete air force base. These jet fighters entered service with the newly established *Esquadrão* 702, also referred to as *Os Escorpiones* and in September 1970 commanded by Captain Azabuja. The unit was a part of *Grupo Operacional* 7001, which also included 701 Squadron *Moscordos*, equipped with T-6s, Do-27s and Cessna 185s, as well as *Esquadrão* 703 *Os Vampiros* which fielded Alouette and Puma helicopters.

Besides flying strikes against enemy bases and armed-reconnaissance missions, the Fiats were also used for reconnaissance missions, equipped with K-20 camera-pods. These not only enabled photographing of areas beyond Mozambique's frontiers but also aerial mapping the entire part of the country that adjoined Zambia.

Close-support sorties, however, were almost unheard of, mainly because of poor cooperation between the air force and army. Portuguese soldiers were not only inadequately equipped for long range penetration patrols, but the truth is, any meaningful kind of liaison between pilots and ground forces was rare. Also, there was never any real effort made to improve the situation.

***

FRELIMO's military wing thus continued extending its influence southwards along the Zambezi River—even if sometimes at a much higher price—but its fighting cadres were unable to penetrate much beyond the frontier regions of Cabo Delgado and Niassa, where the Portuguese had been well-prepared to meet the threat.

In 1971, the Portuguese launched two additional offensives, Operations *Garotte* and *Apio*, which like *Gordian Knot* soon became embroiled in conflicting objectives.

Both began with artillery and air bombardments, followed by well-coordinated heli-borne assaults, mine clearance and consolidation on foot. No question, there was heavy damage caused to FRELIMO's infrastructure in the north but the Portuguese military was unable to get to destroy the guerrilla capability of infiltration.

Effectively, this resulted in General de Arriaga's critics concluding that his predecessors had achieved exactly the same results at much less cost and effort.

The Portuguese had a tough time in trying to clear Tete Province of an enemy presence that, with time, became more pronounced. Obviously, there was considerable Rhodesian pressure—together with active Rhodesian cross-border military support—but it was simply not enough.

Essentially, Lisbon's top brass in Mozambique—in spite of considerable military success in Angola—seemed to lack the fundamental understanding of what guerrilla warfare basically involved. In fact, many observers noted that by the time they were appointed to the East African territory most had seen good service in Angola and Guinea, but some of these senior officers refused to accept that Mozambique was different to both. For a start, the Portuguese military authorities in Mozambique—acting independently of other commands in Africa—never really integrated anything learned from British experiences in Malaya, or even what the United States was then doing in Vietnam.

Part of the problem lay with the unpleasant reality that Portuguese actions were based on decision-making of local commands, which usually needed days if not weeks to prepare for anti-insurgent operations on receiving information about local activities of insurgent groups. It was rare that a unit would act immediately on a tip-off, with the result that by the time operations were launched, the birds, as the saying goes, had flown.

Also, attacks were only undertaken in daylight hours, Portuguese soldiers by and large were reluctant to sleep rough in the bush. Additionally, the treatment of locals very often constituted criminal activity with suspects beaten and sometimes killed, whether they were enemy sympathizers or not. This was something that would never have been tolerated in Portuguese Guinea during General Antonio de Spínola's term of office on the west coast of Africa. Nor were matters helped by the predilection of Portuguese soldiers to destroy anything in their path during operations: that would often include livestock, crops, villages and the rest…

Locals would be routinely rounded up for questioning and anyone acting in what might be regarded as a "suspicious manner" would be taken into custody. Those attempting to escape would be shot and listed as "fleeing terrorists." If someone did manage to get away, it was a rare event for troops to attempt a follow-up: it was just too much effort.

Consequently, it was not surprising that anybody who actually experienced the vagaries of such "search and destroy" excesses on the part of government forces went on to become fervent supporters of FRELIMO.

***

Meanwhile, the Portuguese Air Force started utilizing its aircraft for chemical and psychological warfare.

In December 1971, and again in May 1972, Portuguese transports dropped millions of leaflets over southern Tanzania, attacking President Julius Nyerere and purporting to represent the views of internal opposition.

On April 30, 1972, six South African-registered crop dusters flew from Johannesburg to Nacala, and then on to Mueda, from where they operated with a Portuguese Air Force escort which suggested tight security. Their task, it only became known publicly years later, was to deprive guerrilla forces of their food supplies by crop spraying the powerful 2,4-D-based herbicide Convolvotox onto any area that might have been identified as being used by the enemy.

The South African-registered crop dusters were usually escorted by Harvards, one of which was brought down during the course of one such operation by anti-aircraft fire from a village across the Rovuma River, in Tanzania. Three days later, the Portuguese hit back with G-91 jets attacking the village involved with 50kg and 100kg bombs.

The South African pilots involved in the clandestine operation left Mozambique after another escorting T-6G and one of the crop dusters were hit by ground fire on April 17, 1972.

***

Cooper states that by 1973, the Portuguese Air Force had deployed in Mozambique almost 60 fixed-wing and rotary aircraft. These included 16 Fiat G-91s, 15 T-6s, five Noratlas transporters and seven C-47/DC-3 transports as well as 14 Alouettes, and two Pumas.

He goes on: Clearly the air force was at this time more active than ever before, and the Fiat jets of 502 and 702 squadrons flew dozens of combat sorties each month.

Correspondingly, from early 1973, regular FRELIMO units active in northern Mozambique—well-supported by China—were taking delivery of substantial numbers of SA-7 MANPADs. The first of these Strelas were encountered in action by Major Costa Joaquin and Lieutenant Macario while on operations in northern Mozambique, though the weapon is not known to have caused any losses to aircraft. What the presence of SAMs did do was force Portuguese pilots to change tactics.

The only Fiat known to have been lost in the course of combat in Mozambique was the G-91 "5429," flown by Lieutenant Emilio Lourenço: his aircraft was destroyed while flying a strike against FRELIMO positions due to a premature detonation of bombs it carried on March 15, 1973. The pilot was killed.

The air force suffered another loss on January 8, 1974, when a Douglas C-47B "FAP-6161" (14134/255579) crashed near Vila Cabral, under circumstances that were unspecified. Also, additional Fiat jets might have been damaged in a spectacular attack by FRELIMO mortars against an air base (in this case, AB.10) in 1974. The rebels managed to infiltrate a security cordon and set fire to the local fuel depot. Three replacement G-91s were subsequently delivered on board FAP Boeing 707 transports.

The attack on AB.10 actually came as no surprise. By late 1973, enemy units were operating not far from Beira and early 1974 the rebels launched a major offensive southwards, exploiting slackening Portuguese resistance, especially after the army coup in Lisbon that toppled the government.

By that stage, the war had cost Portugal many thousands dead and 30,000 wounded or disabled. As a consequence, the Portuguese military was increasingly demoralized to be fighting what many soldiers regarded as a fruitless war thousands of kilometers from home. Additionally, morale had hit rock-bottom and many professional soldiers were faced with unenthusiastic conscripts and anti-war subalterns, not counting growing indifference at home.

There was also increasing hostility from many of Mozambique's permanent White residents—some of whose families had been living there for centuries and with whom the army had little sympathy. Local colonists quite often questioned the courage, morale and integrity of the military: they also viewed the army's increasing reliance on Black troops with great suspicion."

The war simply had to have severe adverse effects on the already weakened Portuguese economy, especially as the defense expenditure rose from 25 percent in 1960, to more than 40 percent by 1967. Portuguese citizens ended up among the most heavily taxed in Europe.

Furthermore, international criticism damaged Portugal's international prestige, putting the government under fierce pressure. There were many who believed that the time had come for Portugal to vacate its African possessions.

Eventually, negotiations were organized to agree a ceasefire and terms for independence and a ceasefire in Mozambique came into effect on September 8, 1974.

The exodus of mostly White Portuguese settlers started almost immediately, keeping the FAP busy for months to follow. Aside from flying thousands of civilians back to Portugal, Portuguese Air Force transports also evacuated all the G-91s of the 702 Squadron to Angola, while those of 502 Squadron were shipped to Portugal by sea.

CHAPTER 10

The Alouette III—A Magnificent Flying Machine

Of the many wars I have covered over half a century, there are few sounds more inspiring—usually while waiting at a military base somewhere in Africa, than that of an "Alo"—an Alouette III helicopter "winding up" and preparing to lift off. A few of the inkslingers would sometimes refer to that build-up as "the sound of freedom."

This was something I experienced many times: at Luanda's Craveiro Lopes Airport when the Portuguese were still around; at heavily fortified bases in the *Dembos*, further towards the north and the Congolese frontier; and once on the road that links Tete to the Malawi border post in Mozambique—when one of these helicopters was called in to extract a truck driver who had been wounded in a landmine blast.

When writing about the Alouette III, a helicopter that punched well above its weight for more than half a century, it is always Africa's conflicts that come to mind. These modest, almost frail-looking French-built choppers raised the rumpus just about everywhere they were deployed, especially at Bissalanca Airport on the outskirts of colonial Bissau. That strategic former Portuguese Air Force base in Portuguese Guinea (today Guiné-Bissau) sported an array of planes that included Fiat G-91 jet fighters, Douglas DC-6 and Nord Noratlas transport planes as well as a host of other fixed-wing aircraft.

What really caught your attention were the "Alo's"—almost terrier-like—landing and taking off; some with small squads of combatants, ammunition belts slung macho-style over their shoulders and automatic weapons held high. There would sometimes be still more bringing in casualties from a recent action in the interior.

Looking back at Lisbon's three colonial wars in Africa in the 1960s and early 1970s, it's a reality that without the more than one hundred French-built

Aerospatiale Alouette III helicopters—deployed almost from the start of hostilities—those conflicts are likely to have ended much sooner than they did.

Miniscule by today's standards of a combat gunship, the average Alouette III could comfortably carry a pilot and four or five soldiers, depending on weight and how much kit they were carrying. In the early stages of these conflicts, a few pilots tried lifting off with six soldiers and ended up stripping the gears.

Once Lisbon's forces had left Africa, the Rhodesians followed with the identical helicopter; some deployed as gunships or G-cars and others for command and control. The Rhodesians used some of the experiences and tactics developed by Portuguese aviators in Angola and Mozambique as their guidelines.

South Africa followed suit in its own 23-year-long Border War along the Angolan frontier and therein rests a host of stories.

***

Neall Ellis, who—by the time he'd ended his career in the South African Air Force—held the rank of Lieutenant-Colonel, flew these machines throughout most of the war. In the process, he admits, he came under fire many times and was brought down only twice by ground fire.

I flew many times in several conflicts with "Nellis" (as his friends call him) and we ended up becoming close friends. Together with our wives, we even ended up watching each others' kids grow up.

Thereafter, he went on to fly a lone Mi-24 gunship that was well past its "use by" date, and leaked when it rained in Sierra Leone's rebel war (where I also spent time with him). These extraordinary experiences were eventually recorded in my book *War Dog*, a seminal book on contemporary mercenary activity, published by Casemate Publishers more than a decade ago.[1]

As Neall told me, after he'd qualified on Alouettes, he first had to do a bush tour in South West Africa (today Namibia), before being posted to Rhodesia's guerrilla war. But that changed as hostilities intensified on both sides. As he reckoned, "the experience in the Rhodesian Air Force did help greatly towards effectively operating in an extensive and protracted insurgency along Angola's southern border."

The numbers of helicopters that were involved in South Africa's Border War are interesting. There were 125 Alouette IIIs spread out between the South African Air Force and the Rhodesian Air Force; with a handful donated by the Portuguese forces after Lisbon had pulled its forces back to Europe from

Angola and Mozambique. Additionally, the South Africans deployed 17 Pumas and 14 Super Frelons.

In total—during its 23 years of border conflict—the SAAF lost five Alouettes from enemy engagement, and obviously a couple more from accidents, technical and pilot error. There were also four Pumas downed by enemy fire and one from own forces fire (Operation *Savannah*). It is notable that not one helicopter was taken out by SAM supersonic missiles which, towards the end, were fielded in considerable numbers in Angola, courtesy of the Soviet Union.

It was not that SAM-7s (or Strelas, their NATO designation) were no good; essentially it was the tactics employed by both the South Africans and Portuguese forces in Africa that prevented them from being effective. Ellis explains:

> Firstly, it is not easy to shoot down the Alouette, mainly because it is a small moving target and, secondly, we tried our best to fly at a minimum speed of 65 knots and stay above the effective range of small arms fire. The operating manual states we should orbit above 800 feet when in a contact, but the guys used to fly lower, often at tree-top level. However, when the volume of ground fire became too intense, our boys tended to fly proportionally higher…
>
> The other important aspect is that the Alouette is a very basic machine with very few high-tech moving parts. I know of one instance when an engine took an AK-47 round in the casing to the combustion chamber and just carried on flying. When the pilot landed to refuel and was obliged to shut down the engine, the engine seized. Until he'd turned everything off, he had no idea there was a problem.
>
> Essentially though, the main reason why so few helicopters were shot down in Africa's wars is because of the flying techniques we employed (mostly low level) and the fact that it is not easy to hit a moving target.

In answer to a question about the enemy deploying SAM missiles (or MANPADs in contemporary jargon), Neall Ellis offered the following prognosis:

> I had many SAMs launched at me. In fact, I think more than 13—and there could have been more that passed to the rear.
>
> The South African Council for Scientific and Industrial Research (CSIR) developed counter-measures, such as new types of a special external paint that restricted the Infrared (IR) signature of a chopper. Then they developed a shield over the engine to prevent SAMs from locking onto the hot metal.
>
> One needs to remember that the SAM-7s intrinsic design was such that it was attracted to hot metal rather than heated exhaust gases. With the new shields, these were directed upwards into the rotor downwash, which created a "blurred" heat signature and as a consequence could not enable the missile seeker head to focus on a single heat source … it was actually very effective.
>
> The bottom line with regard to using the Alouette III operationally, is that it remains difficult to pass comment because that French helicopter—used as a gunship—was all that the South Africans had. Because of the government's apartheid laws, the United Nations had

imposed arms sanctions against Pretoria and only the French were willing to sell them arms on the open market. At that time, much else was clandestinely acquired, but not choppers.

At the same time, you have to consider that this is a rugged helicopter, very basic and reliable. It was easy to maintain and even major component changes in the field could be accomplished when necessary. It would obviously have been nice to have a faster gunship—such as the Squirrel—to keep pace with our Puma's, but in terms of outside visibility and from a pilot's point of view, there are not many helicopters that can compare.

I know of a couple of incidents where the helicopter took many rounds and the pilot was able to escape the contact area before either coming down or making a forced landing. When I was shot down, there were 57 holes of various calibers just about everywhere, and I still managed to fly for some distance before the engine seized.

I'm aware too that many Portuguese aviators who flew the Alouette in Angola and Mozambique had their share of stories, some depicting quite remarkable near-crashes or taking the kind of punishment that modern helicopters simply would not survive.

Typically, troops would be flown into selected landing zones that were reasonably close to guerrilla camps. Maintaining an adequate distance from the enemy was vital; if the insurgents suspected that an operation was about to be launched against them, they would evacuate the camp.

The five-seat configuration of the "Alo" meant that it was customary, with companies such as the Paratrooper Special Groups (*Caçadores-Paraquedistas*), for squads of 20 men to be deployed in five helicopters. There was close coordination between other FAP units for heli-drops involving paratroopers. The Alouette was highly efficient at providing close cover (top cover) for ground forces either going into the attack or countering ground fire.

While helicopters had been used by the military in many wars—usually in support or Medivac roles, as with France in Algeria and Britain in the Malayan Emergency—Portugal was the first European nation to arm their rotor craft and take them into battle. They did so in all three of their African wars; initially in Angola, followed by Portuguese Guinea and finally Mozambique.

In 1944, almost two decades before Portugal took their rotor craft into action, the Sikorsky R-4 became the world's first helicopter to go into mass production—and was the first helicopter in United States military service and also to operate from the deck of a ship. After a few modifications, that helicopter became the YR-4B and in April 1944, became the first helicopter ever to fly in combat. Lieutenant Carter Harmon used his YB-R4 to successfully rescue four men who had crash-landed in extremely rough terrain.

In Africa, a quarter century later, Alouettes were at the forefront in this role and to the surprise of many critics, these helicopters soon became indispensable in that capacity.

The "Alo", with its side-firing ability, was the ideal counter-insurgency weapon; well-suited to the war in Mozambique in which the Portuguese found themselves. It could orbit a suspect position and visually acquire an enemy secreted under relatively thickly foliaged bushes or trees. Its lack of speed was offset by its ability to linger over a target.

In its "Overseas Wars," the Portuguese eventually launched their air assaults with clusters of six or seven Alouette IIIs, each carrying paratroopers or commandos, quite often with the support of jet- and propeller-driven aircraft. These were sometimes complex operations but those involved soon became remarkably adept at providing the required back-up during attacks.

The Portuguese practice was for the soldiers to make their exits with full gear and in the hover—the subject of many famous combat images of the war.

The deployment of these troops was invariably covered by a heavy machine-gun poking out the open port sliding door. Once the objective had been either seized or overrun, the choppers would move in again; first to take out the wounded, and then the rest of the troops.

The end of Lisbon's African colonial wars in Africa did not halt the careers of these little craft. The last of Portugal's SE3160 Alouette III light utility helicopters were withdrawn from service in April 2020.

As I was to observe, and echoed by Robert Craig Johnson: the risks of combat flying over the Portuguese colonies escalated dramatically in the late 1960s and early 1970s, largely because the Soviet Strela shoulder-fired missile finally became generally available in the guerrilla-controlled hinterland.[2] Johnson continues:

> The SAM-7 proved extremely capable when it came to detecting the exhaust systems of piston aircraft, and, while high-performance jets could out-fly the relatively low-performance Strela if warned in time, piston-engine types were almost always hit before they could react. Large aircraft, like the B-26 and PV-2, might survive a hit, because the warhead was small. But Do-27s and T-6s were invariably doomed. Losses among these types increased alarmingly.

In South Africa's Border War, Neall Ellis, then serving at the "Sharp End" and at the controls of an Alouette during a major contact that ended with 300 enemy dead, was fired on three times by SAM-7 Strelas during Operation *Super*.[3]

That action took place in the exposed, arid terrain of the Kaokoveld, close to the Angolan border. Major Ellis (as he then was) only had a second or two to react after spotting the meters-long flashes from the missiles as they were being launched and—though evasive reaction time was minimal—the warheads swept past within meters of his machine. They were obviously not armed with the proximity fuses found in later versions of these MANPADs.

Still circling the area, his engineer was able to knock out the launch sites on the ground with some well-placed salvoes with his 20mm heavy machine-gun.

Throughout all these African wars, it was notable that though lightweight, underpowered and comparatively low speed, these tiny aircraft were able to take a remarkable amount of punishment from Triple-A ground fire. Most times, they still managed to return to base, occasionally with their tail booms or a rotor hanging by a thread.

Clearly, the French-built Aerospatiale Alouette III helicopter played a seminal role in all of Southern Africa's conflicts. Although superseded by larger, faster and more modern rotor craft, there are still Alouettes flying in several security and military units all over the world.

Among the 50-odd countries still using them are: Austria (20-something with the Austrian Air Force); India (over 200 still in service in the Indian Army, Navy and Air Force); Bangladesh; Albania; Angola (20); Pakistan (25); the French Navy (18 or 20 on active service); Greece, and more than 50 in various security roles in Malaysia.

It is notable that the last and 1,437th Alouette III left the Marignane assembly lines in France in 1979, when the main production facility was closed down. However, approximately another 500 were to be manufactured under license in Romania, India and Switzerland. In fact, Hindustan Aeronautics Limited of India (HAL) continues to license-build Alouette IIIs as the "Chetak", a two-ton class helicopter that is even more advanced than earlier versions because it can seat seven. More recently, the Namibian Ministry of Defence as well as Suriname in the Caribbean, placed orders.

Historically, it is interesting that one of the first Alouette IIIs to come off the production line in France took off and landed in July 1960. There were seven people on board and it reached an altitude just short of 5,000 meters in the French Alps near Mont Blanc.

What is also noteworthy is that helicopters, deployed as an extension of the military fighting arm, only came into their own not that many years before.

While the British initially formed the Far East Casualty Air Evacuation Flight in Malaya with three Westland S-51 Dragonflys in 1950—an unsuccessful venture, as it transpired—it was the French in Algeria that first strapped men onto litters on either side of the fuselage to deliver support fire in the mountains behind the Mediterranean. It was a somewhat primitive effort for what it was supposed to achieve and involved an early version from the same factory, Alouette IIs, but it worked.

From then on, the French worked vigorously towards the implementation of the helicopter gunships (as we know them today). Some of the early Alouette IIs were delivered to the Portuguese Air Force, whose own wars in Africa had taken off only a few years after France's bitter civil war in Algeria had ended.

Today, many pundits actually rate the Aerospatiale SA-316 Alouette III as arguably the most successful counter-insurgency machine ever built outside the United States.

There were many other pilots in the SAAF who served alongside Neall Ellis in what was increasingly referred to as the Angolan War; Arthur Walker being one of the most prominent. He is the only man to have been awarded two of the highest decorations in the South African Defence Force; the Honoris Crux in Gold (or HC-Gold). The same decoration also comes in silver and bronze, depending on the measure of bravery of the recipient.

Walker was also involved in one of the most savage firefights of the entire Border War period in South Angola, where he won the first of his bravery medals in gold at Cuamato. It was his job to provide top cover for the men fighting on the ground with his gunship. It was also possibly more than a coincidence that he was with the parachute unit deployed—Charlie Company—which was the first go into battle against a fairly well-equipped and organized enemy. They were dropped into position by a squadron of Puma helicopters.

However, to quote the famous maxim: "No battle plan survives a contact with the enemy," the 1981 Battle for Cuamato ended up providing a slew of unpleasant surprises for both South African ground and air forces. Basically, the intention was to use the deserted village as a forward logistics base from where, shortly afterwards, an area operation was mounted to seek and destroy a suspected guerrilla camp. The target included SWAPO's western headquarters.

On the afternoon of 15 January, six Alouette helicopter gunships and four Pumas flew 80 miles to a position roughly 20 miles or only minutes' flying time north of the Angolan border, to set up for the operation due to commence the next morning. Apart from the Parabats, there were also troops from 32 Battalion, the elite army unit that accounted for more enemy losses than any other in the SADF.

With Charlie Company, the troops on the ground were in the process of securing the perimeter and checking out the surrounding area, when the call came: contact had been unexpectedly made with a fairly large enemy force and there had been casualties. One of the patrols had come across a previously unknown Angolan Army strong point, just a few miles north of the village that gave its name to the two-day fight.

That first contact came just before last light and, as Arthur Walker told me years later: "There was no clue that this base even existed … it certainly wasn't on any of our maps. Our much-vaunted military intelligence, fundamentally speaking, was lacking."

That first call was soon followed by another, together with more details of the initial clash: two of the reconnaissance troops had been wounded and one man killed. A helicopter extraction was requested. Walker continues:

> Captain Mike McGee and I went off in our two 20mm gunships to secure a landing zone for a Puma (it had already arrived at Cuamato from Ondangua) and would be tasked to extract the casualties. But we'd hardly got properly orientated when Mike and I came under extremely heavy anti-aircraft fire, both 12.7mm and 14.5mm heavy machine-guns backed by clusters of RPG-7s—scores of them.
>
> We'd already observed in our approaches that the open ground with sandy soil and light grass cover in the suspect area below was traversed by Soviet-style zigzag trenches, straight out of the Red Army Manual. Also, we spotted numerous firing emplacements and positions for 82mm mortars as well as berms and banks that appeared to provide extra cover: all that, together with underground bunkers.
>
> Additionally, a complex mesh of tracks traversed the entire area showing where the Angolans had moved back and forth, making it all the more surprising that the strongpoint had never been identified from the air on earlier air force reconnaissance flights. Thorn trees that were normally dotted haphazardly across the bush had mostly been cleared to provide extensive fields of fire ... or for fuel, leaving only occasional clumps of bush.
>
> Our troops on the ground used yellow smoke to mark their positions and then Mike and I went in to attack the base to suppress what was now a hell of a lot of Triple-A fire coming up at us. Essentially, our role was supposed to soften up enemy defenses so that the Puma could head in and uplift the wounded, but this had suddenly become a dangerous situation and it was only a question of time before one of us would be hit.
>
> Now it was now getting dark, the sky filled with tracers ... all quite dramatic, especially for anybody watching from the ground.
>
> I estimated that there was something like 120 to150 Angolans dug in around this previously unknown base. It was pretty obvious to everybody that the enemy was well armed, with some of the larger automatic guns firing an effective 300 rounds-a-minute. Against these weapons, the Alouette gunships had their single, laterally mounted 20mm cannons, which had to be fired from a low and relatively slow orbit for accuracy.
>
> We'd spot the muzzle flashes and tracers would follow; a powerful barrage of fire and it all seemed to be headed in our direction almost in slow motion, just like in the movies. Then suddenly, the stuff was whooshing past our heads ... all desperate stuff.
>
> Of course we'd be firing back at them, aiming "down their tracers" towards their muzzle flashes ... wouldn't have worked in the daytime, though...
>
> My gunner was Sergeant Danie Brink, and he took on the anti-aircraft guns until we ran out of ammunition (the gunships normally carried 150 rounds each), which was when I broke out of orbit and called Mike on the radio and told him that I was heading back to base to re-arm.
>
> In my mind we hadn't yet given up the battle, even though it was already twilight. Then Mike suddenly came back and said that he was taking a lot of hits and moments later, in a quiet voice, told me that he was going to crash. We'd been hovering at about 500 feet while still in orbit, but that was a mistake—under those conditions it would have been best to get down low and fast.

However, as was established days later in the subsequent debrief back at headquarters, Mike McGee, in his rapid descent must have become disoriented, which might be why he thought he was headed into the dirt.

In the half-light I couldn't really see his chopper, so I turned around to look for it, put on all my lights and told him to fly towards me. But hell, that had the immediate effect of us now attracting enemy fire and it was coming in from just about everywhere. However, that simple action did give my wing man the opportunity to recover and I began escorting him clear of the battle zone.

As our two gunships moved away, it was time for some serious evasive maneuvering. I used a succession of sharp turns and altitude changes to maximum effect and it worked. Mike followed me back to the base where we landed and shut down to both re-arm and re-fuel. More important, we had to reassess the whole bloody situation and I soon realized that it was pointless to head out again because we couldn't have a bunch of gunships orbiting in the dark. At the same time, the position where the South African casualties were lying was too close to the enemy, a mere 200 meters or so from their lines.

By the end of the first day's action, five of the attacking force had been wounded, as well as two from Charlie Company, lying dead. All had to be evacuated in the dark back to the main army base in the Cuamato village on foot.

While all this had been going on, we still hadn't assessed who or what exactly was down there, or been able to make a reasonably accurate guess about total enemy strength. Obviously, the target base was not a relatively low-key guerrilla camp but pretty strategic and no question—a very well-equipped Angolan Army base.

It was a big mistake on our part!

***

The Alouette III helicopter served in the South African Air Force for 44 years or almost half a century. Collectively, records in Pretoria's military archives indicate that they flew more than 346,000 hours.

Asked how the "Alo" compared with the Soviet Mi-24 (Hind in NATO's books) that came later, Neall Ellis stated that there is no way you could compare the two helicopters. The Hind was developed as a tank killer (and often referred as such) and with an all-up weight (AUW) of 12 tons compared to the AUW of 2.2 tons of the lightweight Alouette IIIs. Ellis continues:

Also, in terms of speed, the Hind is a much speedier craft, cruising at 140 knots while the French helicopter could cruise at around 105 knots empty, but when fully loaded with the 20mm cannon or with four troops on board, we would manage just 85 knots. In a "trooper" role, the chopper could remain airborne for roughly an hour and the gunship perhaps 30 minutes more.

The Hind of course—another helicopter that I have flown in for many years, usually in the gunner's seat under the front bubble—is able to remain aloft for just over two hours, and also carry a ton or more of men and equipment.

Fundamentally, the Hind is a much more sophisticated helicopter than the Alouette III, equipped with air conditioning and an effective autopilot. Plus it was designed as an armed gunship helicopter, whereas the Alouette was created primarily for utility work. We were the ones—together with the Portuguese and the Rhodesians—that remodeled it into a gunship.

It should also be mentioned that the standard Alouette III was fitted with a 545-liter tank and burns just under a 44-gallon drum (200 liters) per hour. At the same time—with the load we were carrying—we simply couldn't fly with a full fuel load.

So, when armed with the 20mm cannon (effectively, the gunship), we worked on a flight time of 90 minutes and the trooper with four fully kitted and armed soldiers, we reckoned on an hour of fuel, which meant a range of about 110 nautical miles.

The Zambezi River—Focal Point of the War

Mozambique's rivers—and also Lake Malawi—came to play a series of critical roles during the course of the colonial war. FRELIMO guerrilla elements started their campaign by pushing southwards from their Tanzanian bases across the Rovuma River, while still more infiltrated across that vast body of fresh water previously known as Lake Niassa (today Lake Malawi).

Much of the terrain traversed by these insurgents was wild and undeveloped, which helped foster the opposition's decisive argument that while Portugal had laid claim to the country centuries before, in the years since they had done almost nothing to foster human and economic advancement beyond the more populated coastal regions.

For all that, the war went on and obviously, with so few soldiers, police and militia on the ground—only several thousand to start with, building up to a military presence of about 60,000 in a country almost 10 times as large as metropolitan Portugal—there was no way the influx of hostile elements could be controlled; never mind halted.

Granted, there was much effort devoted to stemming the tide, coupled to an array of preventative measures that included ambushes, attacks on known enemy routes and positions. An extremely efficient intelligence system prevented the trickle from becoming a flood, but the truth is, Mozambique as a country was simply too vast to properly control and administer.

Then, when Zambia allowed FRELIMO cadres access to Mozambique's expansive western regions in March 1968—much of it centered on the Zambezi River—the war entered a new and troubled phase, especially since work had already started on building the giant Cahora Bassa Dam, an enormous project by international standards. When completed in 1974, the new man-made lake—at roughly 8,500km²—was a third larger in full flood than the capacity of either the great Aswan Dam in Egypt or Zimbabwe's Lake Kariba.

Some idea of the problems faced by Lisbon after President Kenneth Kaunda allowed revolutionaries to strike at Mozambique targets from Zambia only emerged after the 1974 army mutiny in Lisbon.

FRELIMO's command structure in Dar es Salaam had set its forces the task of either trying to sabotage the construction of the dam or, at very least, destroy as much of its electrical infrastructure as possible, meaning transmission lines and the steel towers which supported them. In this, the rebels did have their successes, coupled of course to innumerable landmine and ambush attacks: it was all part of the revolutionary drill and ultimately proved effective enough to take a steady toll in men and equipment within government ranks.

The guerrillas had much to their advantage in operating along the extensive Zambezi riverine system. Though it passes through regions that lack the kind of almost impenetrable triple-tiered jungle found along the Congo or the Amazon rivers, the Zambezi starts its journey to sea 2,400km to the west in the hinterlands of the upper Congo, and can be as wild, turbulent and dangerous as either.

For much of its length, the river is flanked by raw African bush, and there is an awful lot of that. Travel up or downstream from the great dam and the visitor—or soldier on patrol—is greeted by great strips of tropical bush or jungle country studded by immense stretches of sometimes impenetrable reeds and rushes, all of which attracts a wide variety of wildlife. There are more hippos and crocodiles than you can imagine, while elephants swimming against the current from both banks, still remains as much a regular feature as they were when Mozambique fell under Lisbon's jurisdiction.

I visited both the upper and lower reaches of the river many times and recall staying at a lodge between the Kariba and Cahora Bassa dams for a week. I was intrigued by everything around and kept a close eye on the opposite bank of the river with binoculars, following the antics of huge herds of buffalo, more impala than you could count and an astonishing variety of other animals, including lion. After dark, you couldn't miss their growls, punctuated by an occasional roar. Obviously, Portuguese troops on patrol further downstream would have had similar experiences to recount.

We were greeted each day by large herds of elephant. In fact, these beautiful creatures were constantly around our camp, sometimes keeping us awake at night as they shredded bushes, shrubs and trees around the main structures while feeding. The same situation held for great numbers of hippos. We had three or four pods of these boisterous hulks which we could comfortably view from the safari camp—at least 80 or 100 of the beasts all told—and they really came to life after dark, displaying a gusto that enthralled.

With the onset of the Rhodesian War, the Zambezi Valley soon became a battleground—as well as transit zone—for "liberation fighters" who crossed the river to launch their guerrilla struggle, in exactly the same way they did when Mozambique's new western front was opened for them by President Kenneth Kaunda, a friend and intimate of Tanzania's Julius Nyerere.

What we now know, many years after that colonial war ended, is that part of the reason for the recall of General Kaúlza de Arriaga as commander of all forces in Mozambique was that, despite some successes in the north (*Gordian Knot*), the Portuguese Army was facing increasing problems elsewhere and in particular, having to extend their already heavily taxed campaign unexpectedly to the Tete region. Truth is he was not coping with the country's immediate problems and those around him—and his superiors in Lisbon—knew it.

Either that, or Mozambique would have been cut in half as the guerrillas pushed hard eastwards along much of the length of the Zambezi. Additionally, the rebels were now attacking out of Zambia.

Opening the new front presented numerous imponderables and, as former United States Navy aviator Captain John Cann tells us in his PhD thesis completed in London 1996, the Zambezi was far from both army headquarters in Nampula and the seat of the civil administration at Lourenço Marques. Indeed, he suggests, Tete had been almost completely neglected by the Portuguese.

The southern regions, he declared, were remote and under no real threat, despite the location there of the major Cahora Bassa Dam project, begun in 1968. Infiltrating through Malawi and waging a selective terror campaign against tribal leaders in the Tete region, FRELIMO infiltrators caught the Portuguese—and de Arriaga—completely by surprise.

Obviously, the new guerrilla thrust demanded desperate measures and a crash program of *aldeamentos* was initiated. Three years later, in 1971, there was a newly appointed military governor in place and the dam completely ringed by what was intended to be 64km of "impenetrable wire and minefields" backed by a reported 15,000 troops. Jack Cann provides an appreciation of the situation:[1]

> Unable to pierce the new defenses, FRELIMO resorted to attacking the 443-kilometer route by which concrete was brought to the dam site. It is also possible that the change of tactics owed something to the benefit the dam might provide an independent Mozambique, although guerrilla spokesmen were careful to stress the value of the project to South Africa in terms of energy production.
>
> To leave the project entirely alone, of course, would also have created the impression that the Portuguese were invulnerable. For a short time, the attacks succeeded in inducing

the Portuguese to fly in concrete supplies, but work was never seriously interrupted and the project was six months ahead of schedule by the middle of 1972.

So successful was its defense that a civilian governor was reappointed in September 1973 while the guerrillas were reduced to occasional and largely futile long-range bombardment by 122mm rockets. Indeed, the guerrillas were generally resorting to long-range weapons more and more throughout the colony, the 122mm rocket first appearing in January 1973.

But the Portuguese appear to have concentrated to such an extent on defending Cahora Bassa that the remainder of the Tete region became a springboard from which the Rhodesian guerrilla movement ZANU (Zimbabwe African National Union), with whom FRELIMO closely cooperated, could start serious attacks into Rhodesia in December 1972.

***

In its own peculiar way, the Zambezi River has always played something of a role in the history of Mozambique. In the early colonial period, it was navigable well into the interior, with fairly large boats penetrating as far west as Tete.

Gold had already become lucrative centuries before and was of interest to both the trading Arabs and Portuguese adventurers who used the Zambezi to reach the gold mines of the legendary Monomotapa Kingdom in present-day Zimbabwe, which, ancient legend has it was linked to the Queen of Sheba.

That gold is said to be the source of much wealth—including ivory—that reached Egypt and the Arab kingdoms of the Persian Gulf during the Middle Ages.

The slave trade followed, aided and greedily nurtured by Arab privateers who encouraged African leaders in the interior of this vast continent to wage war against lesser tribes and deliver captives—men, women and children—who could be traded as slaves. There has been a good deal of research into this controversial issue and among conclusions reached is that more than 50,000 slaves were exported from Mozambique to Brazil, the Spanish Americas and the French colonies before 1800.[2]

By the middle of the 19th century, *Achikunda* slave armies emerged that would capture, kidnap and sell human beings for export, even though all forms of slavery had already been abolished in Europe half a century before.

Adjacent to the river's coastal delta there were (and still are) huge plantations that included sugar cane, bananas and other semi-tropical fruits. Although today virtually unknown, in their heyday the Sena Sugar Estates of Mozambique, formed one of the most expansive sugar plantations in the world and became home to the largest sugar factory in Africa. By 1960, some 14,000 people made their living on the estates.

Nearby is the Marromeu Complex, the region that was and remains vital for the national economy of Mozambique because it provides subsistence for hundreds of thousands of rural villagers. It also lay in the path, early 2019, of Intense Tropical Cyclone Idai—one of the worst on record—that affected enormous tracts of East and Central Africa and which resulted in more than a thousand deaths. That is the official tally; most authorities who became involved downplayed the numbers. Since a region half the size of Britain was affected, most of it remote and outlying and without communications even under normal conditions, the actual figure is probably several times that.

Nobody that survives along the banks of the Zambezi River—or adjacent to it—has anything but respect for this great river, if only because almost every year more stories emerge of disasters in its main steam or along its banks. Most are usually confined to isolated or distant places with few roads and almost no communications links.

Certainly, the Cahora Bassa project ended up controlling the river's flow and halted the impossible flash floods that would sometimes kill thousands, but even today, with the great dam in place, the populace treads lightly in the valley, as did the Portuguese Army when they were operational in the region.

Obviously, the army—and the guerrillas that opposed them—used those and other waters as and when required. There were even large ocean-going craft brought in to patrol the shores of Lake Malawi, hauled overland from Nacala in a multi-wheeled tank carrier loaned to Lisbon by the South African Army. It was a monumental project that took months, across bush tracks and through many river valleys, but the naval boat finally got to its destination and provided good service.

Being a seafaring nation, the Portuguese were pretty good on just about all large bodies of water, including the Rovuma and Zambezi rivers and Lake Malawi, but occasionally they slipped up, once very badly so.

Very little has appeared in print since the Mozambique war ended about what was arguably one of the biggest disasters Portugal was to suffer in any of its African wars and this one involved the Zambezi River. What has emerged was published largely on social media, including a report written by José Conteiro in his blog *O Portomosense* on April 2, 2009.

He tells of a large river barge, the *São Martinho* that was doing a routine crossing on a downstream part of the river late in the afternoon of June 21, 1969, roughly five years before the end of the war. There were an estimated 150 Portuguese troops on board, all of whom had embarked at Chupanga, a rural town a couple of hundred kilometers directly west of the port of Quelimane on the coast.

Company strength, the men with all their operational gear were being ferried to Mopeia on the north bank of the river. Also on board were almost two dozen army vehicles, including Unimog and Berliet troop carriers that would have taken the men to their final destination.

Nobody is certain why the barge capsized though, clearly, somebody did something reckless, because nothing like that had ever happened before and certainly not on that scale. There was talk about incorrect stowage on deck, probably of some of the trucks that were being ferried across. A report was issued and lists the names and origins of many of the soldiers who died. It included the comment:

> It was the greatest cost of human casualty of the entire history of the colonial war, but not much is known about the circumstances in which it occurred, namely, because there was only one subordinate officer on board, and he was a militiaman in charge of his subordinate graduates.
>
> The information offered is very sparse. In that accident died our countryman José Manuel da Silva Franco, soldier nº 02180467 of the artillery company nº 2387, mobilized by the RAL3. His captain was the artillery captain João Luís da Cunha Tavares da Silva, but he was not on board.

It took a while on that momentous day for the news of the disaster to emerge. First reports were filed by a radio operator at what was termed the "Aerodrome of Maneuver 73" (AM 73), a support unit at the Tete air force base, but this information, declared one of the investigating officers was "fragmentary and mismatched."

For several hours, all that was known was that there had been "a terrible disaster in Mopeia, across the Zambezi River," but because communications were desultory, specifics were sparse. Gradually more information filtered through, but by now the news had been reported to every military headquarters in the country, including to the commander-in-chief.

The radio operator near Tete kept transmitting but finally it had to be conceded that with it getting dark, rescue efforts would be abandoned until morning.

The only good news to emerge was that plans were in hand to send several Portuguese Air Force helicopters to the area from their bases in Tete and Beira, but that would be at first light. Nobody in authority was prepared to comment why, when the news first came in—and with several hours of daylight still available—choppers were not immediately dispatched.

Later, still more news arrived that while about a third of the men in the *São Martinho* had managed to reach safety on both banks of the river, "the great force of the current caused many bodies to be dragged downstream and would never be recovered," even though a ship from the nearby sugar plantations was helping with the search.

Another report added: "In spite of everything, the bodies of our ill-fated compatriots have been collected by the ship *Mezinga* of the Sena Sugar Estates … the operation was coordinated by port captain, Fernando Manuel Loureiro de Sousa."

What subsequently emerged in an extraordinarily lengthy official investigation was that very little was known about the circumstances in which the tragedy occurred. There was talk about storms, but the event took place in June, mid-winter in the Southern Hemisphere, and anyway even harsh winds—if there were any—are hardly likely to cause a large ferry to capsize.

The report concluded that those died were claimed by the river "due to an unfortunate maneuvering error."[3]

CHAPTER 12

Rhodesia in the War in Mozambique

In February 1971, a secret strategic military alliance was created between South Africa, Rhodesia and Portugal and referred to as the "Council of Three." This arrangement coordinated much of the behind-the-scenes military, security and supply activity between the three countries, then either at war with liberation groups or, in South Africa's case, about to become involved in hostilities in South West Africa, a war that was to last 23 years.[1]

That was followed up two years later when Portugal's commander-in-chief in Mozambique, General Kaúlza de Arriaga, reached a "Gentleman's Agreement" with Prime Minister Ian Smith's Salisbury government, which enabled Rhodesian forces to strike at hostile targets up to 100 kilometers inside Portuguese territory.

In an unpublished biography of Selous Scouts founder, Lieutenant-Colonel Ron Reid-Daly, Hannes Wessels, well-known for his hard-hitting book on the Rhodesian Special Air Service, *A Handful of Hard Men*, disclosed that by the time all these developments had taken place, the Rhodesian Army had already been active militarily in Mozambique for several years.[2]

Throughout 1968, he declares, the Rhodesians became more involved in helping their Portuguese counterparts in Mozambique, who were then battling the FRELIMO insurgency emanating from Zambia and Tanzania. In the main, he states, the Rhodesians did not have a very high regard for their Portuguese-speaking colleagues in terms of military ability and, conversely, the Portuguese saw their colleagues from across the often-undefined frontier in a very different light.

Ken Flower, head of Rhodesian Central Intelligence Organization (CIO), remarked in his book *Serving Secretly* how de Arriaga "had seen for himself how our soldiers lived rough and tough in the worst of the Zambezi Valley for weeks on end."[3] This was in total contrast to metropolitan

Portuguese soldiers in Mozambique who rarely moved from their bases or their transport after dark and remained dependent on regular supplies of bread and wine.

Flower added that he had heard General Costa Gomes say to his military attaché: "But do the Rhodesians really expect us to follow their example; living like animals merely to confront guerrillas?"

The attaché replied: "No, senhor. It is the example that is quite magnificent and it suits the Rhodesians who are Anglo-Saxons, but they don't really expect that sort of behavior from us Latins."

It was Reid-Daly who also commented that while the Portuguese were not up to Rhodesian standards, that was to be expected. He went on:

> Many were from poor backgrounds and did not really have much at stake in Africa. But as a people I was very fond of them; they always went to great lengths to make us welcome with the little they had to share. I thought some of their professional officers were damn fine too. I became very friendly with Colonel Rodrigo da Silveira who was an absolute gentleman and a good soldier.
>
> On one occasion we had found tracks of over 40 gooks and I told Rodrigo I needed a few of his men. He asked how many and I said four. With that he leaped out of his chair thinking I'd lost my mind. Loudly he insisted I take at least forty. I explained myself and he agreed to call his men onto the parade ground whereupon he explained the situation to the men and asked for volunteers. A deadly silence followed with his troops desperately trying to avoid making eye contact with me or him. Eventually, after much remonstrating a few hands waved warily in the wind and four volunteers came forward.
>
> Once we were out in the field however these chaps gained confidence and we made good progress using a helicopter to help us leapfrog on the spoor. Eventually we made contact and killed two of the enemy. The Portuguese guys were absolutely ecstatic. Following on from this I found a very large base camp which had just been evacuated. This came as quite an unsettling revelation and I realized our problems were bigger than we thought. If the enemy were moving in these numbers so close to our border, we had a major problem.

In truth, much Rhodesian criticism of Portuguese war efforts in Mozambique derived from their sense of the latter having let the guerrillas into Rhodesia by an army for which they had growing contempt.

The other effect centered on the defenses surrounding the Cahora Bassa Dam, which was to force guerrillas to move elsewhere, and as we have seen, they had done that by 1972. In fact, FRELIMO was beginning to penetrate further south as well as east from Tete, although in small numbers. The Vila Pery region was infiltrated about then and the Beira region in the following year, with the Beira railway coming under attack as its importance to Zambia declined following the closure of the Rhodesian-Zambian frontier. Mozambique rail traffic ceased at night and armored mine detectors or *zorras* were placed in front of trains.

As the Rhodesian forces had increasing success in preventing sabotage of the Beira line, so FRELIMO switched their efforts to the Moatize line into Malawi.

There was also some skepticism in Salisbury about Lisbon not making use of large numbers of "freelancers"—mercenaries—who were easily available and would have substantially bolstered Lisbon's military machine. The reason rested largely on pride, yet even the British have never been averse to recruiting foreign volunteers within their ranks, including the famed Royal Gurkha Rifles that have served the Crown for two centuries over and above thousands of Commonwealth volunteers who were found in every possible niche in the British Army, Navy and Air Force.

Mozambique, on Rhodesia's doorstep, had every opportunity to observe, in its day, one of the best examples of government coordinated mercenary activity.

In Chris Cocks' book on his wartime experiences while fighting for the Rhodesian Light Infantry, *Fire Force*—still, to my mind, the best work to emerge from that conflict—he makes the case for the Rhodesian Army having been second only to the French Foreign Legion in assimilating large numbers of foreigners into active combat units (there was also a Spanish Foreign Legion).

As Cocks tells it, the Rhodesian Light Infantry (RLI) had a bigger proportion of expatriates than any other in modern times.[4]

> There was a wide diversity of characters in 3 Commando. By tradition, most foreign volunteers served in the ranks and at one stage, I was the only born Rhodesian in 11 Troop.
>
> There were Americans of course, many of them Vietnam veterans resplendent with impressive arrays of medals, but we were not overly impressed by such dazzling displays and told them they looked like Christmas trees. Understandably, they ignored our taunts and wore their decorations with pride.
>
> Also, Canadians, Australians and New Zealanders, some of whom had fought in Vietnam. And we had Frenchmen, Belgians and Germans too, many of them ex-Legionnaires. Earlier on there had been a lot of South Africans, but their numbers began to dwindle as their own bush war intensified in South West Africa and Angola.
>
> The majority of overseas recruits came from Great Britain and Ireland from a variety of regiments like the Paras, the Royal Marines, Special Air Service and the Brigade of Guards. The British adapted well to Rhodesian conditions and many served with distinction and were decorated for valor.
>
> All foreign volunteers, in the main, were professional soldiers. It is true that a few liked to think of themselves as mercenaries (or mercs) but they weren't really … if they had been, they would have been soldiers "without fortune" if only because they got the same pay and served under the same conditions of service as Rhodesian-born regular soldiers. Like everyone else, they paid income tax to the Rhodesian Exchequer. Added to that, they were allowed to remit only a small percentage of their salaries to their own countries.
>
> The volunteers came for many and varied reasons. For some it was the action and adventure. For others it was glory. Many came in the belief that they were fighting to stop

the spread of international communism. And there were a few who were there just for the love of killing…

One of the more illustrious figures was British national André Dennison who, before arriving in Rhodesia, had served with distinction with 22 Special Air Service Regiment in Borneo. His exploits, penetrating dense jungle on patrol in South Asia with the legendary Sergeant Eddie Lillico, had earned him high praise from General Walter Walker. He was then detached as part of a contingent of 80 British officers and senior NCOs seconded to the 3rd Battalion, the Malaysian Rangers. After that there were stints in Europe, Cyprus, the Malawi Rifles, Northern Ireland and elsewhere.

Major Dennison joined 2nd Battalion Rhodesian African Rifles in October 1975 and commanded A Company until he was killed in action almost four years later.[5]

***

Ron Reid-Daly, then an acting captain with the Rhodesian Light Infantry, was the first Rhodesian officer to be attached to Portuguese forces. Others involved included some Rhodesian SAS specialists who were seconded from time to time, and their comments about the way in which the Portuguese were fighting their war in Mozambique (and, ultimately, why they eventually lost it) are illuminating.

From Reid-Daly's experience with the British SAS in Malaya where he served with distinction and was awarded an MBE, he soon made it clear to his superiors in Salisbury that the Portuguese brass in Mozambique had no real understanding of the nature of guerrilla warfare. They were certainly far behind anything that the British had experienced in Borneo, Malaya, or even Kenya during the Mau Mau Rebellion.

That was surprising, Reid-Daly reflected later, because many Portuguese Army commanders had already seen good service in Angola and Guinea.

The counter-insurgency pattern was the same each time. Some intelligence of insurgent activity would come in and the local garrison commander would spend days getting together a force of several hundred men who would make a huge cross-country sweep, often 500-men strong.

"They would never act immediately on a tip-off, with the result that when an operation was at last launched, the rebel concentration was long gone."

Although Reid-Daly, by then promoted to Lieutenant-Colonel was considered by his peers to be critical of the Portuguese war effort in Africa, and specifically what was going on in Mozambique at the time, his views were largely empirically based.

As he told me: "I was there. I saw it for myself. I went to war with these people, so I was in a very good position [to see] both the insurgent threat as it developed and the people who were defending: I was dealing with the Portuguese fighting man and I was impressed with neither."

He had his own views about Lisbon's *aldeamentos* program—that of resettling rural communities into organized camps, something that was already in full swing in all three of Lisbon's African provinces. Large sections of the civilian population were moved *en bloc* into areas where they would be under Portuguese control and, in theory, out of reach of the insurgents. The justification for this policy, ostensibly, was that it denied the guerrillas the ability to wage war because there "would be no popular indigenous support and no food, which was supposed to be essential for survival in the bush."

But the system never worked. Numerous surveys done after the war showed that the rebels were still managing to communicate with their comrades behind barbed wire and, in some cases, even fed by them: the same food they received from their putative jailers.

For all that, the bulk of the war—apart from what was going on in Tete Province—was confined largely to the north of Mozambique. Lourenço Marques—the capital city with its tourists and bright lights and from where almost all of us scribes operated—might have been in another African country.

***

In actual combat conditions, there were times when the South Africans and the Rhodesians found the Portuguese both clumsy and inept.

There were some notable exceptions—like the great Oscar Cardosa—but generally, army patrols in Mozambique were too large. As Reid-Daly pointed out, something like 30 or 40 men at a time would go into the jungle, and this at a time when his own people had become accustomed to four-man "sticks" and in the process were achieving good results.

Most failures, the Rhodesians believed, resulted from a lack of regular professional troops and the fact that most of these boys from the metropolis neither understood Africa nor wished to be in what they referred to, as one soldier declared to me, "this dreadful tropical hellhole." Letters home were full of such comments and worse.

Even more disconcerting, as hostilities continued, the traditional trust between officers and the men under them started to deteriorate. In a sense, it was almost a repeat of the Vietnamese syndrome, though as far as is known, there was never anything as dramatic as a "fragging".[6]

There were many reasons for this imbroglio and Ron Reid-Daly listed a few.

For a start, he pointed out, radio communications were poor, which was probably one reason why the troops in the field tended to work in such large numbers. "They were terrified of being overrun by the enemy, which, he suggested might be expected of such unprofessional soldiers."

Again, he reckoned, their radio sets were large and unwieldy American instruments designed rather for vehicles than the backs of soldiers in the bush, and quite a number probably dated from the Korean War period. As a result, communication with base was a long and complicated business. At one main base the Portuguese were using antiquated German sets from World War II.

Many of Reid-Daly's observations are insightful. During all the operations in which the Rhodesians took part in the Tete Panhandle, he recalls, the Portuguese were found to be completely base-bound. They fought much as the Americans had fought in Vietnam. The upper command was quite happy to let the insurgents control the bush while the Portuguese held onto the towns, communications links and strong points.

Reid-Daly said that in Tete, patrols should have been launched that lasted anything from four to six weeks and supplied by air. That idea, when he first propounded it, was regarded as preposterous by the upper command. At that time, the Portuguese would not consider anything beyond three days, spending nights in camp if at all possible.

The Rhodesians—already regarded, it might be recalled, as masters of counter-insurgency warfare—always emphasized the need to dominate the bush by night as well as by day. Although most Portuguese officers agreed, they rarely did anything about it.

The ability of FRELIMO to move freely after the sun had set was clearly illustrated by the number of mines—both anti-tank and anti-personnel—they were able to lay. This freedom extended all the way from the northernmost Rovuma River six or eight hundred kilometers southwards to the great Zambezi River, on the banks of which the city of Tete stood.

During one morning's clearing operation in the Mueda area, Portuguese sappers cleared 189 mines along a 10km track, about a third of them Soviet TM-46s. The rest were anti-personnel mines (APs). I was to see a bit of this for myself in the short three-day safari that I completed from Tete to the Malawi border in 1971 where roughly 50 mines were laid along the route we traversed.

Fortunately, almost all were detected before they did any damage, but one or two trucks triggered blasts.

There were other problems, recalls Reid-Daly. Physically, the Rhodesians regarded the average Portuguese conscript as "a poor physical specimen." They couldn't march any distance without frequent rests," he said. Most of these young men had come from poor backgrounds, and although they were put through their first physical training session on the day they joined the army in Portugal; there were many that were barely fit or strong enough to meet the fairly rigorous demands of their officers. Again, there were exceptions, some quite exceptional.[7]

One of their worst faults on the march was that the column was noisy and straggling. In one report, Reid-Daly wrote: "They talk loudly instead of maintaining silence, which even FRELIMO knows is one of the first principles of counter-insurgency warfare." After dark, he found that when an ambush had been set up, Portuguese soldiers would cough and fidget. "It was as if they were warning the enemy to keep clear, so that they would not be compelled to fight. Clearly, this was an impossible situation."

On the other hand, some of the *Flechas,* parachute and Black commando regiments were excellent operators in the bush. Most were superior to FRELIMO, and many of the kills in Mozambique were attributable to them and to the air force.

While most operational plans were carefully prepared by the brigade staff, Reid-Daly discovered that they seldom allowed the battalion commander scope for flexibility or personal initiative. It all had to be done according to the book. There was even a marked reluctance to change plans in spite of fresh information received and other developments as the operation progressed.

A sorry example of this was the failure to capitalize on the discovery— towards the end of 1967—by one of the helicopters during an operation, of a large insurgent camp about 500 meters across in the mountains near Cahora Bassa. It was only days later that an infantry attack was launched: the Portuguese officer responsible wasn't prepared to change either the original plan or the sequence of events he and his colleagues had earlier mapped out.

Reid-Daly was with them when this happened. He insisted that they scrape together another body of men and try an immediate vertical envelopment. That would have been possible, because there were eight Alouette helicopters available that together with the troops they ferried in, could have done some serious damage to the enemy. But the operation only got off the ground several days later, and because of delays it produced a lemon.

Reid-Daly believed that the Portuguese soldiers with whom he came into contact on these operations were not as well equipped as he would have thought, considering the nature of the war. Apart from the standard G3 rifle of 7.62 NATO caliber, they had no illumination flares, no claymores and none of the elementary means of protection found as a matter of course in most armies of the world. "Also, the average grunt from Europe simply had no idea how to handle smoke grenades to call up helicopters, or how to use small mirrors to attract the attention of aircraft—many little things that most bush fighters take for granted in remote or isolated areas."

Whereas the Rhodesians maintained excellent liaison between pilots and ground forces, that never existed in Mozambique and no one ever took steps to improve the situation. Their commanders were sometimes not even talking to each other. It was the same kind of real or imagined superiority that I had observed at close quarters in Angola's embattled Sector D in the *Dembos* jungles north of Luanda, which stretched all the way to the Congo.[8]

Another device taught by the Rhodesians and eventually taken up in Mozambique was to set up radio relay stations on hills, which also served as observation posts. Rhodesian officers began to take into the neighboring territory some of the elementary equipment that was lacking and which attracted great interest. Reid-Daly even ran a course showing his Lusitanian counterparts how to make a simple claymore mine from a ploughshare.

He and other Rhodesian officers also explained to them the principle of a stopper group and its role in a frontal attack. They needed to work hard at it, for the Portuguese choice of positions was usually bad; they rarely planned escape routes, and were simply not trained for the kind of bush warfare which, by then, had become second nature to many Rhodesian and South African units.

For instance, the very idea of taking a prisoner immediately after a skirmish was sometimes not favored. Although not all FRELIMO captives were shot, the Portuguese would argue that they ought to have been. It depended on the attitude of the officer in charge at the time. On more than one occasion Reid-Daly stepped in; it took a long time for the Portuguese Army to understand the need for interrogation and the importance of military intelligence. PIDE, Lisbon's all-intrusive secret police, was always calling for prisoners, which sometimes resulted in friction and occasionally an exchange of harsh words with the military.

The Rhodesians noted that Portuguese military vehicles, the West German Unimog and the French-built Berliet—both of which formed the mainstay of communications in the bush—were excellent, as was their maintenance. Like their uniforms, of which the troops were issued two per tour of duty, it was all they had and they looked after them. But that was not the case with their weapons.

Perhaps because the G3 was virtually proof against stoppage, few Portuguese soldiers bothered to clean their guns, either before or after an operation. They would smile among themselves at the Rhodesians who took great care of their rifles all times. One young captain told Reid-Daly that the last place he had seen a man actually cleaning his rifle every day when not ordered was Goa, the Portuguese colony on the Indian subcontinent. He had done so after he'd been captured by Indian troops.

Morale among Portuguese forces was seriously affected by the lack of facilities for the evacuation of casualties. That was due mainly to the shortage of operational helicopters. Also, while most of the camps had medical officers, most were conscript students who had only the bare minimum available for their needs. A man injured by a landmine would usually have to be moved to an airstrip, where a small plane could be landed. Depending on how remote a base was, that could take a day. Many Portuguese soldiers died of wounds because of such delays.

The Rhodesian officers found it curious that the Portuguese in Mozambique had never developed reconnaissance patrols. They would seldom reconnoiter a position beforehand, or use aerial photos for intelligence purposes once a known FRELIMO camp had been pinpointed. Instead, they would deploy Special Forces in an operation which would often include the necessary primary reconnaissance with the attack, very much a hit-or-miss affair.

Reid-Daly spent some time with one of the *Flecha* units; he became a close friend of Oscar Cardosa, who was brought from Angola to establish the *Flecha* concept in Mozambique. Unlike so many of his fellows, Cardosa proved to be an excellent soldier and tactician.

While the *Flechas* worked in smaller groups, they also lacked enterprise. They were composed mostly of captured terrorists, turncoats and local recruits and were paid bounties for kills, captures or recovery of weapons. Their training was hard and simple and discipline was draconian. A petty misdemeanor would be treated as a serious offence. At the same time, they did make excellent soldiers. Their ability to shoot straight with a rifle was unmatched even in the Rhodesian Army; they either got one- or two-inch groups at 50 yards or they were thrashed by their officers.

The *Flechas* considered a 40km patrol between sunrise and sunset as normal, in spite of the difficult mountainous and jungle terrain. Some Rhodesian SAS men who worked with them were amazed at their ability to keep going and were themselves hard-pressed to keep up.

They were also militarily correct in their actions; they would cross a river or other obstacle by first sending two sections tactically across, checking the area and then bringing the rest of the group through. During the entire day they had only one break for a smoke, that respite that most soldiers regard as a natural right.

The Rhodesians achieved some success in Mozambique. They managed to teach some units how to run a proper operations room and to set up an efficient Joint Operations Command. Trackers gradually began to come into their own, and here members of the SAS played an important part. Unfortunately, in the long term there were simply too many Portuguese and too few Rhodesians to have any real effect on the war.

But they never really succeeded in goading the Portuguese into effectively following up tracks after a contact. Under Reid-Daly, they would often refuse outright to go into the bush unless a large force had been mustered, and then with additional helicopter support. The result was that FRELIMO units were able to snipe at Portuguese patrols almost with impunity. They knew that their adversaries would rarely detach men from their columns to go after them.

To the conscript army, capturing a FRELIMO camp was the pinnacle of success, even though it might have been abandoned because the rebels had foreknowledge of the attack or could hear them coming. Holding ground was the ultimate achievement, even if they abandoned that ground an hour later.

Reid-Daly recommended on his return to Salisbury that RLI units should be allowed to work with the Portuguese, not so much for political reasons, but rather to demonstrate what ordinary young soldiers were capable of achieving when properly led and trained. He was aware too that the presence of Special Forces like the SAS might have been regarded by the Portuguese command as an attempt by the Rhodesians to "show them up," with consequent ill feeling.

In the opinion of most Rhodesian and South African soldiers who came into contact with the Portuguese Army on full operations, the quality most needed was initiative. As it was, independent enterprise among the officers was almost entirely lacking. Occasionally a brilliant officer would be encountered—a professional soldier who knew the war, the enemy, the ground on which he was fighting and capable of inspiring his men to better results; but that was rare.

Towards the end of the war, discipline became lax, and the average Portuguese soldier, while respectful to their officers, except during the final phase of the conflict when the entire army was pulled back to the metropolis after the army mutiny, was sloppy in both dress and bearing and slack in military operations.

Often a battalion commander would be of the best type imaginable, but he would lack good professional officers to support him. Senior commanders usually had only a handful of regular officers, supplemented by many more *milicianos* (the title accorded temporary officers from universities).

Notably, Prime Minister Caetano, who succeeded the ailing Salazar, admitted once he was in exile in Brazil that "we had no organization capable of directing the army in operations." Most of the Portuguese defense structure was haphazard and piecemeal, he said, which, as Porch declared in his authoritative work[9] meant that the army, simply put, was "ill-equipped to cope with a long war."

***

A fascinating insight to the kind of conditions likely to be encountered by the Portuguese Army in Mozambique also came from Reid-Daly.

As he explained, the Portuguese and the Rhodesians were fighting the same kind of insurgency on both sides of the Zambezi, so the terrain in the valley, largely jungle and overgrown, was similar and unforgiving. Conditions could be exacting, he admits, in summer months especially when you had additional issues like malaria and the tsetse fly to deal with.

The incident described by the man who was to become the founder-commander of the Selous Scouts, one of the best tracking units in any man's army, took place in November 1967. At the time he was serving as Training Officer in the 1st Battalion, Rhodesian Light Infantry in his first post as a commissioned officer. Occasionally he was required to deputize for commando commanders who were on leave, or on course at the School of Infantry.

During their absence Reid-Daly would take their commandos over on border control operations and it was during one of these stints that he had an unusual experience which, had things turned out otherwise, might have resulted in catastrophic consequences. The program was centered on bush survival, something about which this officer was outspokenly critical when it came to his allies, the Portuguese Army. Lieutenant-Colonel Reid-Daly takes up the story:

> It was already well into summer when I was ordered to command the Battalion's Support Group for a six-week border stint at the northernmost corner of the country where Rhodesia, Zambia and Mozambique shared common borders at the junction of the Luangwa and the Zambezi rivers. A temporary military base large enough to house a company or even an RLI commando had been built behind a police post known as Kanyemba, which was a pleasant place set in picturesque surroundings on the banks of the Zambezi.
>
> Whoever sited the post obviously had the natural beauty of the place in mind but very little else. Tactically, in event of an attack, it was a potential death-trap, which we all knew would happen at some time or another because this was quite an important infiltration region.

Things were rough in the bush: troop deployments were carried out by vehicles along atrocious bush tracks, or by boat skimming up the Zambezi River. The Mpata Gorge which formed my northwestern limit was considered uncrossable because the Zambezi stormed through almost year-round, its passage constricted by the ravine. Further downstream, below that obstacle, the river spreads out again, and in the process, slowing it down.

The width of the Zambezi River in this region is considerable, almost a mile in places and the Rhodesian military, taking cognizance of the lack of any kind of watermanship among the insurgents, considered it unlikely that they would come through there.

I went up to this point by boat, landed and looked around, not at all impressed with what I saw. The promontory was littered with piles of junk from the rubbish pits of previous patrols that had been dug up by wild animals. We could see that there had been fires lit all over the place, which told me that some of these units had been casual in their observation duties, at night especially. They'd used fires either to keep warm, or more likely, to keep prowling animals at bay.

I didn't see much point in traveling up the Zambezi River in full view of the Zambian side to take up what should have been a clandestine observation post.

So, on my return to base, I studied the 1:50 000 scale map pinned to the wall of the operations room looking for a land route to what we referred to as The Gates, our name for the gorge. There were no properly surveyed maps of this part of the Zambezi Valley at the time and the men on the ground had to make do with sheets of paper covered with a military grid system.

I now understand why the previous commanders had used boats to position their patrols there; but I was determined to find a way to insert a patrol without the whole of Zambia— and of course, the enemy—being aware of it.

A careful study of the map showed that the nearest accurate jump-off point for the patrol to enter the area was the western corner of a bush airstrip which lay south-east from The Gates and served Kanyemba. I worked out a compass bearing to the top of a high range of hills known as Kapsuku. If the patrol's map-reading was accurate, they'd find themselves at the headwaters of the Euguta River; all they had to do was follow the river down through the hills to the Zambezi.

The total length of the patrol was 17 map kilometers, a distance which should easily be covered in a long daylight march, or about 12 hours. However, taking account of the fact that this was the hottest period of the year with temperatures around noon running at something like 90 degrees Fahrenheit (roughly 32 degrees Celsius), it was not going to be an easy march. In addition, each man was carrying a load, the lightest of which clocked in at almost 30kg. All these factors, coupled with the kind of terrain that included steep gradients, made me accept that the patrol might have to sleep out one night and reach The Gates only the following morning.

Orders were issued for the task ahead. At dawn the patrol debussed at the airstrip in preparation for an early start so that as much ground as possible could be covered in the relatively cooler part of the day. I checked the patrol commander's compass bearing and pointed out a clearly visible gap in the mountains that formed the headwaters of the river which would lead him to The Gates.

The patrol set off and I returned to my operations room to monitor other counter-insurgency units deployed on the valley floor.

We worked to fixed routines, which required patrols to adhere to a strict radio schedule. They would call their control station (headquarters) at 07h00 hours, noon and then again at 16h00 hours and provide us with routine sitreps or situation reports.

I heard nothing from this particular group throughout the day and by last light, I was starting to feel a bit uneasy. Failure to observe radio scheds did occasionally happen, so I left it at that for the time being, aware that there were many reasons which could affect communications. These might range from mechanical failure to a faulty radio or possibly screening by mountains. Still, I had a nagging feeling that all was not well. Before getting my head down, I advised Brigade Headquarters that I might need a helicopter for a casualty evacuation the next day.

The following morning's 07h00 radio schedule still showed no sign of the patrol. I summoned the boat crew and headed upriver, stopping along the banks of the Zambezi in a bid to reach the patrol by radio. It just so happened that one of our Canberra bombers on a cross-country map-reading exercise passed overhead. I called him up, gave him the approximate map coordinates and asked him if he could deviate slightly from his course and give The Gates patrol a radio call. He returned a few minutes later to report nothing heard or seen of the patrol.

It was now 12h00 and I knew that we had something serious on our hands. I returned to Kanyemba base, called up Brigade Headquarters and requested the immediate use of a helicopter. But that was easier said than done because in those early days of border control, we had the same kind of problems that the Portuguese faced. Getting a chopper was a major exercise and Heaven only help the field commander who called for one only to discover that there was no emergency.

Flying time to Kanyemba by helicopter was about three hours and as arranged, an Alouette arrived at 15h00 hours. I gave the pilot a quick briefing while his technician refueled and loaded onboard as many water bags as could be found in the camp. Then, together with my medic, we headed off into the bush to try to locate these chaps.

We reached the location that the patrol should have passed through and though we circled for a while, there was no sign of the squad. The pilot then headed over the next range of hills.

Suddenly he cursed and then banked sharply. Something had caught his eye, and then I spotted it. It was an astonishing sight: there was a bunch of men running around in the bush below, all of them stark naked.

We landed and they came running. We actually had to fight them off as they desperately tried to get at the water bags.

Although it was late in the afternoon, the sun still radiated an intense heat, as it always does in the Zambezi Valley. There were many patches of forest in the area, but in November, few of them have leaves and the parched soldiers had almost no shade to shield them from the sun.

It was obvious that this patrol had reached its limit of endurance. Had we not pitched up that afternoon, I'm pretty certain that several would have been dead by morning.

I flew the soldiers back to camp in relays, where, on touching down, they rushed to the showers, where they'd stand or lie down under the cold flow of water. At the same time, being youngsters, it was astonishing to see how quickly they managed to recover, their mouths wide open, taking in as much as they could.

In the debrief that followed, it appeared they had missed the gap. But instead of pushing on north towards the great river, they'd wasted valuable time trying to find the Euguta River to follow down to The Gates. Climbing up and down steep hills with the sun beating down had exhausted them all. Even worse, the exercise generated thirst.

What had happened was they made good time on the first day out and had their map-reading been more precise, they would probably have reached the Zambezi River that evening, thus achieving the objective. Instead, an element of panic apparently crept in when some of the men thought they were lost. It became more serious when they found they had no comms with base.

Had I taken them in hand before, I'd have been able to tell them that anxiety and fear often make a man sweat profusely. All this, plus some heavy physical toil while the patrol cross-grained exceptionally difficult terrain in their bid to find the river soon exhausted their two standard water bottles. Dehydration set in rapidly.

I asked them why they had taken off their clothes and their reply was interesting. They found that dehydration had made their skins become paper dry and they simply couldn't stand their clothes rubbing against their skin. The only obvious relief was to take everything off, which they did. Some, in desperation, even tried to drink their own urine, disguising the taste by mixing coffee powder with it.

I noticed that the younger soldiers had been the worst affected. It was clear that the older men had a tougher mental outlook and were much better able to cope with the stress. It was a good lesson and we took it to heart because we'd only just begun to teach bush craft in the Rhodesian Army and this particular group had not had any of it.

When we flew to recover the group, we passed over an astonishing range of wild animals. In fact, a herd of elephants together with hundreds of impala: all were in clear sight of the patrol. Had the men been properly trained, their water problems would have been over: the average impala provides about two liters of water from its stomach and an elephant holds on average, 36 liters.

Later, during 1973, when the bush war began in earnest, I was given the task of raising and training a special multiracial unit, the Selous Scouts. Bush survival and tracking formed an important part of the operational training of these men because it gave them tremendous self-confidence in their abilities to survive and live comfortably in the African bush. Indeed, once put through their paces, they found nothing unusual in carrying out long-range, two-man reconnaissance patrols over distances, sometimes, of hundreds of kilometers.

These two-man patrols, comprising a Black and a White soldier, would be dropped by parachute (high altitude, low opening) often 200 kilometers from the Rhodesian border in hostile country and operate behind the lines for up to six weeks at a time. It was a tribute to their training that they never ran into problems from a bush survival point of view…

As Lieutenant-Colonel Ron Reid-Daly was to comment in later years, the Portuguese Army knew none of this. Nor was anybody in either Lourenço Marques or Beira interested enough to learn, even though the offer was repeatedly made both by himself and other Rhodesian Army officers who spent time in the bush with their allies from Europe.

Had they done so, he ventured, an awful lot more lives might have been saved.

CHAPTER 13

The Landmine War—Ultimately the Deciding Factor

"Our targets multiply. When they open more roads, the enemy creates more targets for us. When they bring more cars, they enlarge the field of action of our sabotage units. When they concentrate in the bush, they make easier their own annihilation."

CANDIDE MONDLANE, FRELIMO

In an astonishing development, decades after Lisbon's Mozambique war had become history, that country was still grappling with an almost overwhelming problem that involved landmines. Many were laid by the Portuguese, but after the colonial war ended, many more went into the ground at the behest of the Maputo government in its decade-long effort to combat RENAMO rebels.[1]

Who then would have believed it possible to use rats to detect those same landmines and neutralize them? Exactly that is still taking place in remote parts of this former Portuguese East African colony. The rodents are termed "Hero Rats" and some are almost the size of cats. They are able to sniff out live ordnance buried in the ground and have been doing so for years. In the process, the creatures have saved countless lives.

While the Mozambique civil war ended decades ago, one of its enduring legacies is the number of landmines spread about the country, together with the skeletons of hundreds of mine victims, often left untouched for years because nobody has been brave or stupid enough to enter the minefields to recover the dead.

Employing rats to identify landmines emerged by a rather curious process. It was common knowledge in the old days that the ancient Chinese could diagnose tuberculosis by the smell of a person's saliva on a flame or hot rock. Afrikaners use the word *tering* to describe the smell of tar, which is the same odor that TB patients exude, and in Africa the disease is endemic.

Somebody came up with the idea that if it were possible to actually smell TB with our inefficient human olfactory senses, then dogs—and possibly other animals—might be able to detect it at a much earlier stage. That was when "Hero Rats" were brought in for trials.

It is significant that in Tanzania—where less than half of TB patients are diagnosed before death—these rodents detected almost a thousand cases of tuberculosis in 2008 and 2009. An NGO group there subsequently estimated that the rats prevented at least 14,000 transmissions.

Bart Weetjens, the moving force behind another non-governmental organization that calls itself APOPO—a Dutch acronym meaning Anti-Personnel Land Mines Detection Product Development—believed it possible that if rodents could detect disease, they might also be able to point out bombs since explosives almost always permeate intrusive odors.

Previously, the Belgian-born Weetjens spent several years involved in landmine recovery in Third World countries. In the spring of 1995, he learnt that scientists were studying the use of gerbils in bomb detection, but they were using a system involving brain electrodes which Weetjens found unsustainable.

Instead, he declared, he wanted a locally based solution that might empower communities, like impoverished societies in Africa. That was when he was reminded of TB experiments involving "Hero Rats."

What is notable in this regard is that the International Campaign to Ban Landmines is on record as stating that from 1999 to 2009, landmines and related devices were responsible for 73,576 casualties worldwide. Campaign data from 2007 say there were 5,426 recorded casualties in that year alone, with almost a fifth in two dozen African states, among them Mozambique, Zimbabwe and Angola.

In effect, landmine warfare, while an insidious means of destruction, is nothing new. In his memoir, *Seven Pillars of Wisdom*, T. E. Lawrence revealed his most effective tactic. Landmines, he declared, were the best weapon yet discovered to make the regular working of the Turkish enemy's trains costly and uncertain. It is generally accepted that but for Lawrence's pioneering use of precisely placed explosives, the Arab Revolt might have failed.

These bombs did not fail in more modern times for a succession of guerrilla movements ranged against a Portuguese Army fighting for survival in Africa. Indeed, but for landmines, Lisbon might still be something of a force in Africa today because it was these hidden killers—to which there was no effective answer until South Africa developed a range of "mine-protected" vehicles—which demoralized Lisbon's soldiers like no other single feature of the wars.

In Afghanistan until recently, the insurgents were using similar weapons against Coalition forces. Instead of referring to them as landmines, they are called IEDs—for "Improvised Explosive Devices"—and vehicles, as opposed to trains (as in the Lawrence era), were targeted. The effect was just as devastating and the statistics are sobering. The number of landmines being used in Asia, and the share of casualties for which they are responsible, dwarf anything ever seen before by the American military.

Robert Bryce, in an insightful article for the American publication *Foreign Affairs*, stated that during World War II, three percent of United States combat deaths were caused by mines or booby-traps. In Korea that figure was four percent. By 1967, during the Vietnam War, it was nine percent, and the Pentagon began experimenting with armored boots.[2]

More pertinent, says Bryce, from June to November 2005, IEDs laid by insurgents in Iraq were responsible for 65 percent of American combat deaths and roughly half of all non-fatal injuries. Though conditions were not as serious for Portugal in its African conflicts, mines had the required debilitating effect for Lisbon's guerrilla adversaries.

***

Dr John Cann, the American historian we met in earlier chapters made an incisive study of Lisbon's landmine problem, and the effect it had on movement and transportation in regions where hostilities predominated.

Ground Transportation and Mine Counter-measures affected several Portuguese units; first in Mozambique's north where it was comparatively easy to bring these bombs into play, and later in the central regions along the Zambezi River, the Cahora Bassa Dam and Tete, its nearest large town.

Almost all Portugal's military posts in these regions had to be supplied by truck because there was no other practical means to deliver heavy items; rail lines were restricted by the route that they took, and airlift by weight limitations. Cann goes on:

> If Portugal was to win its war, then the trucks with their supplies must reach their destinations in sufficient numbers to provide for the soldiers. Truck passage not only had to negotiate an enemy but also some of the most primitive and daunting territory in the world, and thus travel by truck could be a slow and grueling process in most areas. Paved roads were easy routes but tended to connect the principal towns and not the villages and the more remote sites, outposts that were important in keeping the insurgent separated from the population.
>
> To deliver supplies to the more secluded areas required a fleet of supply vehicles negotiating not only the paved highways but poor roads, tracks, and trails. In many cases these latter pistes could degenerate into rutted tracks through deep sand. Vehicles could and

very often did become stuck in these primitive roads, requiring hours to extricate. During the rainy season unpaved roads became quagmires of soft mud and sand and were virtually impassable. In the dry season they remained a problem, although the dry river beds baked hard and provided a solid roadway. Some of these trails could follow a dry water course for as much as 50 kilometers.

Trucks traveled these routes generally by convoy when enemy contact was expected. The convoy might be all military or a combination of commercial hauliers and military. When entering an area of known or probable insurgent presence, the trucks would be assembled, and the drivers briefed on convoy procedure for driving, being ambushed or detonating a mine.

Mines were used increasingly in all of the theaters as the war progressed. Initially the guerrillas were inept in using them, but their proficiency improved over time, as they acquired the skill of safely handling and effectively placing the devices.

As he tells us, their use eventually far exceeded that in other insurgencies for the simple reason that mining of the road system in the interior was far and away the easiest way for the insurgents to disrupt the Portuguese ground logistic system and create an opportunity for the ambush of a truck convoy. Ultimately, widespread mining prompted the Portuguese to adopt a series of counter-measures in the modification and operation of their vehicles and in demining procedures.[3]

Lisbon came up with a variety of "solutions," the majority either impractical or unwieldy. Mozambique's interior was always a rigorous experience for those involved there and even tougher on their equipment and vehicles.

Anything devised to counter the landmine threat had to slot into those parameters and as South Africa was later to prove in its own wars in Africa's south-west, only specially designed vehicles built with extraordinarily resilient steels would do.

But all that cost money and a series of dedicated research establishments manned by engineers who had been specially trained for the task. While the war lasted these demands were simply beyond what Lisbon could afford at the time.

Obviously, as losses mounted, the Portuguese Army did what it could to try to negate the threat of mines but it was an almost impossible task. Roads were primitive and unpaved and the guerrillas came and went almost as they pleased because, as we have seen, the majority of government forces were either camp-bound or unwilling to go after the enemy in their own backyard.

Initially, army trucks were made as safe as possible in the event of encountering mines. Since the Berliet truck was designed and built for resupply, it was the first choice from a safety angle: its wheels were well in front of the cab so that the mines would be detonated ahead of the driver and passenger, with the engine providing protection from the blast. As Cann explains, the bonnet and the metallic top of the driver's cab were removed, in part because the bonnet sometimes had a habit of acting as a guillotine and decapitating the driver and passenger in a mine explosion. If not removed, the force of the explosion would also throw them both upward against the cab roof causing severe injury.

The floor and bed of the truck were laid with sandbags to protect the occupants from shrapnel emanating from the explosion. It was also important for occupants to keep their arms and legs inside the vehicles to achieve maximum protection from the sandbags. Then convoy organization and truck operating procedures were adjusted to accommodate the threat: the lead vehicle—traditionally a Berliet "mine crasher" truck—followed by a Mercedes Benz Unimog troop carrier with 50 meters regarded as the standard separation, with the remainder of the convoy following behind.

On sandy roads convoy drivers would tend to follow immediately in the tracks of the vehicle ahead to be certain of a safe and tested path. Troop carriers were positioned throughout the convoy, and a Berliet concluded the train.

Progress was generally irregular, depending on what obstacles the escorts found in the road. There could be debris, a suspicion of a mine, or a broken truck. When night came, the vehicles would form a laager, only to be on the road again at first light.

The convoys would only travel at night if they met an oncoming convoy that had cleared the road ahead. It would then be important to cover the sanitized route as quickly as possible before the insurgents had the opportunity to plant new mines.

The road tarring program made mining much more difficult for the insurgents. Planting mines under a hard-surfaced road meant carefully removing a section of fringe, digging a hole for the mine, and then replacing the section over the explosive. It all had to be artfully resurfaced to conceal its lethal charge and while no road was fully immune, the insurgents preferred the sandy tracks.

Convoys along these bush highways sometimes employed a lookout who would attempt to assess the situation in the road ahead. If in his judgment he felt that here was a risk of mines, then the convoy would halt, and a team of from four to eight men would alight from the trucks.

These men would begin a line abreast search in the path of the vehicles with pointed probes or lances called *picas*: wooden rods of about two meters in length with a metallic 50-centimeter point, the name of which was derived from the lance used in bullfighting. These *picadores* or "trail blazers" were rotated every 20 minutes with all soldiers detailed to the convoy taking a turn.

The job, naturally, was tedious besides being dangerous and required uninterrupted concentration. After a mine had been discovered, a combat knife was gently used to clean sand and earth from around the device. If the charge appeared to be booby-trapped (which happened increasingly as hostilities wore on) then it was destroyed in situ.

Often anti-personnel mines were employed with the anti-vehicular type and placed either around it or on the side of the road, the purpose being to frustrate convoy procedures where personnel would abandon the trucks and seek shelter elsewhere to avoid the effects of an ambush.

By freezing personnel in their vehicles—with the omnipresent threat of anti-personnel mines, the insurgents would obviously increase their chances for an ambush.

With time, the Portuguese found that the *pica* in the hands of an experienced *picador* was the most efficient and reliable method of locating mines. It was also cost-effective.

Specially trained dogs were valuable aids in detection, but were by no means as reliable as the *picadores*. Many mechanical road flagellation systems were also tested, but they were cumbersome and expensive, and none matched a team of four experienced *picadores*. Also, they were mostly either too cumbersome or weighty to take into remote areas, where traveling even for ordinary four-wheel-drive vehicles was difficult.

***

A valuable insight to the kind of mines that were deployed in Mozambique (and in other Southern African guerrilla conflicts) comes from a publication put out by Human Rights Watch under the auspices of the Arms Project Africa Watch and titled *Landmines in Mozambique*.[4]

Landmines were deployed by the parties to the conflict in Mozambique in a variety of ways, frequently in violation of the Landmines Protocol. FRELIMO regularly disseminated landmines in a random and indiscriminate fashion. This was sometimes used as a tactic to deter infantry attack and reconnaissance patrols, but civilians were often the main victims of randomly laid mines. Records were rarely made of randomly disseminated landmines, an irresponsible action without regard for the welfare of the civilian population.

Nevertheless, a local army mining officer provided Oxfam with a list of 34 locations mined by FRELIMO with about 500 mines. While many of the mines may have since been cleared or detonated, it will be necessary to inspect each location.

The great majority of mines in Mozambique appear to be of former Soviet or East European origin and were laid by both government troops and RENAMO.

The anti-personnel mines found in the largest quantity in clearance operations and inspections of arsenals are former Soviet PMN, POMZ-2 and POMZ-2M mines. Other types are present in smaller, but still significant, quantities, as can be observed below.

Anti-personnel Mines

Soviet Union

PMN Source: U.S.S.R: Soviet State Arsenals. Type: Anti-personnel blast. Initiation: Pressure. The PMN, a very common mine, may be responsible for more mine-related deaths and amputations throughout the world than any other mine. Although easily detected, this mine device has a large explosive content (240 grams of TNT) and requires as little as 0.25kg of direct pressure to initiate an explosion. Injuries from this mine can often be fatal.

PMN-2 Source: U.S.S.R: Soviet State Arsenals. Type: Anti-personnel blast. Initiation: Pressure. The PMN-2 differs from the PMN most notably in that the delay arming mechanism is irreversible and there is no known neutralization technique.

PMD-6M Source: U.S.S.R: Soviet State Arsenals. Type: Anti-personnel blast. Initiation: Pressure. This mine employs a wooden box body with a block of cast TNT initiated when 1–10kg of downward pressure on the box forces the pin out of a MUV-2 fuse. The design has been widely copied. After having been buried for some time, this mine becomes unstable and finally ineffective once the wood rots. There is a high metallic content in the fuse, aiding detection.

POMZ-2 and POMZ-2M Source: U.S.S.R: Soviet State Arsenals. Type: Anti-personnel fragmentation. Initiation: Tripwire. Both types consist of a cast iron fragmentation casing mounted on a wooden stake. The casing contains a 75-gram charge of TNT and a fuse (normally an MUV fuse) which protrudes from the top of the casing. A tripwire is connected to a striker-retaining pin in the fuse. A pull of approximately 1kg on the tripwire will release the striker and initiate an explosion. The POMZ-2 has six rows of fragmentation; the POMZ-2M has only five. Both mines have an effective killing range of up to 25 meters.

OZM-3 Source: U.S.S.R: Soviet State Arsenals. Type: Anti-personnel bounding fragmentation. Initiation: Remote, pressure, pull, or tension-release. This mine can be initiated by electrical or other remote control, or, depending on fusing, by pressure, pull, or tension release. Following initiation, the mine base explodes, expelling the main charge to a height of 1.5 to 2.4 meters before it explodes. Height is determined by a tether wire. The charge throws metal, from an inner fragmentation shell, with an effective radius of 25 meters.

OZM-4 Source: U.S.S.R: Soviet State Arsenals. Type: Anti-personnel bounding fragmentation. Initiation: Pull or pressure. Derivative of OZM-3 (above), but cannot be fired electrically.

OZM-72 Source: U.S.S.R: Soviet State Arsenals. Type: Anti-personnel bounding fragmentation. Initiation: Pull, pressure, or remote. This mine is fired by either electrical remote control or a pull or pressure fuse. As the mine is fired a propellant charge blows it upwards until a tethering wire is drawn taut which detonates the fuse at about 1 meter above the surface. The main charge explodes, sending the steel shrapnel in all directions. It has a lethal radius of 25–30 meters. When an electric detonator is used the mine will explode immediately. In this role the mine will normally therefore be placed above ground.

MON-50 and MON-100 Source: U.S.S.R: Soviet State Arsenals. Type: Anti-personnel directional fragmentation. Initiation: Remote or tripwire. The MON-50 is a virtually identical Soviet derivative of the U.S. claymore with a lethal range of 50 meters. The MON-100 is a larger version of the MON-50. The cylindrical casing has a face diameter of 220mm and contains 450 pieces of steel fragmentation mounted in 5kg of plastic explosive. The killing area is reported to be 100 meters.

China

Type 69 Source: People's Republic of China. Manufacturer: China North Industries, Beijing. Type: Anti-personnel bounding fragmentation. Initiation: Pressure or tripwire. This mine can be set to explode by pressure or tripwire. On detonation it bounds to 1.5 meters before exploding, discharging approximately 250 metal fragments over a lethal radius of more than ten meters.

Type 72 and 72B Source: People's Republic of China. Manufacturer: China North Industries, Beijing. Type: Anti-personnel blast. Initiation: Pressure or anti-disturbance. This small, nearly all-plastic anti-personnel mine is one of the most frequently encountered mines in the world. Because of its low metal content, it is very difficult to detect. The 34-gram explosive charge is small, but is sufficient to produce severe injuries. The Type 72 and 72B are externally identical, but whereas the Type 72 operates only by pressure, the Type 72B also has an anti-disturbance mechanism, so that the mine will explode when it is handled or disturbed in any way, making it extremely unstable.

Czechoslovakia

PP-Mi-Sr Source: Czechoslovak State Factories. Type: Anti-personnel bounding fragmentation. Initiation: Pull or pressure. Initial activation of this metallic-cased bounding mine may be by pull-fuse using a tripwire or by pressure-fuse. These fuses set off the propellant charge which, after a three-second delay, causes the mine to leap upwards to a tethered height of one meter before detonation. The casing of the mine acts as fragmentation.

East Germany

PPM-2 Source: Germany (former GDR). Manufacturer: Former East German state factories. Type: Anti-personnel blast. Initiation: Pressure, electric charge. The integral fuse is delay-armed, pressure initiated and electrically fired and utilizes a central spring-loaded "snap column" to transmit pressure on the pressure plate to the piezocrystal.

Yugoslavia

PROM 1 Source: Yugoslavia (ex). Manufacturer: Federal Directorate of Supply & Procurement. Type: Anti-personnel bounding fragmentation. Initiation: Pressure. It is pressure that pushes the cylinder down, freeing the retaining balls, which allows the striker to hit the percussion cap. This ignites the delay element which burns for approximately 1.5 seconds and then ignites the bounding charge, which in turn ejects the mine 0.7 to 1.5 meters above the surface of the ground (as limited by a tether wire). The main charge then explodes, causing fragmentation which is lethal to a radius of 50 meters and dangerous to a radius of 100 meters.

A Personal Experience of the War in Mozambique

Notes from my diary, February 16–18, 1973

While Portugal fought its military campaigns in Africa, the town of Tete—a large sprawling place that even today is totally dominated by a huge suspension bridge across the Zambezi River—came to represent one of the last embattled outposts of an imperial tradition that had lasted five centuries. When I visited the place in the early 1970s, it was an epoch that was about to close.

I'd gone through Tete with Michael Knipe—at the time the London *Times'* man in Southern Africa—and we discovered an archetypal Portuguese-style town similar to those found all over the southern half of the continent. These were critical times in what the European media would term "Africa's Liberation Wars" and difficult times for the town of Tete especially. It was a tough place where hostilities sometimes started at the edge of town as soon as the sun had disappeared over the great river and the jungles to the west.

Mines eventually took the biggest toll. In fact, there wasn't a day when we didn't spot vehicles being towed in from the countryside or hauled back to town on low-loaders after they'd been ambushed. Many more trucks were blown up by landmines and most times, their cargoes were either removed *in situ* or, if too big—like mining equipment—destroyed and the damaged vehicles abandoned.

Moving through Mozambique during wartime was one of the most fascinating phases of this observer's life.

Michael Knipe and I had traveled overland through Rhodesia—then also beleaguered—and the idea was that he would return to Johannesburg when I kept on heading north. It was my intention to head through the Tete Panhandle, first to Malawi and then on to Lusaka in Zambia—also a Black African country technically at war with the "White South." My final destination this time round was the Congo.

But first I had to wait for the next convoy and, for a short while, Tete became my base. It was an unpleasant little sojourn. Wrapped round a dirty crossroads on the banks of a great African river, Tete could easily have passed for a film set depicting the early years of the great American trek to the west. The only real difference was a very occasional modern-looking building and a tall communications aerial on the hill that overlooked us all. There was nothing to remind us that the settlement was one of the first inland trading posts established by Portuguese mariners who sailed up the river from the Indian Ocean in their shallow-hulled galliots in the 15th century.

What little development there was, remained centered on the couple of thousand men of the 17th Battalion, as well as helicopters and ground support squadrons who had nowhere else to spend what little they earned. The glass and glitter of Lourenço Marques (Maputo today) lay more than 1,600km to the south.

The only hope for Tete, one sensed, was the big hydroelectric dam then being built in a huge gorge on the Zambezi River more than 160km upstream. That construction promised progress, but as we now know, it was only finished after the war had ended. By then the majority of the Portuguese had decamped, bags and all, back to Lisbon.

At that stage though, the Portuguese did all they could to build the Cahora Bassa Dam, which was to create the second biggest man-made body of water in Africa, after Egypt's Aswan. For their part, the insurgents hurled everything they had at the colonials in their efforts to stop construction. Along the way, an awful lot of lives were lost.

Twice each day, starting at dawn, open trucks carrying two lurching platoons left Tete to guard the shipment of supplies, men and equipment that were headed for the remote Cahora Bassa gorge. The road had been metaled, which meant that the mine threat was minimal. But not the ambushes, which seemed to keep some kind of an intermittent pace with the convoys and inevitably, took a daily toll.

Tete's Barracks Square was where all military activities were coordinated. Writing about the place, British writer James McManus recalled that it looked "absurdly Beau Geste." From there too, patrols around the town would set out before dawn each day and check all routes for landmines which, we were soon to discover, were often responsible for the first casualty of the day.

Security in and around Tete was tight. Journalists like Michael, James McManus and I, were rarely welcome. In my case, I suppose I was fortunate because I'd been given a letter of introduction to the local commander. And anyway, having covered the war in Angola, it was inevitable that I'd become "one of them." That invariably happened after the metal cap of the first bottle of hard stuff had become garbage.

In spite of the drinks and apparent bonhomie, talk about the guerrilla role in the conflict was always guarded. It was almost as if the enemy didn't exist. Casualty figures were "secret" and when there was an "incident," we would observe that such discussions in the officers' mess were in hushed tones.

The general approach to the war was different to what you would find in other conflicts. One got the idea that the Portuguese liked to think—and some of them actually believed—that it was all a rather temporary business. That is what they'd tell us: it would "soon" be over. It was a patronizing approach that annoyed because none of us was exactly brainless. In any event, things in Mozambique were very different from what I'd already experienced in Angola and Portuguese Guinea. There, at least the Portuguese Army got to grips with the threat.

To their credit, they acknowledged that it existed.

***

The convoy left Tete at dawn. In a straggling line astern, the trucks rumbled across the river, halting briefly at the tollgate at the far end of the bridge. There were machine-gun emplacements at several points along the structure, some of them illuminated by a string of searchlights that swept continually across the water below.

One by one, the sleepy-eyed drivers paid the toll and moved along the last 20–25km of tarred road to Moatize. There, under military supervision, we would assemble for the remainder of the journey to the Malawi border, almost 160km to the north.

Some of the trucks in our column were bound for Blantyre, the capital of Malawi, the tiny country that formed a northwestern border with Mozambique. Others were headed even further north, where they would again cross into Mozambican territory and where the war was at its worst.

The majority of vehicles traveling with us were eight- or 12-wheelers, including a number of low-loaders from various Johannesburg factories that hauled freight bound for the Zambian Copperbelt. The drivers were a motley bunch, most of them professional haulers, some White, the majority African.

That said, there were very few of them who might have been indifferent to what lay ahead. Their guffaws and uneasy, conscious swaggering as they gathered in groups prior to us setting out, were typical of traveling groups who were under a bit of strain. Quite a few of the drivers had been shot at and just about everybody knew somebody who'd been hurt. Not too many killed though, it seemed. They'd all survive, they confidently told each other. Then they'd smile and nod their heads. What a helluva way to earn a living…

"They kill one man last week. *Mulatto*. His truck he go up … Boom!"

That came from a swarthy trucker from the Madeira Islands. It was lost on many because of his poor English. Nobody made any comment but most continued doing what they'd been busy with or looked down at the cups or tin mugs. Some of the drivers kept drinking, even though the sun had barely cleared the thorn and baobab trees clustered to the east beyond the railway station and coal dump at Moatize.

The man who spoken had a lot to say during the three-day convoy run. He'd done the trip often enough apparently and made the point that he preferred to travel somewhere near the rear of the column.

"Better others hit the *minas*, than me," he quietly commented when nobody else was listening, using the colloquial word for the ubiquitous bombs. All that we knew about him was that he was bound for a settlement in the interior which had been attacked in the past. His cargo was his own business, and he said so. It was that security thing again.

Apart from two buses packed with African tribal people of all ages, there were about 35 trucks assembled at Moatize. Most were taking supplies through to Malawi and carried Rhodesian identity discs. These would later be replaced by Zambian tags for the final leg of the journey.

There were two private vehicles on the road with them: our Land Rover that had Dutch registration along with a medium-sized English car on its way to Zambia. The driver, a young Englishman from York, was under contract to one of the mines and had brought his car back with him from long leave in Britain.

He had been forced to cross the Tete pedicle after waiting for six days at the Kasangula Ferry in Botswana. He said he preferred risking landmines and ambush a thousand miles to the east, to testing President Kaunda's largely untrained and undisciplined Zambian Army. He had made that choice after hearing that a drunken bunch of soldiers had fired on another civilian car which had tried to approach the river to cross southwards.

***

Portuguese bureaucracy and a tenacious enemy ended up playing havoc with our schedules. We were told the journey would take eight hours; it lasted three days. Our trucks and their escorts were left standing in the tropical heat of the Zambezi Valley for four hours before we eventually pulled out.

Just before we left, a flock of uniformed officials—some of them soldiers but others obviously civilians even though they were wearing khaki and displayed badges of rank—approached the convoy. The ritual that followed was tedious. Names were checked against lists, vehicles against registration plates, passports perused, cargoes vetted, instructions issued and questions asked. Weapons, tape recorders, radio equipment?

"Anybody here with binoculars?" somebody shouted. The reply was negative all round, even though one of the drivers sported as powerful a 400mm tele-lens for his Nikon camera as any I'd seen back home.

As a final measure, all civilian passengers and drivers were required to sign forms—in triplicate—which indemnified the Lisbon government against loss of life. It also included equipment, freight and all material damage that might be suffered along the way. The document included losses inflicted by the Portuguese Army and Air Force that might result from enemy action.

We signed … anything to avoid further delay.

At this stage Erico Chagas, a young Portuguese Army lieutenant, came forward and introduced himself. I noticed that he'd been watching us from a distance and only then understood why. He needed to get to Munacama, he said. He would travel with us, no doubt because the Land Rover offered the most comfortable ride. There was no question of him asking permission: it was already a *fait accompli.*

Young Chagas was to join his unit in Munacama, about eight to ten clicks from Zobue, one of our destinations in the north. Born in the Mozambique capital and educated in South Africa, he spoke excellent English. Chagas, though barely out of his teens, was one of a type of military men one meets from time to time; tough, seasoned by Africa as well as by conflict. On the face of it, he allowed himself to be flustered by nothing. We were happy to have him: at least we'd be spared further inspection.

The young officer was casual about most things, including the prospect of death. To him, born in Africa and as familiar with the bush as his native trackers, it seemed incomprehensible that he could ever be taken by surprise in the environment he knew so well. And ambush, while traveling in convoy, he stated blandly, was "so much noise." Mines, yes, he stated, but ambushes…

He backed his argument by quoting statistics. The insurgents—he called them *terrorists*—rarely caused damage by firing at convoys from the bush, he said. "Their aim is awful, and anyway it's that old law of survival. Unless someone is firing specifically at you, that you are the actual target, the chances are just as likely that the bullet will hit someone else or go astray."

He was specific about one thing; that we travel as far to the rear of the column as possible. He pointed at the truck belonging to the Madeiran. "We stay behind. He knows the tricks."

The man from Madeira had already spaced himself well down the line. It was his contention, we learned, that the more wheels that passed over the track before he arrived at any spot along the road, the better. "Let the others take the chances," he said, and obviously, it made sense.

More instructions were given to the drivers by an authoritative little man in uniform who had called them together. We were to stay between 50 and 100 meters behind the next vehicle. If the vehicle ahead was destroyed by a landmine, he asserted, the explosion wouldn't affect the following truck. It was necessary, he said, that each vehicle was to follow exactly in the tracks of the truck directly ahead, not to the right of it, nor to the left. He conceded that this might be a difficult option at times because of the dust.

"If you don't," he added impassively, gesturing eloquently as he spoke, "you go up." The Rhodesian drivers laughed among themselves.

There was another issue, he told the gathering, most of whom didn't let the interruption stop them sipping their coffees and cognacs. When he said it was the most important of all, some of the men moved closer to hear a little better.

Should a truck in a convoy be blown up and forced to stop, because then it was policy for the troops to search for other landmines, every individual was to stay where he was.

"There are landmines for trucks," the little man stated, with Chagas keeping pace with a good translation in English, "and there are landmines for people."

He continued: "And when the terrorists lay a mine for trucks … they hope that some inquisitive person might vacate his cab to find out what was causing the hold up." That too, had happened before and there had been casualties, he disclosed. "With landmines, all casualties are serious," were his words.

He also said that although there would be one or two officers traveling as passengers to rejoin their units up-country, the convoy would be in the charge of a sergeant, whom he then called forward and introduced by name.

***

Perhaps the most impassive of all the people gathered around in Moatize that morning were the Black Rhodesian drivers. They'd heard it all many times

Towards the end of the war, there was an element of despondency clearly evident in the faces and demeanor of defending colonial troops.

PAF Harvard ground support aircraft on ops—note the under-wing rocket pods.

Bush radio communications were inadequate in the deep interior of Mozambique, largely because of vast distances involved.

Portuguese troops set out on a Berliet truck, an army transport mainstay. These vehicles were not protected against landmines.

In Africa conditions are always tough, the wars that are fought in this kind of environment especially so, as is being currently discovered in the ongoing Jihadist war in Mozambique's northern Cabo Delgado region.

FRELIMO party propaganda poster.

All three of Portugal's bush wars needed periods of adjustment—Mozambique probably most of all because of vast distances.

Cahora Bassa today: it was still under construction when the author visited the site on the lower Zambezi River.

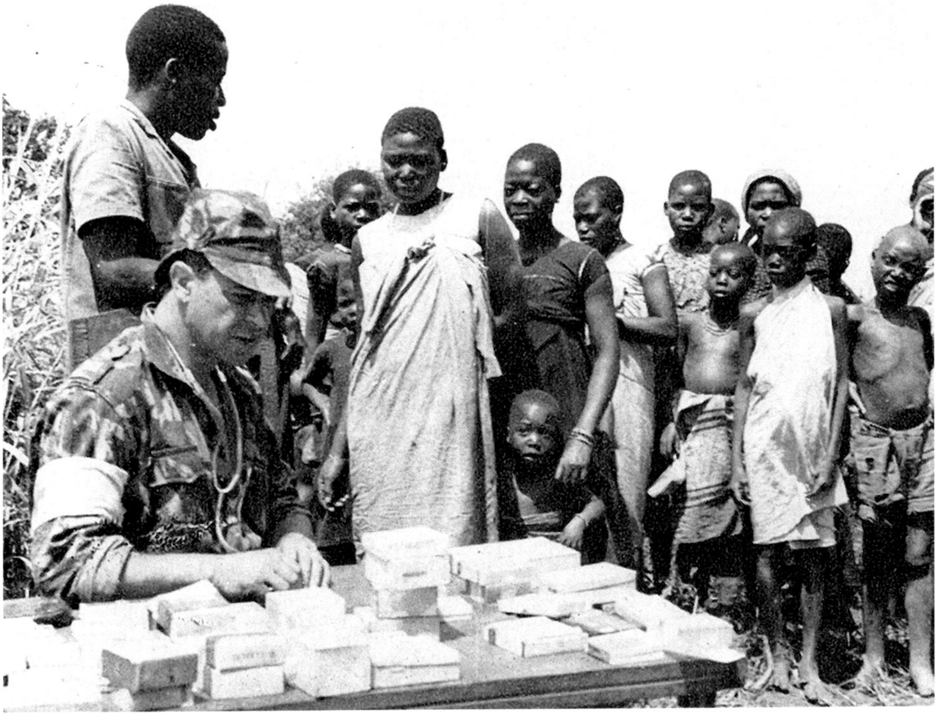

As the war progressed, the Portuguese started to look towards social obligations with regard to the civilian population and the army played a role. But these efforts were largely cursory.

A sad but familiar experience during the war that went on until the very end of the struggle in 1974.

In Mozambique—as with Angola—the principal adversary was always the jungle.

White-led civilian resistance in Lourenço Marques after the ceasefire had been signed took place on a significant scale, but was soon quelled.

Government poster depicting the much-heralded image of a multi-racial Portuguese Army (Author's photo from Luanda).

Samora Machel's statue is proudly placed in a public square in present-day Maputo.

A youthful Portuguese soldier arriving home in Lisbon from the war.

before, both prior to hostilities and now that war had officially arrived in the region.

We got to know some of them quite well in the days that followed and they were a resolute bunch: it was their way of putting bread on their family table and though they didn't like it, they did the work without complaining. We were to discover later that there were times when they knew the ropes a little better than their Portuguese escorts. Some had lost colleagues in previous mine blasts. All were out to ensure that mistakes wouldn't be repeated.

Their heavy vehicles, with their company names painted on them—Swifts, Watson's Transport, United Transport, Heins and others—stood at the vanguard of the procession. A 10-ton Albion truck from United Transport's Malawi office headed the civilian bunch. The driver was carrying Caterpillar spares or something similar and was headed for Zaire. He'd traveled the route for almost two years. For reasons of his own, he preferred to travel up front.

By 10 o'clock that morning, the first army truck that would provide escort rumbled past towards the rear. It was a hefty Berliet, heavily sandbagged around the driver's cab. Because the hood had been removed, we could see more sandbags fitted around the truck's wheel cavities. Portuguese convoys rarely moved about with their hoods intact. Too many troops had been decapitated by these steel sheets in landmine blasts before this rough and ready antidote had been semi-officially implemented.

A short while afterward, more troops arrived, all in regulation camouflage uniforms. Each one of them was armed with a G3, standard issue in Lisbon's African war zones and most times casually slung over their shoulders. A few more had mortar tubes, bazookas and crates of shells and would take up position along the length of the convoy. Just about everybody had additional belts strapped on with grenades and extra ammunition.

The troops generally seemed a happy, lively lot, though there were those among them who were perhaps a little nervous until they got into the swing of things. Few looked as if they'd made the ripe old age of 20. The sergeant to whom we talked later, for instance, was 22 and had already been in Africa for two years. He'd been obliged to interrupt his university studies to fight and made no bones about the fact that he couldn't wait to get back home.

A couple of Unimog trucks roared past from the direction of the railway station and stopped nearby. A man spoke in rapid tones into a walkie-talkie. We were ready to move, said Chagas.

The first trucks rolled forward, a sandbagged Berliet in the van. One of the Unimog troop carriers moved into position towards the middle of the convoy, about five vehicles ahead of us. Its soldiers on the back clustered about a heavy machine-gun that had been mounted on a fixed tripod. An imposing width of steel plating swung about as the weapon rotated on its pivot. Moments later there was a clicking of bolts all the way down the line as soldiers tested their weapons for action.

With another Berliet bringing up the rear, we were at last on the move, but we covered only 18–19km that first day. Almost from the start we encountered evidence of conflict in the area to the north of Moatize.

Barely five minutes from the railhead we had left the last of the surfaced road behind us. Once on dirt roads, a blanket of dust immediately enveloped everything ahead—trucks, soldiers, civilian cars and their passengers—and remained suspended above ground for some time after we'd passed. The heat was oppressive, with thirst a constant companion.

Minutes later we passed an abandoned, broken-down villa, its faded, off-white walls pock-marked by the bullet holes and shell splinters of who knows how many actions. It was almost like the kind of scenario you're likely to see these days in news reports on rural Afghanistan. The only difference was that the dense African bush started right alongside the road and seemed to continue forever.

Then another building came into view, also partly blown. Chagas pointed at a window-sized gap that yawned in one of the front walls, probably caused by a mortar or an artillery shell. He ventured that the building might have been used for training purposes by the Portuguese Army, which was when I said that training must have been intense, for we were suddenly seeing many such derelict buildings.

All were shell-scarred. Many showed signs of hasty evacuation. There were broken beds and burnt roofs and here and there a burnt-out pick-up or tractor lying abandoned somewhere around the back.

Five or six minutes afterwards, the truck immediately ahead of us, still dutifully following the convoy track, skirted a large round hole in the middle of the road. Strips of crumpled metal lay scattered along the verge, which was when we spotted the wheelless and buckled front suspension of a truck that lay discarded in the bush nearby. The rest had apparently been removed by an army recovery unit. Chagas said nothing: a large crater in the middle of the road needed no explanation.

It was the same the further north we traveled: more holes, more of the detritus of war. Twice the convoy stopped and we waited. Being a cloudless day, the sun beat down from a brassy sky with a fierce intensity. Even a light breeze might have eased the discomfort but it was sauna time.

All that happened was that sweat rolled off our foreheads in large, translucent droplets as we sat waiting, impatient and uncomfortable.

"They're checking for mines," Chagas reckoned. He was trying to be helpful. "With mines we must always be careful … you do understand." At this point he told us he had lost three members of his unit as a result of mine explosions in the past three months, including a good buddy with whom he'd gone through training.

The convoy started to roll again but slower than before. Although delays had been expected, we'd never anticipated that the going would be so slow that after the first delay, the drivers never again that day shifted into second gear.

Finally, we slowed to a crawl, where a man on foot would have outpaced the convoy. Some people peered anxiously towards the tall grass on both sides of the road and there was little conversation.

At one stage we passed an abandoned corrugated-iron tsetse fly control station. It too was pitted with holes. "More training?" I asked, and all Chagas could do was smile.

Small wonder then that tsetse bothered us from time to time. Each time one of these insects entered the cab there was desperate flapping all round. Anything that came to hand became an improvised fly swatter and for good reason: the tsetse has a bite easily as painful as a horse fly.

Chagas would view our antics with mild amusement. To him this was just another convoy and there were more tsetse flies in his base in the interior than anybody had cared to count. For most of the time that he spent on the road with us, he buried himself in the English-language papers and periodicals that we'd brought with us from the Cape.

Stop again, roll again, became a kind of set routine. We covered perhaps 5km in the first 90 minutes and then the pace slowed still further. It could have been worse, someone said: at least we had a little movement as the sun reached its apogee and the heat became almost stifling. We were still in the Zambezi Valley

Eventually we were guided by a man in uniform into a clearing alongside the road.

The heavier trucks were pulled into a large oblong laager completely surrounded by bush. The buses and we passengers were pointed to a position towards the center and the Land Rover parked on the perimeter of some shade.

Meanwhile, our escort troops had spilled out in groups and disappeared into a low building which had probably been someone's home in the distant past and where only three of the original walls were still standing. They were precariously holding up part of the roof, or what was left of it, and the structure did offer some kind of cover in an otherwise desolate terrain.

***

The following day started early. Even before the Portuguese soldier nearest us had been able to dismantle his mortar, the Rhodesian drivers were running their engines in preparation for the haul. It would be another long haul, we'd been warned the night before.

There had been activity elsewhere during the night. We'd heard a few blasts in the distance and then, several times, sustained automatic fire. But there was nothing definitive about any of it, or anything to which Lt Chagas could or wouldn't venture. Happened all the time, he shrugged … the war…

Barely five minutes out of our bivouac, the convoy stalled to a halt. Unlike previous hold ups this was a lengthy stop. It culminated in a heavy blast up ahead.

"Landmine," said Chagas. "They must have blown it," he suggested. For the first time in the journey, he displayed a little enthusiasm. "You will see later when we hit a real minefield how they do it."

We traveled into the morning in this fashion and for three or four hours, mines remained the principal preoccupation of the journey for us all. Every few hundred meters the column would stop while the soldiers searched, both on the road ahead and to our flanks. Another explosion followed, a big one, and Chagas said something about it being anti-tank—probably TM-46, the Russian version of the wartime German Tellermine 42. Word came down the line that it had been detonated by the soldiers in the lead Berliet.

All day long we passed holes in the road, some jagged, others barely larger than potholes. Or perhaps they were potholes. Some had obviously been blasted by the soldiers for there was no wreckage about. At other times, large scraps of steel and rubber lying about in disarray provided tell-tale evidence of previous carnage. There was never any talk about casualties, though obviously they had happened.

One area, near a bridge that had been partly demolished by FRELIMO guerrillas, provided a few of the answers we sought. The remains of a burnt-out truck had been blasted onto its side alongside the road, its cab brutally smashed. Alongside the dusty track—only meters away—lay the wrappings of army field dressings, empty plastic plasma bottles and wadding, a few of the latter tinged with coagulated blood that had turned black in the sun and had a covering of flies. The dressings were relatively fresh, which indicated that the event had happened only a few days before, probably on the south-bound convoy. Certainly, it had taken place since the last rains, two or three nights previously, which would almost certainly have washed all this evidence away.

Later a soldier told us what had happened. A Black Rhodesian, he said, working for a transport company out of Salisbury, had been caught in the blast. His legs were badly mutilated and he had large gashes in the head and arms. Because he was losing blood fast, they radioed to base for instructions. Fortunately, the air force had one of its Alouettes deployed in the area and the helicopter landed and pulled him out.

The driver lived, we heard, but he went on to lose one of his legs. What was noteworthy, the soldier said, was that within a couple of hundred yards of the incident, another 39 landmines were uncovered in an expansive operation that involved dozens of soldiers and took a full day-and-a-half. The mines were mostly anti-personnel (AP), causing no more casualties. "Not that time," he smiled.

Two more TM-46s were blown where they'd been planted, he told us afterwards, which was apparently why the truck had toppled over onto its side.

***

And then, for us on this hot February morning, came the moment of truth. Quite suddenly, we were involved in an event that would have had serious consequences for one or more of the vehicles if one of the Portuguese Army scouts, perched precariously on the roof of the lead Berliet hadn't spotted something suspicious on the side of the road ahead.

It was human tracks that he spotted, in an area where there hadn't been anybody living for who knows how long. Having stopped the column and dismounted, he moved gingerly ahead, keeping as close to the edge of the road as the bushes would allow in case there had been more APs laid, which was when he spotted wires. At that moment a series of sporadic shots rang out from a gully on the far side of the convoy: automatic fire and it came in bursts.

The three of us in the Land Rover squeezed as low onto the floorboards as our bulk would allow because we had no idea where the shooting was coming from or who the target might have been. Moments later a few lone shots rang out from another position towards the rear. This was what the Portuguese drivers had earlier referred to as *flagelaçao,* a whipping burst of gunfire and the quick getaway.

Seconds later it was the escort that answered. They ripped off a stream of tracers in a broad arc across the bush to our right. The heavy machine-gun on the Unimog followed, together with a dull plop from one of the mortars, then three or four more. At that point we emerged from our vehicle and found ourselves close enough to watch the resultant explosions a few hundred yards away in the bush.

For a while the countryside was enveloped by an eerie quiet. Even the birds were silent. Then we heard the young sergeant shouting instructions: he told a squad of Black soldiers to take up positions along the length of the column. They were to face outwards, towards the unseen enemy, Lt Chagas explained.

In doing this several of them took their chances in crossing stretches of gravel that had not yet been swept.

***

Because of the problem ahead and the uncertainty of the strength of the force which had fired on the convoy, the next hour saw regular movements of troops up and down the length of the convoy. We watched intently.

Troops on foot moved carefully, where they could. They stepped gingerly in the footsteps of anybody who had preceded them along any stretch of dirt that hadn't been "tested" for landmines. When we eventually stepped down from the cruiser, we followed their example.

When one of the men from up front came down the line and indicated to Chagas that the insurgents had laid a fairly considerable field of mines ahead, he told us to stay put. We were to remain in the vehicle rather than alongside it. The entire area first had to be cleared, he stated, and it was a job which could take the rest of the morning. There were several more bursts of fire from the insurgents, perhaps from a little further away, but by then we'd become accustomed to the sound of gunfire. Each time their shots would be answered by a fusillade of mortar bombs and small arms fire from our lines.

The army eventually cleared the minefield although it took hours longer than anticipated. A total of 14 mines, two round metal TM-46s and 12 anti-personnel bombs, were detected and detonated. By the time it was over there were no casualties—probably on either side. For our part, we'd gambled on the notoriously bad marksmanship of the enemy.

Although Chagas maintained that the aim of the terrorists was poor, he chided us whenever he found that we'd moved a few paces from the vehicle, which was sometimes the only option we had in heat that had become crippling.

"You are taking chances," he'd say. "Unnecessary chances ... this area hasn't been cleared." Then he went off towards to the head of the column and when he returned, he said that he'd asked permission for us to come forward. We could watch the demolition process first-hand from the gun platform of the lead Berliet. I was elated and I grabbed my cameras.

The system that the Portuguese Army used to clear mines was simple. A number of trained soldiers—Black and White—first spent a little while assessing the situation in the road ahead. If they felt that the road surface might conceal mines, a stick of four would disembark and walk ahead, all the while using steel-tipped wooden lances about the length of a golf club to probe the soil. It was soft, recently disturbed areas that usually indicated mines.

The lances were named after the Portuguese bullfight probe, the *pica*. They were a curious anomaly in an age of some of the more sophisticated weapons and electronic mine-detecting devices imaginable. Throughout all of Lisbon's conflicts in Africa, these primitive handheld staffs were always regarded as the most reliable means of detecting buried bombs.

There was electronic gear available for the purpose, all of it with NATO designations. But this equipment was rarely unpacked from its bulky, suitcase-sized containers, principally because it was all but useless along roads where huge amounts of metal debris lay about the track. That included cans, tin foil, spent cartridge cases, spare parts and the rest—all discarded over the years by a minor army of transients like us.

The mine-detecting process was painstaking. It was something regular for insurgents to lay patterns of smaller mines around much larger anti-vehicle bombs in hopes that should the one be found, the others would cause damage.

***

Midday brought up the short distance to the Portuguese Army para-commando camp at Muxoxo. For at least an hour before we reached the camp the unit's helicopters provided air cover against further insurgent forays. Camouflaged Alouettes with heavy machine-guns mounted to port would move at a fair pace above the bush, sweeping low and often doubling back again to previous sites, their heavy machine-guns strafing suspect positions. On more than one occasion the pilots waved as they passed.

Muxoxo provided no surprises. The ramshackle building at its center had once been a farmhouse and was surrounded by neat rows of army tents. That housed most of the garrison. We welcomed the opportunity to buy warm Manica beer at inflated prices. In the world of the Portuguese businessman in Africa, passing trade has always been regarded as fair game.

The men at the camp had a large area to patrol, at least by today's counter-insurgency standards. They were served by a squadron of six Alouettes that air-lifted them to wherever intelligence reports indicated the guerrillas might be working or possibly concentrating their assets.

The unit averaged about four operations a week, mostly during periods when road convoys were expected. They were also responsible for security on part of the railway line between Moatize and Caldas Xavier and these activities often took them far to the south-east.

These were all short, swift "search, find and destroy" sorties which sometimes provided unexpected surprises. During our brief stay, two captured FRELIMO insurgents were brought in. One was an old man hardly able to walk and obviously malnourished. No belligerent this one.

Yet both admitted they'd been linked to a rebel sabotage unit operating out of an area near the rail town of Goa. They had been taken while preparing food for their compatriots in the bush, men whom they admitted had been responsible for a spate of attacks on the rail link which winds its way from Moatize to Beira. They had hardly arrived before a unit prepared for a strike: the attackers were nearby and the crack *Comandos Africanos* unit intended to make contact.

The two captives were first interrogated and then fed. More interrogation followed before they were flown to Tete for a more professional grilling before being transferred to one of the prison camps near Lourenço Marques in the south. After doing a little independent news-gathering of his own, Lt Chagas told us that the men would probably be of some use to the security forces. They would probably be taken back to headquarters.

"They claim they were shanghaied into the terrorist movement and had they offered any resistance they would have been shot," he said. "The trouble is," he added, "they all claim that and they probably would have been had they not cooperated with the *terroristas*."

***

It was late afternoon when we made contact with the southbound convoy at the road junction to Xavier Caldas. Nothing marked the crossroads except for a wooden signpost on which none of the directions were discernible.

We were warned that the area had not been cleared of mines and that we should be circumspect about where we walked. Spent cartridge cases littered the area and its approaches.

While approaching the area we had crossed a small river which had been prominently signposted in Portuguese: "*Zona Armadilhada*: Minefield" it read, in two languages.

This minefield was Portuguese. It had been laid in a bid to prevent the guerrillas from setting charges at the base of the bridge and destroying it. As somebody mentioned while we were hanging about, the measure was double-edged since it also prevented any of us travelers from getting water at a time when our supply was starting to run short. Water shortages on board the buses, we knew, were already critical, especially among the children.

The oppressive heat which had followed us across Africa from the Zambezi Valley hardly made matters easier. Even so, a handful of passengers did make an effort. In a small column some of the men and boys traipsed single file down a path towards the river, each one stepping carefully in the imprint of the man directly ahead.

One of the older soldiers traveling with us later told us that the week before a civilian had tripped a mine. He hadn't been killed, but it did underscore some of the privations that those with very little faced when traveling across the region.

"…poor fellow, he needed water very badly—not only for himself, but also for his family. So he set out on his own in spite of warnings from the convoy commander. As he stepped near the water his foot triggered some trips which hurled a small mine about two meters into the air." The mine was similar to what was known as the "S-mine" during World War II, or what the Americans called the "Bouncing Betty" in Southeast Asia. Lisbon used them willingly throughout the war.

Apparently, luck smiled on the man that eventful day. The mine detonated almost within touching distance, but it was apparently facing the wrong way, if that be possible. The charge ripped apart everything in the opposite direction and he was mildly concussed by the blast.

We waited an hour for the oncoming convoy to arrive. From the start we could see that conditions were much harder in their sector than in ours. A number of times we heard detonations in the distance, but gradually the distance shortened.

Chagas came back not long afterwards to tell us that that convoy had suffered a casualty. Moments later an evacuation helicopter veered overhead and prepared to land in open ground near the crossroads. Ours was the first convoy the pilot reached and he had no way of knowing which of the two columns had triggered a bomb.

Having established that much, he was gone again in moments, having left clouds of dust whipped up by his rotors in his wake. We watched as he sped at tree-top level northwards and a minute or two later, returned, this time at a higher altitude. He was making for Tete Military Hospital.

When the oncoming convoy did reach us, we were told that a man had been killed. He had been second in the line in the *pica* squad, his point man having apparently stepped over an anti-personnel mine, though he didn't know it. The soldier behind was not so lucky and he caught the full impact.

Three other members of the *pica* squad were lightly wounded but they continued with their duties even though their leader was limping badly from a large open cut on the thigh. In the American Army in Vietnam, a wound like that would have meant immediate evacuation to the base hospital. With the Portuguese Army in Africa, such matters were accepted in the line of duty. They didn't even get Lisbon's version of the Purple Heart: there wasn't one.

***

We traveled halfway through the night to reach Mussacana. The road had been cleared by the oncoming convoy and it was necessary to cover the prodded ground as quickly as possible before the terrorists laid more mines. The same held for the passing convoy: they had to cover the ground we had cleared.

But we weren't quite fast enough. A heavy tropical downpour provided the drivers with an almost impossible task in following the tracks of the vehicles ahead, and two more vehicles were blasted. Both were heavy trucks, one from Johannesburg, the other from Salisbury. Both had cargoes on board for Zambia.

It was ironic to us all that those who had laid the mines were actually using Zambia as a base. Now they were helping to disrupt the economy of one of their few allies: another quirk of warfare in Africa.

There were no more casualties. The mines had been detonated by the back wheels of both trucks, giving credence to reports that the insurgents were using a more sophisticated type of landmine recently been brought in from Southeast Asia following the de-escalation of American military involvement there. Only very much later were we to learn that these were ratchet mines.

A curious name: the ratchet mines used by the Cong were usually set to detonate after a pre-determined number of wheels had passed; sometimes 10 or 12, often double that. The fact that the trucks involved were well down the column when they were blasted underscored this development. One of the vehicles was barely 100 meters ahead of us and about a kilometer out of the village of Capirizanje, rain pelting down, when the blast ripped through one of the open windows of the Land Rover. The column halted.

So did we, after which we sat in silence. Only when we started to move again and carefully followed in rows of new tracks created through the bush around the stranded vehicle, could we see that a set of back wheels on one of the low-loaders from South Africa had been shredded by the blast.

Not long afterwards we passed what was probably a quarry alongside the road, illuminated by lightning as we passed. It was one of those tropical storms for which the Zambezi Valley is known, the water coming down in spurts that might fill a bucket in an hour. Three or four flashes of lightning indicated no sign of habitation in the quarry and some of the trolleys that had probably been part of the facility Heaven only knows how long before, lay on their sides. A wheelbarrow without its wheel rested upside down, more detritus of a conflict that had already spanned half a generation.

Mussacana arrived unheralded. We had climbed steadily in the mud and then, suddenly, just before midnight, there were lights ahead. The rain had lifted and, as so often happens in that region only a few hundred kilometers from the Indian Ocean, the settlement lay in a swathe of mist in the mountains above Capirizanje. The ground was sodden, for it had poured here too.

A soldier on guard in one of those improvised machine-gun turrets that these poor soldiers fashioned from a handful of tin cans and some fishing nylon stood perched on high ground shouting a greeting. We replied in English.

At least the beer would be cold…

War Wounded

"Two weapons today threaten freedom in our world. One—the 100-megaton hydrogen bomb—requires vast resources of technology, effort and money. The other—a nail and a piece of wood buried in the sand is deceptively simple, the weapon of a peasant."

LIEUTENANT-COLONEL T. N. GREENE, U.S. MARINE CORPS,
"THE GUERRILLA AND HOW TO FIGHT HIM"

War results in casualties, no matter where it is fought; it has been that way since the beginning of time and Mozambique was no different. While the guerrillas fought to oust the Portuguese colonizers, the country was beset with many problems; a shortage of doctors, nurses, hospitals and rural health clinics among them.

In Africa, it was and still is, tropical diseases—with malaria topping the list—that are the most consistent threat to the life of the Average Joe out there. The colonial war brought more problems.

Landmines were the other most persistent threat, as I was to observe from up close from many road trips in every one of the "Liberation Wars" that ranged from the 1960s onwards. Apart from Mozambique, I covered a lot of ground in Rhodesia during its war, in some frighteningly isolated corners of the country where, even today, the roads have never been surfaced.

I sometimes had my wife with me, as happened when we traveled to the tiny military outpost of Gulu in the south of the country, which lay about an hour's traveling time across bad roads from the main north–south highway linking old Salisbury to South Africa. While there was the occasional convoy, none were running when we wanted to do the trip so we went out on our lonesome and it really became a rather lonely excursion, in both directions.

During the course of the war, I was to visit the home of Italian professional hunter Giorgio Grasselli on his farm near Matetsi in Rhodesia's north-east many times. Often this was hairy because there were constant reports of ambushes and landmine blasts in the area, which became quite a battleground as hostilities progressed. Also, once off the main highway between Bulawayo and Victoria Falls, none of the farm roads in his area were tarred.

It was the same when I traveled from the Mozambique riverside town of Tete southwards towards Beira—this time on my own. Though the road was tarred, heavy bush hung over the road in places and one tended to mutter silent Hail Marys each time open ground was reached.

Looking back, I often surprise myself at the risks I (and many others like me) took. But it was the only way we could get around so we bottled our worries and pressed on, something I would not even consider doing today.

What came across rather sharply with all these events was that there were constant reports of people being either killed or wounded in ambushes or landmine blasts. It was exactly the same where the Portuguese Army was active, not only in Mozambique but in their two other overseas possessions as well.

Obviously, the various military headquarters in the interior were always on full alert for such events, but in a territory as vast as Portuguese East Africa where distances were measured in the number of hours of travel (and sometimes days) to get to a destination, it was often impossible to give proper attention to the wounded. More often than not there were no helicopters available, or these air force elements were stationed too far away to offer any assistance, as I was to see for myself more than once.

When that happened, it was left to the unit medic to save lives, but then again, the training these men received did not cover all eventualities.

Whenever I headed out, not only in areas where there had been armed combat, but also in some countries where medical facilities were sparse—like Uganda, the Niger Republic, the Congo and elsewhere—I would always take along a couple of liters of saline drip. In non-war zones this was because of the possibility of road accidents—the most serious problem in Africa for visitors and residents alike—and naturally, it was not enough to have the stuff in your baggage. You also had to know how to administer a drip…

The most immediate problem in Africa—whether in war zones or not—was invariably disease and here contamination was a constant. While filming in Uganda I contracted typhoid from drinking from bottles of mineral water that had been factory sealed but not properly cleaned. Bad water was one of the most consistent problems European troops deployed into Africa experienced and if not promptly treated, infection resulted in serious illness.

In those days there were bugs and mosquitoes just about everywhere and if you did not take quinine, you went down with malaria, and sometimes the cerebral affliction, as happened after I emerged from the Zambezi Valley and was admitted to Salisbury's Andrew Fleming Hospital. It was my worst malaria attack ever and it took me months to recover: my wife was flown up from South Africa because the doctors did not think I'd make it.

Nobody will ever know how many young Portuguese soldiers died of tropical disease while on active service in the colonies. Apart from malaria, dengue and yellow fever, while not commonplace, were (and still are) found in many tropical destinations. So is trypanosomiasis ("tryps" or more commonly, "sleeping sickness"), transmitted by the tsetse fly, which is found almost everywhere in Southern and Central Africa. Fortunately, not all flies are infected with sleeping sickness.

Meningitis was a regular problem and needed prompt treatment or patients could die. The same went for hepatitis (jaundice), which earlier in these African wars was contracted by an astonishing number of soldiers, until it was discovered that mess dishes and pots were not being properly cleaned by kitchen staff.

But it was malaria that was the most rampant problem and that persists to an even greater extent these days. During the various colonial epochs, some effort was at least made not to leave standing water in containers lying around in urban areas, but there is no control these days.[1]

As a result, there are tens of thousands in Africa that succumb to the disease every year.

In 2019, while this book was being prepared, I lost two friends as a consequence of them being bitten by the Anopheles mosquito, and that in an age when Western medicine is supposed to have contained the problem.

Granted, there are fewer deaths from malaria than there were perhaps half a century ago but it remains an extremely potent killer, usually masked by an onset of problems that closely resemble a cold or flu attack. Tropics or not, people still get the sniffles and these are quite often accompanied by a light fever. It is only when these symptoms are ignored that they can sometimes become life-threatening.

While Lisbon fought its African wars, quinine was an essential prophylactic, very much as it was when British forces were combating the Mau Mau in Kenya and the U.S. Army and Air Force remained active in Southeast Asia.

As Britain's National Health Service declares on its website, it takes only a single mosquito bite (it is actually a stab from the front end of the insect's proboscis) to cause malaria. This can result in an intermittent and remittent fever caused by a protozoan parasite that invades the body's red blood cells, something that happens in many tropical and subtropical regions, Africa especially.

The World Health Organization (WHO) tells us that malaria is still one of the deadliest diseases on Earth: each year more than 600,000 people worldwide die from it. Small wonder then that the WHO directorate in Atlanta, Georgia declared April 25, 2019 "World Malaria Day."

Despite statistics, most people are likely to survive malaria after a 10- or 20-day illness, much less if the new "wonder" herbal anti-malarial artemisinin-based combination therapy (ACT) is taken. It commonly needs only three tablets taken over three days to get the patient up and about again and is my first choice when heading out on safari. That cure is currently widely prescribed in Africa.

***

As in any war, including those in Portuguese Africa, there are two issues of paramount interest to the average soldier. The first is news from home, which is why the mail needs to get through, no matter what.

The second is no less personal, involving as it does his own well-being. Should the soldier be wounded during an action or caught in a landmine blast, he needs to be assured that he will get the kind of medical attention that will enable him to survive.

Israel's Defense Force has this down to a fine art. During routine cross-border forays into South Lebanon when the IDF still held onto the Exclusion Zone—that inappropriately-termed stretch of real estate in South Lebanon that adjoined the Israeli border—it was estimated that if it took a helicopter more than three or four minutes to reach a casualty, somebody wasn't doing his or her job.

American forces east of Suez are equally efficient. Casualties are sometimes lifted from the scene within minutes of an IED having been detonated alongside one of the main roads leading into Baghdad, because there are always helicopters hovering somewhere in the vicinity.

The South Africans tried to emulate that example, but with such huge distances to cover in Pretoria's Border War, minutes would sometimes become hours. Essentially it all depended on where an incident took place in relation to one of the helicopter bases along the Angolan border. Close to Oshakati or Rundu further to the east, and it could be minutes. Across the frontier into enemy-held territory—and depending on whether it was day or night—it often took much longer.

The same equation applies to Coalition forces in Afghanistan, a large country with a limited number of air bases. For all that, if a wounded man can be saved in the Hindu Kush or along open ground leading into Kandahar, he usually is.

Things were very different in Portugal's African wars, though not always because there were not enough willing hands around that could help.

Part of the problem was the availability of medical expertise—or more often than not, its unavailability; Portugal's wars were incredibly low-key compared to what is going on these days in the Middle East, Central Asia or even Libya. The number of casualties as listed in the book *Africa: A Vitoria Traida,* published in Lisbon by *Intervenção* soon after the coup, is indicative.

For a start, in the over 13 years of combat in Angola and somewhat less in Portuguese Guinea and Mozambique, the army lost 3,275 men killed in action and fractionally fewer—3,065—from other causes, which would have included accidents and illness. For some inexplicable reason these totals do not include Portuguese Air Force or Navy casualties which might be why other sources talk of 8,863 military deaths in Lisbon's African conflicts.

As one publication phrased it afterwards, "…in more than a dozen years of war, we lost 8,863 soldiers … *que Deus os tenha em paz, bravos soldados* (may God have you in peace, brave soldiers)…"

However, what does emerge is that the army had losses of about 250 men a year, from either combat or disease. That meant that cumulatively, there were approximately five men dying each week in Africa, which would have been manageable. It also bears little resemblance to the 2,000 men that France lost every year in Algeria over an extended time frame of seven years; or to the thousand South Africans killed in 23 years of combat on Angola's frontiers.

Clearly, the official statistics quoted do tend to underscore the fact that by keeping the casualty rate low, Lisbon was handling the medical side of the war quite well. At the same time, though, there are two schools of thought here: the first being that with more and better-trained resources, the number of deaths could have been much lower. The second was linked to an almost culpable disregard among some medical personnel in the field to pull out all stops for those in their care, which I was to see for myself, but more of that later.

Also, my own sources suggest that about three-quarters of those troops who succumbed to illness or disease had contracted malaria. As the Americans discovered soon enough in Vietnam, you can hand out as many prophylactic tablets as you'd like, the biggest problem is getting the men to actually swallow them.

On the issue of sick and dying soldiers not getting the attention they deserved from Portuguese Army medical staff, those few scribes who were able to put a foot inside some of the military hospitals in Portugal's African domains were able to form opinions of their own. They were not always flattering, specifically in Mozambique.

While conditions in the largest military medical establishments in places like Luanda, Bissau, Beira, Nova Lisboa (Huambo today) and Lourenço Marques (now Maputo) were exemplary, it was not lost on some of the critics that these were the showpieces of Lisbon's wartime effort. All *major* medical installations in the overseas provinces were kept in good order, but the same could not be said for the rest.

My personal observations were limited to what went on outside the capitals of Portuguese Guinea and Mozambique, the latter especially, and my modus operandi for getting through the door was as a South African aid group gathering funds for medical supplies for Portuguese troops. Fund-raising efforts in South Africa were quite successful, to the extent that there was a constant flow of medicines and drugs going from all major cities down south to the three provinces. Larger items included ambulances, suitably emblazoned with the name of the organization, as well as X-ray machines that were usually delivered overland, to much fanfare on arrival.

Because of my South African connections, I was able to get into some of these medical establishments at a time when they were very much off limits to the Fourth Estate, and what I uncovered as a consequence was disturbing.

While all of Lisbon's African cities had adequate medical supplies, there were shortages, sometimes critical, in the interior that included items as mundane as bed linen and gurneys. Worse, nobody appeared to have any interest in rectifying matters: it was always "somebody else's department." Nor were these isolated incidents. I visited several military hospitals in the interior and it was much of the same each time.

Conditions at Tete Military Hospital, for instance, were appalling. While there weren't an inordinate number of troops on the injured list, we were gobsmacked at the condition of some of them. Though it would have been difficult to lay specific blame for these inadequacies (because I was not around long enough to do an intrusive investigative study), my initial observations with regard to modern medical methodology, hygiene, sanitation, equipment and inattentive medical staff were sobering.

In one of my reports, I described conditions—witnessed at the time by Michael Knipe of the London *Times*—as barbarous. An American observer who accompanied one of my groups as far as Tete, condemned conditions at the local military hospital as "symptomatic of another epoch, probably pre-World War I." We would emerge from some of these establishments aghast and talk about the experience afterwards in whispers.

While there were exceptions, especially in the bigger centers, much of what we were able to view from up close made the American TV series *MASH* look like the Mayo Clinic by comparison. There was a consensus among us all: if one of us had the misfortune to take a bullet or be injured by a landmine, the others were to get the injured party out of Mozambique as quickly as possible—cost was to be the last consideration. We even agreed that if it happened, we would pool resources and order a charter flight from Salisbury if there was no other way. The last thing any of us wanted was to end up as a patient in one of those wards...

In almost the entire country, the troops were exposed to malaria on a day-to-day basis. The same situation at the time held for Rhodesia, yet the two countries might have been on separate planets. In spite of quinine, malaria took a steady toll in lives lost in the Portuguese armed forces throughout the Zambezi Valley.

Similarly, many Portuguese soldiers contracted hepatitis, again because of abysmal hygiene in the cooking areas and latrines. Israeli studies of the disease among their own units in the field discovered fairly early on that one of the principal causes of jaundice was due to fat residues in kitchen dishes. More to the point, this was information available in medical journals all over the world; somehow, nobody in Portugal seemed to have noticed.

The hepatitis theory was immediately quashed by some of the Portuguese doctors to whom I spoke. Jaundice, they argued, was everywhere: this was Africa and flies had always been a problem. One got the impression that fresh ideas were a closed door and that nobody seemed to care. In some camps in the interior there were even inadequate supplies of fresh water.

Portuguese Guinea, it seemed, offered a more efficient medical quotient to those serving there, largely, one suspected, because the commanding general took a personal interest. Unannounced and most times unheralded, General Antonio de Spínola—always a stickler for the right thing—would arrive at hospitals or clinics under his command. There he'd spend an hour or two, not only talking to those in charge but doing the rounds of the wards, the kitchens, emergency rooms and the rest. He'd spend time talking to the wounded, always lending a sympathetic ear, and interested in trying to right wrongs.

If he found something amiss, God help the offending party. While he or she wouldn't be put on the next plane home—there were too many Portuguese servicemen praying for that option—that individual would be charged and, likely as not, placed on extra duties.

If there was a second offence, it might even be the brig. In that enervating climate—coupled to short rations and possibly no mosquito nets—this kind of punishment could be harsh. However, as we all know, fear tends to engender efficiency and it didn't happen that often.

***

It was while transiting Mozambique that I was given the opportunity to spend several hours at the military hospital at Tete. It was February 1973 and the Portuguese, always meticulous with their records, will be able to check this event—one of the most horrendous I'd experienced in any man's war.

During our tour of the hospital wards, Michael Knipe and I discovered a soldier alone in a ward with terrible leg and abdominal wounds. "Landmine," he said, using the English term, his face contorted by pain. The stench in the ward was overwhelming; it hit us like a foul wet rag when we entered the building.

The youngster was perhaps 18 years old and obviously in terrible distress. His pain must have been awful because he blacked out twice in the 20 minutes or so that we were there. Even to this inexperienced observer it was obvious that gangrene had set in, more than adequately amplified by the stench, which is symptomatic.

Being on the spot, we were able to collar the Portuguese doctor who accompanied us and, pointing, asked him what he intended doing about it: the man would die if his wounds were left untended. Barely acknowledging that there was a problem, he dismissed our suggestions with a shrug.

We nevertheless persisted because it was obvious that something had to be done and this was clearly some mother's son, never mind that he'd been serving in the Portuguese Army.

On pulling back the bedclothes, we could see that part of the youngster's upper thigh that had not been wrapped in bandages had turned an evil shade of greenish-black. Clearly embarrassed, steps were soon afterwards taken by the hospital authorities, but we were never to discover what treatment he eventually received; we were not allowed anywhere near the ward again.

My sentiments at the time were something in line with a pox on the homes of the medical personnel who were responsible: an abhorrent situation that was not being dealt with by staff who, to our minds, could not care a damn. It would have been very different had it been one of their sons lying there…

Interestingly, there were other Portuguese present, including some junior doctors and orderlies who shared the experience, but it wouldn't have been worth a nickel for them to have countermanded their senior medical officer.

One sensed that such things had a seriously debilitating effect on morale. More to the point, it would be interesting—decades later—to establish exactly who was in charge at the time. More to the point, did the young man with gangrene in his leg came out of that horrific experience alive?

***

During my time covering Portugal's wars in Africa, for more than a decade, I was constantly in and out of Lisbon. I had learnt to accept that—because driving standards on the country's roads were so dismal—there was probably more chance of my becoming a road casualty in cities like Lisbon or Luanda than in any war.

I held that view until I got to Lebanon during that civil war: I had always rated Portuguese traffic as the world's worst, but…

I also discovered that the high number of driving deaths among the Portuguese was not surprising; the average Lusitanian driver, even these days, takes more risks on the road in a week than most Americans or British do in a year. Some of us hacks long ago decided that on the face it, the Portuguese seemed imbued with some kind of death wish, which was why they drove the way they did. Locals call the malaise *loucara*, a fatalism or super optimism that was also reflected in the way they fought their wars.

That said, there was none of the regimentation or militarism of the Germanic races, but some Portuguese soldiers more often than not did what they had to and would emerge from these frays as unusually valiant fighters. I was to experience it many times while with their forces over several years in all three of Lisbon's overseas territories.

***

The following casualty figures were provided by official Portuguese sources some years after the war ended:

Table 15.1: Casualties among Portuguese armed forces in Africa (averages)

	Guinea	Angola	Mozambique	Total	Average/day
Killed in action	1,084	1,142	1,039	3,265	.80
Other causes	791	1,529	755	3,075	.76
Total dead	1,875	2,671	1,794	6,340	1.55
Wounded in action	6,161	4,472	2,245	12,878	3.16
Accidents/casualties	2,167	6,595	6,279	15,041	3.69
Total casualties	8,328	11,067	8,524	27,919	6.86
Disabled	-	-	-	3,835	.94

Statistics relating to the Portuguese Navy and the Portuguese Air Force were unobtainable.

The figures listed are: Guinea from May 1, 1963: Angola from May 1, 1961, and Mozambique from November 1, 1964 and in all three theaters of military operations up to the end of the war in 1974.

In the case of Portuguese Guinea, 4,016 days were used as a basis for calculation: 4,746 in Angola and 3,647 in Mozambique, giving an average of 4,076 days.

From 1961 to 1973, the total number of troops in the three theaters of operations reached 1,392,230, which corresponded to an annual average of 107,095. The indices for this annual average and for the average duration of the war were calculated on 4,076 days.

According to Field Manual 101-10-1 (1072 of the United States Army and based on relevant figures for World War II in Europe) the indices corresponded to a theater of operations in classical non-nuclear warfare. If these figures are applied to the total number of troops deployed throughout the duration of the war in the Portuguese overseas territories on a daily basis, it would be equal to 61,112 killed in battle; 240,083 wounded in battle with 707,154 casualties through accidents or sickness. World War II lasted for seven years, while Portugal's colonial wars went on for almost double that.

CHAPTER 16

Why Portugal Lost its African Possessions

As we reach towards the conclusion of this volume, Charles Guillain's description of Mozambique in the early 1800s comes to mind.[1]

He referred to the Portuguese colony as a "dusty corpse only preserving its form thanks to the immobility of the environment in which it found itself," and goes on: "There was no lack of carrion crows and undertakers around the 'Portuguese mummy' in 19th-century Mozambique, but in the end, Lisbon would chase them away and find sufficient subterfuges and even the strength to breathe life into the flesh which had escaped corruption."

Although the end was to come suddenly with the 1974 "Carnation Revolution" that overthrew the Portuguese government and handed independence to its overseas possessions, the reasons why Portugal was ousted from its colonies are many and complex. The principal one is that, as with so many autocrats, Prime Minister António de Oliveira Salazar—after decades of running the show almost single-handedly—ignored the advice of those who told him that the writing was on the wall with regard to Lisbon's colonial possessions in Africa. The international community had reached a turning point, they said, adding that that was why Britain and France (followed soon afterwards by Belgium and Spain) had offered their African colonies self-rule.

Unperturbed, Salazar rejected this advice and insisted on doing things his own way. Not long thereafter, in one of his rare public pronouncements, he declared that the provinces in the *Ultramar* had been under Lisbon's rule for centuries and would stay that way. While he accepted that the war in Angola had become a reality, such things had taken place often enough in the past and the troublemakers were always defeated, was his response. The people responsible for "the current phase of troubles" would similarly be put in their place…

There were other reasons why Salazar remained intransigent. First in line was the incontrovertible fact that Portugal was broke: after Albania, it was the second poorest nation in Europe and Lisbon needed its overseas provinces to balance the books. More salient, he would argue, the African colonies were part of one great family, suggesting that the one would never survive without the other.

In retrospect, those deliberations held little water, but then Salazar was the boss. Also, he was supported by powerful financial, industrial and security interests (including an extremely efficient secret service). Consequently, while he remained alive, there was nobody either intrepid or daring enough to counter his dictates.

Those of us who knew and understood the nature of the problems the Portuguese were facing, were very much aware that without its African possessions—or *Império Português*—Lisbon would be deprived of the prominence it had achieved as a major colonial power. It was not lost on anybody close to Salazar—or his supporters—that the nation's expansion had strong historical roots, having started with the conquest of Ceuta in North Africa in 1415 and eventually extending all the way across the globe. For centuries Portuguese banners had fluttered from mastheads, from Brazil in the New World to Macau on the Chinese mainland.

In addition, there were other possessions. These included Portuguese Timor in Indonesia, Goa in India and other outposts all the way to Africa where, cumulatively, Lisbon was in control of three territories twice the size of Germany and France together. By 1571, a string of naval stations and islands along the coasts of Africa, the Middle East, India and South Asia linked Lisbon with Imperial Japan on the far side of planet.

It was impossible for anybody in Lisbon to suggest to the old man that the time had come to abandon the country's proud colonial heritage, and that it could be done at the stroke of a pen. His answer, as always, in harsh tones was that the glorious *Ultramar Português* "is here to stay."

Add to that the "wisdom of the day" in the upper echelons of Portugal's High Command, which was twofold: first, you simply do not negotiate with the enemy, especially when they are in a position of strength. That they were for much of the time: the Soviets were supplying all their needs and doing so free of charge. Second, those in charge within Lisbon's corridors of power passionately believed that in Mozambique—where the Portuguese were stuck with inferior leadership and a terrain far too big to effectively control with so few troops on the ground—the great Cahora Bassa Dam and the sudden discovery of enormous oil and gas deposits, would eventually change everything.

***

Portugal's wars in the three overseas provinces were not "great conflicts" in the classical, historical mold.

Essentially, they were regarded in more pragmatic terms as battles that were being fought in order for the nation to survive. This applied to both sides of what was always a badly demarcated front. Of course, it helped that Portugal was one of a dozen founding nations of the North Atlantic Treaty Organization (NATO), and though some help came from its partners, the country remained indigent and ill-equipped.

The guerrillas were even poorer. While the liberation groups received succor and weapons from the Soviets, China, Cuba, Yugoslavia and their allies, those involved in the actual fighting were most times rarely experienced enough—both mentally and physically—to use what they had to good advantage. For all that, this series of three African colonial conflicts lasted 13 unforgiving years.

Inadvertently, I'd had some experience of one of those wars while traveling overland through Angola in the mid-1960s on my way back to London. I'd used connections to get a visa that allowed me to travel almost the entire length of the country—south to north—from Ovamboland in South West Africa to Luanda, from where I was able to fly to Pointe Noire in Congo-Brazza.

Though battles were being regularly fought in the overgrown tropical *Dembos* to the immediate north of the capital, hostilities in the south were rare. At the same time, there were troops, military camps, armored personnel carriers and warplanes just about everywhere. I was even briefly arrested as spy on the main road north out of Lobito and spent the night in a cell, until I could show the following morning that apart from my British passport, I had another travel document that had been issued by South Africa.

A few years later I went back as an accredited correspondent and almost every time things were different: sometimes the Portuguese Army was on the front foot, other times its performance was dismal. There seemed to be a constant downside lurking somewhere in the eaves—more often than not involving landmines—a threat that Lisbon was never able to effectively counter.

From that initial phase I wrote my first book, *The Terror Fighters* (published in 1969 by Purnell, a British company), as well as a multitude of articles that reflected a series of disconcerting impressions about a war that seemed at the time almost impossible to win.

On my return to South Africa after that first visit to Angola, I addressed a large audience of interested people in the Johannesburg City Hall. Many of them regular or reservist military personnel, including several dozen generals and staff officers who occupied the entire first row below the platform from where I delivered my talk.

What was significant about that gathering, was that after a month-long sojourn with various Portuguese Army and Air Force units, I managed to convey (together with a selection of slides) something that foreshadowed a few of the formidable problems that South Africans would themselves have to face in the not-too-distant future.

Both at my talk and in the blurb on the dust jacket of that first book, published shortly afterwards, I warned that the Angolan War, only a few hours' flying time from Johannesburg, was historically significant to all Southern Africans in the long term. My exact words were succinct: "It is not generally realized that on its outcome—one way or the other—may depend the future of the entire Southern African subcontinent."

As might have been expected, my "gloom and doom projections" were afterwards raised in Parliament in Cape Town and in the process I made some lasting enemies, including the loquacious South African foreign minister Pik Botha. He suggested that I had lost my mind and he was furious that I had actually dared to challenge the perception—within the confines of the National Party—that the security of South Africa was inviolate. It was a bit like Rhodesia's Ian Smith declaring that, as a country and a political entity, his former British colony would last a thousand years.

I went back to cover Lisbon's wars quite a few times and after more spells with Portuguese military units, it gradually became clear that while the guerrillas, insurgents, freedom fighters—call them what you will—while not making great inroads with their "Liberation Wars," were very much on the ground; fighting, resisting, destabilizing and intimidating those who did not share their revolutionary views. More concisely, it was incontrovertibly evident to anybody who wished to see (and given the opportunity of doing so), that those ragtag bands of bush combatants were getting on with the job of trying to drive the Portuguese out of Africa.

The Portuguese military, in turn, while coping with most of it, were having a hard time trying to get to grips with an exceedingly elusive enemy who, though not nearly as well trained as themselves and lacking modern-day military experience, could sometimes be astonishingly forceful. What eluded many of Lisbon's commanders on the ground in Africa was that the average insurgent—for all his or her shortcomings—was often a good deal more determined to achieve victory than the defenders. Obviously, it helped immeasurably that they could cross borders from neighboring territories, while the Portuguese Army was hardly ever allowed to follow up in hot pursuit once they had scooted back to their safe havens.

The few times that Lisbon's forces did launch cross-border attacks, the hullaballoo raised by the United Nations took ages to dissipate. The South Africans, who fought a significant part of their Border War in the country from which the South West African People's Organization (SWAPO) operated, most times did not give a hoot what the UN or any other country might think about such intrusions. In contrast, the Portuguese almost always played it by the book.

As hostilities progressed, with the fog of war often becoming as impenetrable as the tangled rain forest or savannah terrain in which it was being fought, I would sometimes try to envisage what would happen should the guerrillas gain the upper hand.

From Day One, when the first few thousand rebels streamed into Angola in long, irregular columns from the Congo—a country already in dreadful turmoil after being rushed helter-skelter into independence by Belgium; self-government for which it was woefully unprepared—the war in Angola always appeared to see-saw back and forth. There was a lot of evidence that those primitive fighters (and yes, they were primitive, mostly untrained, and only issued with boots a year or two into hostilities) had the fortitude to go on indefinitely. Portugal, in contrast, a country run by a dictator, did not. In short, the guerrillas had absolutely nothing to lose, and the Soviets who provided all the succor the rebels needed, knew it.

Projecting that same scenario onto what was happening just then in South Africa, it should have been staring the nation in the face that if Lisbon did not hold out in its colonies, first Rhodesia and then the Pretoria government would be next in line.

***

In many ways, Portugal suffered numerous problems never envisaged before the start of the Angolan war in 1961.

While most Portuguese Army conscripts were happy enough with their lot to start with, that enthusiasm started to wane as hostilities dragged on. Here one needs to be reminded that conflict in Angola lasted twice as long as American forces were deployed in Vietnam.

Then two things started to happen. The first was that many young men approaching call-up age opted to discreetly slip across the border into Spain and seek work elsewhere in Europe to avoid being drafted into the army. Not long afterwards, regular soldiers—facing another tedious stint in Africa—also began voting with their feet. It was never a massive exodus—in fact, available figures put the number of desertions from the military at 25,000 during the course of hostilities in Africa, all active serving soldiers—but a serious enough loss in trained manpower to hurt.

It became so bad that by the time the wars ended in 1974, there was hardly a bar or restaurant in Paris, Amsterdam or Berlin that was not or had not been employing Portuguese youngsters either in their kitchens or in service roles. Moreover, there was no stopping them because the frontier with Spain was all but porous and there were numerous places where you could just walk across the border. Many of these men left their homes clandestinely after receiving their call-up papers, and notably, those losses were over and above the 25,000 actual deserters.

Douglas Porch tells us in *The Portuguese Armed Forces and the Revolution* that as the war continued, more commissioned ranks began to slip away. He maintained that while some of those who took the gap were politically motivated, many more were spurred on by economic considerations. Then there were those that failed to return from holidays abroad…

In 1973 there followed the incident involving 15 engineering cadets—all regarded by the establishment as the "cream of the nation's Military Academy." After completing their four-year course, the entire class strolled across the frontier into Spain.[2]

Those losses apart, by the time the wars in Africa ended, more than a million Portuguese men and a small number of women, mostly in medical roles, had served militarily in Africa. The majority returned home totally disillusioned with what they believed had become a futile effort that was wasting the lives of their compatriots. This became more pronounced with time, to the extent that many serving troops were becoming outspokenly hostile towards the system.

For Lisbon there were two additional problems. Though the country was ruled by a right-wing dictator who abhorred the left, there was no way of stopping individuals embracing radical political causes. As a consequence, the Portuguese Communist Party had a field day. It was actually an open secret that many members of the officer corps were hard-line socialists and that there were communists within the ranks who openly espoused Marxism and slept with copies of *Das Kapital* under their pillows. While that might sound absurd, it happened.

The second issue was far more serious: convincing the average young Portuguese recruit who had been called up to fight a faraway guerrilla war in Africa that he was battling for a noble cause in protecting his nation, something the Americans also faced during the Vietnam War. It might have worked on home soil, but stuck out in some distant pestilence-ridden jungle outpost thousands of kilometers away from home, it simply did not make sense.

In this regard, one has to bear in mind that Maputo (or Lourenço Marques as it was known in the old days), lies 8,400km from Lisbon and, in today's world, getting there involves a direct flight that takes less than a day. In the 1960s, the journey lasted three weeks or more by ship. Getting to Luanda, though closer to Europe, was an equally tedious slog. Consequently, the first question most conscripts asked on arriving in tropical Africa was: "Why the hell are we here?"

When I tackled one young lieutenant in a camp in the north of the country, he retorted with comments like: "What's all this bullshit about? This is Africa, and it's neither my home nor my country." In the overall picture, I discovered soon enough that all the majority of these young soldiers wanted was to go home, with the result that few were prepared to risk their lives while on active service.

Unbending, the *raison d'être* provided by those in charge of this largely civilian conscripted army was that Angola, Mozambique and Portuguese Guinea (along with Lisbon's islands and far-flung outposts), were all one marvelously cohesive integral entity: in effect, a single country, and that they were required to protect that which was integral to their historical heritage. London said something similar when the American colonists revolted between 1765 and 1783...

So, it was averred by their superiors, by being posted to a military base near the Congo border or somewhere equally remote in Mozambique, you were actually fighting for the "Motherland." It used to be called "Fatherland" but that abruptly changed after 1945, for obvious reasons.

Naturally, that rationale had its opponents and while the majority of Lisbon's youth might not have made good students or lacked the wherewithal to study further, they were not naive. A jungle strong point in some isolated outpost along the Zambezi, where the lions would get you if wandered into the darkness at night to have a pee, was not home. Nor were the shores of

Lake Malawi, used to good advantage by the insurgents to clandestinely infiltrate their own forces.

In fact, as some of these European combatants were heard to argue in the latter stages of the war, the soldiers of the Portuguese Army were the interlopers, not their purported enemy.

***

One of the curious observations made by hacks covering Southern African conflicts during the final quarter of the last century was how very differently the armies involved in these regional conflicts went about their business.

For a start, the Rhodesians preferred to operate in small groups in the bush, usually four-man "sticks" as they were dubbed. Despite small numbers, these armed quartets were remarkably successful at getting to grips with the enemy. A "stick" would observe an enemy patrol from a distance, usually somewhere on high ground, or make contact if the numbers were not disproportionate and it would not be long before a helicopter-led Fire Force would arrive on the scene (usually a Rhodesian Light Infantry squad). Or they would be dropped in at very low levels from Rhodesian Air Force Dakotas.

For their part, the Portuguese almost always regarded small-unit operations in the African bush as tantamount to suicide. Their preference was invariably fighting groups of a couple of dozen men.

And whereas the Rhodesians and South Africans would send their patrols out for days, sometimes weeks, the average Portuguese Army bush patrol rarely gravitated far enough from their bases for them not to be able to sleep in their beds. The attitude, by and large, was that the bush was for wild animals and, of course, the enemy, but then the majority of these soldiers from Europe knew little about the African bush.

Portuguese Special Forces, in contrast, were in a class of their own and they could mix it with the best, Black or White. Their African troops, which included the *Flechas,* African Special Marines (*Fuzileiros Especiais Africanos*) and the specialist, all-Black *Comandos Africanos*, all fought brilliant campaigns and were held in deep respect by all. It actually surprised Southern African Special Forces like the Recces or the Rhodesian SAS—sometimes embedded with Lisbon's forces—that that tradition was not being emulated lower down.

Still, that was the way the Portuguese had always fought their wars, their officers would say, and theirs was not to question why…

In contrast, the only White faces in the ranks of the guerrillas in the Mozambique war were handfuls of Russian, East European and Cuban advisors as well as the very occasional government defector. There was also a bevy of British journalists who propagated the cause, including the British writer Basil Davidson and the ultra-radical *Mzungu* David Martin. Occasionally a member of the French left, customarily a follower of Regis Debray or some other revolutionary, would discreetly show face.

In the eyes of guerrilla central committees, said one neutral observer at the time, a White Portuguese defector would always be exactly that: a White Portuguese, even though, over the years, there were quite a few Portuguese soldiers and airmen who deserted and crossed the line.

Curiously, desertion figures for the Portuguese Army in Africa were modest; there were only 103 men who defected throughout the 13-year period of the war in all three African territories.

While the intent of a fugitive from the Portuguese Army might have been sincere, rebel leaders considered these defectors of more value outside the fighting zone—preferably behind the Iron Curtain or, in the case of the PAIGC—the Freedom Army in what was to become Guiné-Bissau (under the control of the exiled, communist *Frente Patriótica de Libertação Nacional* [FPLN] that had its headquarters in Algiers).

A constant preoccupation with the possibility that some defectors might be double agents was a trait—not necessarily peculiar to either FRELIMO or Guinea's PAIGC High Command—almost certainly inherited from the Portuguese. In this regard, the movement's internal security could almost be equated to that of PIDE, Lisbon's ultra-efficient secret police. Equally ruthless, an individual might easily be liquidated if even suspected of collusion with the other side.

Other differences between Southern African conflicts included casualty evacuation procedures, which were to become a critical issue as the wars progressed. As discussed earlier, if a South African soldier or airman was wounded, every effort would be made to get him out of the bush and into hospital as quickly as possible: more often than not that involved a helicopter.

There might be a full-scale contact on the go involving scores of men, but once it got down to fundamental life-saving, the air force would detach a chopper or a small plane to haul the man out. In contrast, a wounded soldier in the Portuguese Army would obviously be cared for by his buddies and clearly, if his condition was serious, a helicopter might be requested. However, the possibility of one being available was generally remote, which was not surprising, as there were three African wars on the go and not nearly enough aircraft or helicopters to cope with demand.

It was also probably true, said one of my American colleagues who visited Africa at the time, there were probably more helicopters in the air over parts of New York State or Greater Los Angeles as might have been operational at any one time in all of Mozambique.

The unit medic would do what he could while his patient was being moved overland, but obviously, that took time. It was not unusual, if treatment was delayed in the tropics, that any serious torso wound would result in septicemia setting in within hours. Landmines were another problem, with the result that more often than not the medical profession would be hesitant about traveling on dirt roads.

Then, as Michael Knipe of the London *Times* and I found in Tete, Portuguese military hospitals were sometimes not worthy of the appellation.

One can only contemplate the lasting effect on army morale, especially since this sort of thing, as in any war, quickly does the rounds back at base.

***

There were numerous other reasons for Portugal's colonial demise, all of which warrant examination. Economic issues feature prominently.

For a start, historical development of the "Overseas Provinces"—the *Ultramar*—had always been pitifully slow and it was only in the second year of the Angolan War that Prime Minister Salazar began to address some of these issues.

In Lisbon's African colonies, the administrative accent had always been on cheap labor, which meant keeping the populace relatively uneducated. While the majority of the combined populations spoke Portuguese—as they still do today more than a generation after the bloody transition—there was heavy emphasis on what was termed the "Great Society," but little effective authority was ever vested in the provinces. Most important matters were invariably referred to Lisbon, far away, and in any event a dictatorship.

Moreover, the African colonies were subject to the bidding of legions of functionaries who—with the military or the law just outside the door—oversaw everything from local government to administration of the civil service, education, health, trade, commerce, industry, utilities and the rest. In the boondocks it was even worse: the local *Chefe do Posto* (district head) was the dominant force and his word was law!

In theory, Angola being an immensely wealthy region with Mozambique not far behind, there should have been more than an abundance for all their citizens, whatever their color. In practice, Africans were relegated to a subservient level of second-class citizenship that would sometimes make conditions in apartheid-ridden South Africa seem benevolent by comparison. Forced labor was commonplace, as were public beatings. If a suspect died in jail, questions were rarely asked.

Government rule was not only brutal but also repressive, coupled to heavy-handed press censorship (both in the metropolis and in the African colonies). Forced labor was exacted on a massive scale, with many of the country's roads built using either forced or prison labor.

The Portuguese secret police was almost a government in itself. Its methods were cruel, and in some respects, could sometimes compare with those of the Nazi SS or Iran's SAVAK during the rule of the Shah. There was rarely any quarter afforded those suspected of colluding with the enemy, with the result that the guerrillas soon employed equally brutal tactics against anybody linked to the administration.

Additionally, while everybody was supposed to be governed by a single, universal set of laws, there were different criteria for Portuguese nationals and ethnic Africans. Blacks could be arrested at whim, even for trivial offences. Not paying the mandatory head tax or perhaps using bad language in the presence of a Portuguese woman could result in a jail term. Similarly, anybody encouraging labor unrest for better wages was charged with sedition and imprisoned. Since the entire country was ruled by decree, any kind of political activity by either Blacks or Whites was ruled illegal and those involved prosecuted.

Harsh laws were imposed by equally uncompromising bureaucrats. Sometimes mindlessly brutal, these officials were rarely made to account for their actions, even when lives were lost. Coupled to that, wages for Blacks in Angola, Mozambique and Portuguese Guinea were among the lowest on the continent.

Not surprisingly, living conditions throughout this expansive overseas empire were dismal, for African people especially. Lisbon would always argue that in the long term, it was better for all because nobody starved. Nor did they, but by the end of World War II, this political scenario was also a clear-cut recipe for revolt.

What Lisbon had not initially factored into the colonial equation was communications. What was going on elsewhere in Africa by the 1960s could obviously not fail to have an impact on Portuguese citizens of all races. How could it be otherwise, when Lisbon suddenly had to deal with a number of former British and French colonies now in control of their own affairs, several of which were neighbors.

These included Senegal, Malawi and Congo-Brazzaville along with other societies that were passionately opposed to any kind of Portuguese presence on the continent: Guinea, Tanzania and Zambia. Some were soon to support the guerrillas in their ongoing wars and permitted revolutionary groups to operate from their soil.

Even so, the Portuguese government believed it could deal with those imponderables and it actually might have been able to do so, had those belligerent neighbors acted on their own. But the Cold War had taken effect, and both Moscow and Beijing believed there were good prospects to be had in Africa.

Consequently, as we now know, it was politics that became intrusive and the word "freedom" ultimately dealt the death blow to any aspirations Lisbon might have had of holding onto its African possessions.

Portugal's Forces Leave Africa

It was politics that finally put an end to any aspirations the Portuguese people might have had of holding on to their African possessions. But before that, we witnessed the old paradigm of colonial conquest followed by African resistance, burgeoning nationalism, the struggle for independence and then finally liberation.

It had happened in Algeria, French Indochina and a century or more before that in South and Central America, so there was nothing new to the imbroglio when it hit Portugal's possessions on the continent of Africa.

For those of us who can remember, numerous images out of Lourenço Marques in the final days of Portuguese rule stirred many emotions: regret, confusion, frustration, desperation and even revolt.

Following the army mutiny in Lisbon on April 25, 1974, there was talk of a counter-revolution and even a handful of hard-liners in both the capital and Beira who attempted to take over the Mozambique government. For a short time, hospital emergencies in major centers were running on double time, and newspapers were full of reports and photographs of casualties that resulted from opposing factions making contact, both in the cities and beyond.

For the average man in the street, Black or White, the war was over and on the face of it, there was no argument. Samora Machel's guerrilla army had ostensibly won the final battle, though there was very little that was militaristic about the outcome: the country was handed to them on the proverbial platter by a bunch of radical soldiers turned politicians in Lisbon.

Though long-term consequences only began to materialize some time later, one can only speculate how the architects of the *Revolução dos Cravos* ("Carnation Revolution") would have felt had they known that their actions—all very carefully planned beforehand—would have resulted in hundreds of thousands of deaths, most of them innocent civilians.

Look at the facts: Portuguese Guinea—renamed Guiné-Bissau before the ink was dry on documents signed by the oppressed and oppressor—plunged headlong into a civil war that ended with the slaughter of just about everybody—men, women and children—who had been linked in any way with the recently departed colonial regime. If you were thought to have had some kind of link with the hated oppressors, even washing their laundry, you were dead.

The same with Angola, only that carnage was on a much vaster scale and the civil war that followed lasted almost a quarter century. It eventually encompassed a group of a few hundred South African mercenaries, almost all Special Forces operatives, who ended up serving within the ranks of their former enemies. With characteristic vigor, they pursued their trusted erstwhile ally Dr Jonas Savimbi and his ragged band of guerrilla fighters and with unerring efficiency, killed them.

Taking prisoners of war never entered the equation. Those cadres that surrendered were gunned down wherever and whenever they were encountered and what is astonishing here, is that every single one of these actions indubitably constituted war crimes. Yet not one of those responsible (nor anybody within the Angolan military who called the shots that resulted in the kind of officially sanctioned brutality which counters everything the Geneva Convention stands for) has ever been brought before the International Court of Justice at The Hague to answer charges.

Nobody is certain of the numbers of fatalities; some put the tally of all of those who died in this post-colonial struggle, civilians included, somewhere in the region of half a million, give or take a hundred thousand. In fact, if disease and debilitation caused by starvation and the privations of war—as well as landmines—are taken into account, it was probably a good deal more.

The same goes for the civil war in Mozambique between FRELIMO and the anti-communist insurgent forces of the Mozambican National Resistance (RENAMO) which started in 1977. With liberal assistance, first from Rhodesia and thereafter from South Africa, that horrific conflict only ended in 1992—but it still flares up sporadically when the rebels feel they been sidelined or have a grudge to air.

At the end of the day, the rebels in that vast East African country fringing the Indian Ocean, caused far more damage than Mozambique ever suffered during its 10-year colonial struggle. But as the highly revered Bill Deedes commented, while still editor of the *Daily Telegraph*, some years after the Portuguese had left Africa, "Who really gives a damn?"

Certainly, nobody in Lisbon did.

***

The truth of the matter is that Portugal's struggles in Africa should never have ended the way they did.

The original vision among Lisbon's ageing leaders to improve the political situation—either at home or abroad—or to strengthen the Portuguese military equation in Africa, was unquestionably blinkered. If ever there was an example of political leadership having atrophied while in power, it could be viewed on the banks of the Tagus, especially since Salazar had been in power since 1932 (his iron-clad authoritarian rule lasted more than three decades, one of the longest in contemporary history).

When Marcello José das Neves Alves Caetano succeeded him in 1968—the last prime minister of the *Estado Novo* regime—the same people who supported Salazar ended up in the Caetano Cabinet. Effectively, there was no change in political form or content.

Yet, despite the label of it being the "new" state or society, Africa was always dominant in the minds of both Salazar and Caetano and, curiously, there were times when South Africa also became the focus of attention. Portugal's friendly "neighbor" at the southern tip of Africa was occasionally viewed with great suspicion by Lisbon's hierarchy.

Salazar, it emerged long before he died, was obsessed with an incipient threat of a Mozambique unilateral declaration of independence (UDI): in other words, cutting ties with Europe and going it alone in Africa very much like Rhodesia had done in 1964. This later became something of an obsession; Salazar believed there were people in Mozambique plotting with Pretoria to overthrow the Lourenço Marques establishment.

Matters weren't helped by the many South Africans who wished to invest in the Mozambican economy. Although it was permitted at first on a modest scale, it was only in 1966 that any considerable foreign investment was allowed into the overseas territories: too late.

Also, because of his UDI fears, Salazar permitted little real economic development in his Portuguese possessions. He was wary of foreigners with large wallets becoming too influential among his more distant subjects.

At the same time, it is also a reality that while Mozambique remained firmly committed to everything Salazar stood for, Angola was the one overseas province where the possibilities of a break from the Motherland had been mooted for decades. Had the war not arrived, Angola might ultimately have followed Rhodesia's example.

Douglas Porch, in his book *The Portuguese Armed Forces and the Revolution* mentions an air force colonel in Angola who said:

> In 1965, most of us already thought that Angola should become an independent and racially mixed country like Brazil. We saw that we could not win in the colonies. It was impossible to continue. Freedom had to come gradually because the people were not prepared for it. The military would be very useful in preparing the political solution. It was a task which we could not do in two months, but in six or seven years. We had to prepare the government and the local governments. The army had to maintain independence, build up the armed forces and so on…[1]

Similar circumstances started to evolve later in Mozambique where the Portuguese authorities in command were stuck with inferior leadership and a terrain that was far too big to effectively control with so few troops on the ground.

***

Ultimately, the downfall of Portuguese interests in Africa lay with the country's armed forces. To start with there was a good deal of discontent among members of the Portuguese military over conditions of service.

Troops normally spent two years on military service in Africa, customarily followed by six months at home and then another two years in the provinces. As might have been expected, that practice had a crippling effect on morale. As with Rhodesia, people with jobs who were sent on active service lost seniority or experience with their companies and obviously, domestic life sometimes suffered severely.

Things were not made easier by manifest hostility between regular soldiers and the large number of conscripts, particularly within the junior and middle ranks of commissioned officers. The old-timers resented the fact that many university graduates, fresh in uniform, were given ranks that had taken them years to achieve.

The MFA or Armed Forces Movement (which eventually organized the army putsch of April 1974) recognized that no political development was taking place either in the military or in the African territories. General de Spínola actually said as much in his book *Portugal and the Future*.

As we have already observed, there were also powerful radical elements at work within the regular army. Many officers were known to be socialist and quite a number outspokenly communist. They espoused these doctrines quite openly, yet they were allowed to continue to serve their country as dutiful patriots, in part because some of their senior officers were of similar mind.

Brigadier General Willem van der Waals, the penultimate South African military attaché in Luanda prior to the Portuguese leaving Africa, has his own views on developments:

> The military coup in Portugal took the entire international community by surprise, none more so than South Africa whose politicians refused to believe that a relatively primitive "barefoot bunch of revolutionaries" could ever achieve victory against a well-armed and organized European power. This was a measure of hubris for which Pretoria would pay dearly for much of the two following decades.
>
> To well-informed observers however, the news was not completely unexpected. One of the general officers prominent after the coup as a member of the military junta was General Francisco da Costa Gomes. He was destined to become Portugal's second post-coup president and it was during that early transitional phase that Angola would inexorably slide into civil war in 1975.[2]

Like most others familiar with what was going on in Africa just then, van der Waals was acutely aware that Angola would be stuck with its own brutal destiny once the new quasi-Marxist establishment in Lisbon went on to abandon its responsibilities, which it did to grand fanfare on November 11, 1975.

He goes on: "I worked closely with Costa Gomes after he became commander-in-chief of the armed forces in Angola in May 1970 and I found him soft-spoken, shy and a regular visitor to his troops in the field. Strange to relate in the light of subsequent events, it was he who significantly changed the military situation in Angola. He arrived at a critical time and when he left two years later, the military crisis had dissipated to such an extent that optimists believed that the war had been won. However, there were doubts in certain quarters concerning both his sincerity and his loyalty."

Shortly after Costa Gomes' appointment, a senior Portuguese officer remarked [to van der Waals] that the new commander-in-chief was a communist who had been sent to Angola to prepare the ground for a handover. To some, his military successes dispelled any doubts. But having done some research of my own, I discovered that after the outbreak of hostilities in Angola in 1961, Costa Gomes had been involved in an abortive coup against the Salazar government. So, these doubts persisted. As van der Waals declared:

> Returning from Namibia a few days after the coup in April 1974, I was in contact with military intelligence in Pretoria. Two years earlier I'd submitted a report forecasting the possibility of decolonization in Angola. At the time, it was accorded little attention, but now all that material was analyzed afresh.
>
> In particular, note was taken of a letter written in March 1972 by Costa Gomes' predecessor, General Almeida Viana to a member of the Angolan Legislative Council in which he referred to a conspiracy in Portugal, after which Angola would be left to the "vicissitudes of the times."

> Could the seemingly spontaneous events of the spring of 1974 have been planned two years before? [They would obviously seriously affect Mozambique as well.] There is no hard evidence to support this contention, but it is known that conservative elements of Portuguese society, including the top structure of the armed forces were very much concerned at that time about Caetano's liberalization of colonial policy.
>
> He was even called Portugal's de Gaulle, so something was indeed brewing.

Significantly, some Portuguese officers (as with quite a few South Africans of similar persuasion), tended to equate their military efforts in Mozambique and Angola with those of the French in Algeria. Porch drew this analogy by stating that in Portugal (as with France) circumstances for the military coup were provided by a long and exhausting colonial war.

There were crucial differences between the two countries. Many French soldiers serving in North Africa actually believed they were almost within striking distance of victory. They reacted against what they believed to be a betrayal by de Gaulle. Portuguese officers, in contrast, felt that the country was locked in a pointless and cripplingly expensive struggle to maintain a burdensome empire. Portugal's colonial wars continually sapped the nation's strength, making it appear ridiculous in the eyes of the world. They believed the war had ruined the army by flooding it with half-trained conscripts, many of whom, as we have seen, the government attempted to promote over the heads of long-serving regulars.

As Porch maintained, the latent resentment, which gradually built up to "scalding point" in the officer corps, was a combination of bruised national pride and wounded professional vanity; an explosive mixture of sentiments which the Portuguese military establishment shared with revolutionary soldiers in countries like Egypt and other developing world countries.

The Portuguese experience proved that the increasing professionalism of the armed forces could hasten its entry into the political arena rather than discourage it, an issue argued by American historian Samuel Huntington. He perceptively declared that "professional discontent creates shop floor militancy and the coup substitutes for the strike."

In retrospect, it is astonishing that Portugal never considered transferring military families to the African colonies for these extended periods of anything up to five years. It was a rather obvious choice that was never made, because the principal argument against such a step was the UDI bogey: a real fear that too many metropolitan Portuguese sent to the African colonies would then begin to think for themselves ... exactly as the Rhodesians had done.

Then came money, and generally, the military suffered severely when compared to other European military establishments.

By way of comparison, Porch observed that not long after the war started, a full colonel of an infantry regiment stationed in Portugal earned 10,200 escudos a month, which would have been something like US$250. A British colonel earned about double that, while a French colonel took home about five or six percent less than his British counterpart.

Physical conditions too, especially at the "sharp end," were abominable. Military camps at remote corners of the empire were invariably difficult and could be quite unhealthy. Malaria was rife throughout Mozambique (as in Angola and Portuguese Guinea) and so too were other fairly serious tropical ailments.

In some places local tribal people actually lived under better conditions than their "protectors," especially where they were herded together in their Malayan-style protected camps or *aldeamentos*.

At the end of the war, there were those who maintained that for all of Lisbon's problems and makeshift "fix-alls," it was Portuguese Guinea that was the principal cause of the rot that set in among the Portuguese armed forces. By 1972 it had become apparent to even the most sanguine supporter of colonial rule in Africa that the war in this grim jungle and swamp terrain on the West Coast of Africa could never be won. It should have been relatively easy for the Portuguese to withdraw from Guinea. But, as an apologist in Lisbon pointed out, that would have been impossible without abandoning the other two African "provinces."

The so-called "Domino Principle" would take effect at once, he warned, and that at a time when domino theories were being bandied about in Southeast Asia.

Then, as the war progressed, further problems arose. Apart from casualties—which were never really severe—more and more young men failed to answer the call. The strain on Portuguese manpower in 1967 caused the age of conscription to be lowered to 18 and that was followed by the conscript service term to be extended from two to four years by the addition of two more years' compulsory service overseas. However, not all those called up actually served.

In Portugal itself, as opposition to the wars in Portugal grew, so avoidance of the call-up increased. It is estimated that something like 110,000 Portuguese failed to report for military service between 1961 and 1974, either through deliberate avoidance or absence abroad, since over a million Portuguese were emigrant workers by 1974.

In the last call-up, before the April 1974 putsch, less than half of those who had been sent their papers reported for duty. Consequently, as the defense establishment grew, the universities were called upon to provide many more of the junior officers needed to fight. These were enlightened young people, who had observed the dictatorship from up close. They knew what Prime Minister Caetano's legacy had done, and what it was still doing to their homeland.

Few were under any illusions that they would be involved in what the Americans like to call "a just war." Nor were they made overly welcome by regular officers of the army and air force; veterans who'd spent years in uniform struggling up the slow ladder of promotion. In the Portuguese armed forces, any kind of vertical movement could be very slow indeed and often depended as much on family contacts as on ability.

A man rarely attained the rank of colonel before he had reached the ripe old age of 50. The professionals bitterly resented newly commissioned lieutenants and captains who had usurped their positions, or as one prominent commentator in Lisbon subsequently noted:

> The key trigger of the 1974 coup seems to have been much more what many professionals perceived as a challenge to their esprit de corps and their career prospects in the form of an understandable, if inept, attempt by the Caetano government to turn conscript officers into professionals in order to address the growing shortage of professional junior officers needed to carry on the war and lead the large numbers of conscripts without a loss in military effectiveness.

Ultimately, it was these liberal, fairly well-educated officers and their undermining of the Portuguese war effort—both at home and abroad—that led to the formation of the Armed Forces Movement, followed by the 1974 coup d'état.

Within a year Portugal was out of Africa.

***

What followed Lisbon's unilateral abrogation of authority in its African colonies was a disaster, though there were few who recognized it as such at the time. Hundreds of thousands of Portuguese nationals had to look to the immediate option of fleeing while they could still manage to do so. Others, not so fortunate, were caught in the cross hairs of a violent imperial-linked legacy that nobody could have predicted, even though the Congo's troubles had predicated future problems for Angola.

The difference was that while the Belgians abandoned their colonial responsibilities (and we have seen the consequences this past half-century), the Portuguese stayed and fought.

Yet curiously, only 15 years before Angola's travails, the neighboring Congo had collapsed in a fury of African retribution that eventually involved Belgium and its NATO partners in a succession of rescue efforts. Tens of thousands of colonial Belgians fled into Angola to avoid the bloodshed, from where they went back to Europe. Quite a number preferred to stay in Africa and headed for Rhodesia and South Africa.

Obviously, what took place, with the majority of Whites pulling out, totally changed everything in Angola and the civil war that followed independence was only part of it. It took Britain's *The Economist* to put these matters into perspective in a report headlined "The Flight from Africa," published on August 16, 1975, only months before Angola's independence finally happened.

The article is worth quoting even though it was written decades ago and took a radical London School of Economics line, referring to those few Whites who did try to stand up to Luanda's Marxists as belonging to an "underground fascist army" which was ridiculous. Its author does go on a bit about constantly referring to the MPLA as *the* "Popular Movement" almost as if the *Movimento* was the only political party contesting the Angolan election. So much for British fair play … I quote:

> The Portuguese are calling it the greatest exodus in the history of Africa, and they are right. Not even the Congo, where in 1960 the White population fell from 110,000 to 20,000 between January and July, was like what is happening in Angola now. Angola's 500,000 or so White people, nearly all of them Portuguese, have had enough.

Exactly the same sentiments were to be applied to Mozambique after it achieved its independence on June 25, 1975.

In the end, one has to also consider other issues which came to the fore, including the weakness of Portugal as a metropolitan power in the 19th century, contrasted with the strength and expansiveness of the Portuguese Creole communities which in some circumstances confronted Portugal in her obscure colonial wars and sometimes acted as surrogates for Portuguese power. All eventually played something of a role in a tiny chapter of colonial history that sadly, has since been all but forgotten by the world beyond Portugal's traditional frontiers.

The eminent French academic, René Pélissier, who spent his working life immersed in Portuguese culture and history, admitted to a certain admiration of Portugal, which he declared "found ways of achieving so much with so few resources."

He had it right when he stated in one of his volumes, carefully compiled like the rest of his work: "the Portuguese conquest of Mozambique was not achieved by magical incantations at the tomb of Vasco da Gama, but by passing over the tens upon tens of thousands, not to mention hundreds of thousands of corpses which for generation after generation Africa, heedless and forgetful, allowed to be sacrificed to some blind Moloch."

Though he was discussing a plethora of earlier colonial campaigns, what he declared applied as much to the earlier colonial epoch as to the anti-colonial "Liberation Wars" that followed.[3]

His description of the Portuguese armed forces makes clear the extent to which Lisbon depended on the locally recruited *Guerra preta* of the Creoles. Africa, he ventured, was "conquered by its own inhabitants."

So it was too...

The end, when it came, arrived as suddenly as nightfall in the tropics. Once the young officers in Lisbon had decided that the wars had to end, tens of thousands of Portuguese nationals looked very carefully at their options at what was certainly going to be a change of government. Also, it might be a violent transition, as it was in the Belgian Congo in 1960 when that colony imploded.

The immediate reaction of many of these people, some whose roots went back centuries, was to flee, after which the exodus started and quickly gathered strength. To many of them, caught in an African limbo with an uncertain future (the civil war that was to last almost a generation had already started)—Pretoria, which was largely Protestant and with an English- and Afrikaans-speaking people as well as a "lifestyle that many did not understand"—simply did not appeal.

Brazil did, which is one of the reasons why so many Angolans and Mozambicans upped sticks and headed west across the Atlantic to make new homes for themselves and their families.

The consequences were calamitous, especially for the economies and administrations of the former colonies. Nobody gave a fig about what would happen when the Whites—who had the prerogative of all the skilled and many of the semi-skilled jobs in the country—departed. Nor that local government, which included municipalities, also collapsed in short order. Those essential services that remained: hospitals, law and order (which fell under the military, anyway), utilities and the rest continued more or less by inertia because by then nobody was concerned about anything but personal safety.

Lisbon launched its historic rescue effort "Operation *Air Bridge*" in August 1975 and hundreds of thousands of refugees, the majority White, were returned to their original roots in Europe. No question, whichever way this issue is viewed, Africa is that much poorer for it.

For Portugal, five centuries of proud but troubled history on the continent of Africa were over.

Epilogue

After the military putsch in Lisbon which ousted Portugal's civilian government, followed by a ceasefire in all three of the country's colonial wars in Africa, most of the guerrillas emerged from the bush.

They did not exactly lay down their arms because conditions remained uncertain, even though FRELIMO had won the war and the newly created Marxist government set about molding a society in which everybody, Black and White, could be involved.

Many Portuguese nationals, some having briefly protested in the country's two largest cities—Beira and the soon-to-be-renamed Lourenço Marques—decided to vote with their feet. Others tried to stay but many had been too closely linked to the old regime and were given harsh marching orders: they had 24 hours to leave and could take with them only the clothes on their backs and a single suitcase that did not weigh more than 20kg.

All private industry was seized by the state and nationalized, in keeping with the country's new Marxist constitution. The young country, headed by Samora Machel, one of Moscow's closest allies on the African continent, was soon in full stride.

But that lull was only temporary because both Rhodesia (still immersed in its own guerrilla war) and South Africa (eager to deflect attention from its racist apartheid policies) had initiated a new subversive campaign centered on a small group of dissidents opposed to FRELIMO's staunch communist ideals. Many had fought against the Portuguese and had become disillusioned with the harsh tenets of the new regime which they believed were alien to African tradition. Rhodesia and South Africa made contact with some of these nonconformists and in the process, a new political party, the *Resistência Nacional Moçambicana* (RENAMO) was formed two years after the Lisbon coup.

Incorporating a number of diverse recruits brought together by their opposition to the country's swing to socialism, including disgruntled former colonial troops and deserters from the post-independence army and security forces. Rhodesia employed the resources of its Central Intelligence Organization in addition to the country's Special Air Service, which for decades had been linked to the British SAS, to create a remarkably robust fighting unit.

South Africa gave whatever assistance was called for, including enormous supplies of weapons captured in its own Border War adjacent to Angola. That aid included a large body of military instructors, communications equipment and the launching of several clandestine raids on Mozambican rail, road and harbor installations.

Some of the more accomplished RENAMO fighters were sent to South Africa for specialist courses that included demolition and intelligence work as well as training a fully-fledged airborne unit where parachute jumps were conducted at a base in northern South West Africa (today Namibia).

An interesting insight here is that paratrooper recruits were given three static jumps for their training and then sent back to Mozambique by air, their fourth jump being made at night into sometimes hostile territory. None of them argued because, as one instructor said, they didn't know any better and believed that was the way it was done.

By the late 1970s, former FRELIMO cadres were acting as scouts for Rhodesian military units carrying out raids deep into Mozambique; in the process they launched attacks on major settlements and sabotaged infrastructure. RENAMO's political wing also operated a radio station, the *Voice of Free Africa*, which was said to have clandestine CIA links, and which broadcast anti-communist propaganda from Rhodesia.

Fighting increased sharply between 1982 and 1984, by which time the Rhodesian war had ended and South Africa took control. What had started as a decidedly low-key subversive moment, quickly escalated; first into an effective insurgency, then into a major civil war that is thought have caused the deaths of up to a million—mainly civilian—Mozambicans. It created a refugee situation in Southern Africa that lasted well into the new millennium, when a peace treaty of sorts was signed.

A brief resurgence of violence followed in early 2013 and lasted roughly a year, after which another formal accord followed, even though cursory attacks continued from time to time. In a sense, though still active militarily, RENAMO had lost its appeal and finally, a real sense of peace settled across the land.

It was then, late 2017, that Mozambique came within the sights of Islamic State. This Jihadist movement—as well as al-Qaeda—had already turned its attention to Africa by fomenting insurgency in both Somalia and Mali, a former French colony in West Africa.

In truth, Islamic State's war in northern Mozambique is far worse than anything experienced in this distant East African country for centuries. Portugal's colonial war lasted longer and claimed more lives, but what is going on in Cabo Delgado, the northernmost province of Mozambique—known to some as *Cabo Esquecido* or "Forgotten Cape"—is horrendous.

Few are able to view video clips of dismembered men, women and children—the majority decapitated—and left for all to see after one of their "visits" without being sickened by cruelty.

For the third time in just over half a century, Mozambique was facing a civil war that threatened to cripple the country. The only difference was that this one involved a fairly large and extremely well-organized Islamic force that maintains close ties to Somalia's al-Shabaab insurgency because most of their early recruits were trained there.

The new war could almost be described as an "overnight" revolution. It took most people by surprise because for the first two years, while attacks which had originally emanated out of Tanzania increased, the newly arrived Jihadists fomenting revolt kept their heads down and simply went about their business, never claiming any successes; military or otherwise.

All the while, thousands more people of the Islamic faith were moving southwards across the Tanzanian frontier and setting up cells in an area half the size of England: much of this was textbook Soviet tactics, though Moscow was never involved. In contrast, the late Abu Bakr al-Baghdadi, the Islamic State "Supremo," certainly was.

The extent of the Jihadists' murderous exploits which include the routine dismembering of bodies, besides decapitations of those taken prisoner, defies description. Some of these images have been viewed on social media and all are hideous. To some observers they are African versions of the kind of ethnic cleansing we observed not long ago in the Middle East, where Syrian military atrocities in places like Aleppo, Homs and Idlib spring to mind. The only difference is that east of Suez, violence was focused on embattled cities: in this corner of Africa, it is mostly rural or peri-urban.

Indeed, conditions in this northern province defy either description or categorization because the killings are randomly gory, all done in the name of the Islamic State Central Africa Province (ISCAP), in turn affiliated with the Islamic State group that calls itself *Ahlu Sunnah Wal-Jama*, a name often used by Sunni Jihadist groups.

Britain's *The Economist* described it accurately on August 16, 2020: "A smoldering Islamist insurgency has set the province ablaze. There were almost as many attacks by the Jihadists in the first half of 2020 as in all of 2019, which was bloodier than 2018, the first full year of the conflict."

What is notable about this conflagration is that by the time the authorities began to accept that they had a problem—and it took them a year or two even to admit that there was anything resembling a revolution—this African war was following a pattern not unlike others on the continent in recent times. The initial attacks suddenly emerged from nowhere, with nobody claiming responsibility and the local population too intimidated to venture any kind of opinion.

It was the same in Mali in West Africa a decade ago, and with Somalia before that. Some pundits have suggested that South Africa, with its own large Islamic community that is millions strong, could be next.

***

It was Russia's President Putin who first offered to help. Following discussions in Maputo between the two governments, it was agreed that Moscow would send in a large irregular private military company (PMC) known as the Wagner Group: mercenaries actually, who had already seen action in both Syria and Libya. It is no secret that many of its combatants are still serving members of the Russian armed forces, although Moscow denies this.

The London *Times* actually took to referring to this Russian group as "Putin's Private Army."

The Wagner Group entered the country in October 2019, using heavy-lift Russian Antonov AN-124 aircraft—physically larger and allowing for larger payload capacity than Lockheed's C-5 Galaxy—to fly in helicopters and infantry fighting vehicles. All this came with a formidable range of ancillary equipment such as heavy weapons, drones and electronic equipment that included monitoring and communications sets. It was a massive effort and cost millions, not the sort of enterprise normally handled by private companies.

From the start the "Men from Moscow," as they were dubbed by locals, seemed to enjoy complete dominance in the air with their array of Hind helicopter gunships as well as Mi-171Es (medium twin-turbine transporters with weapons mounted which have the same performance as the Mi-8MTV, but with more sophisticated systems fitted). There were unconfirmed reports that one of these gunships was shot down, something the Russians would never admit to…

Almost immediately, the newcomers launched numerous actions against an enemy entrenched in the jungle- and mountain-clad terrain fringing on southern Tanzania.

That much we know. What we do not know is how many guerrilla fighters there were, how they were able to bring their weapons into the country (through Tanzania), or how much truth there is in unsubstantiated reports that the rebels might have been equipped with supersonic ground-to-air missiles or MANPADs. That report followed a Mozambique Air Force Mi-17 possibly shot down by one early in 2019.

For all its gung-ho bluster and swagger, the Wagner Group lasted only three or four months in Mozambique's war before the entire force retreated back to Nacala—from where they had first arrived in the country—packed their bags, loaded all their equipment on more heavy-lift freighter aircraft and went home. The Russians had simply been overwhelmed by a more committed and better disciplined force that also liked to decapitate its victims and place the heads of victims on stakes so there would be no mistaking their intentions.

What is still not clearly understood is how this relatively low-key Jihadist insurgency element was allowed to develop into a crack and potent combat force under the very noses of the Mozambican Army, and within such a relatively short time. More to the point, this was the first time in recent years that one of the major powers has been driven out of a Third World conflagration, even though the Russians enjoyed total air supremacy.

What did emerge was that while the Russian mercenary force was active in a vast area adjoining the Tanzanian frontier, it had totally underestimated the ability of a ragged bunch of bush fighters to counter its every move; the Jihadists were certainly better mobilized and were a lot more sharply focused than the opposition.

It also became clear that rebel intelligence was vastly superior to that of either the Wagner Group or Mozambique's government—which was supposed to operate in conjunction with the mercenary force, but did not—since almost every thrust against them was met with hard-line bush tactics that cost lives.

The most significant factor of all is that the entire region is largely Muslim, with the insurgents enjoying the support—most of it surreptitious—of the local population. Whatever the Wagner Group planned or did, the rebels were informed within hours.

Possibly the biggest problem faced by the Russian air and ground forces—roughly 200-strong—was that they were designated to operate in close cooperation with the Mozambican Army, the *Forças Armadas de Defesa de Moçambique* or FADM. That combination soon turned sour.

During initial ground and air strikes, the combined forces bombed insurgent bases in several areas, pushing them into the remote interior, but the impasse did not last long. The insurgents retaliated by launching attacks on several government military bases in which dozens on both sides were killed.

Following the arrival of the Russians, the Jihadists reinforced their units in Mozambique by rushing in "volunteers" from other East African countries, Somalia especially; this soon led to an intensified series of guerrilla onslaughts. As one hack commented, "the presence of Wagner created an exponential increase in incidents: it was as if someone had kicked the hornet's nest."

By mid-November 2019, several Mozambican and South African sources observed growing tensions between Wagner and the FADM after a number of failed military operations. Joint bush patrols were halted and reports did the rounds in Pemba, Nacala and other cities in the north that there had apparently been a breakdown in trust between Moscow's men and the national army.

It is no longer a secret that Wagner regarded Mozambique's military as not only inadequate, but also badly trained, inefficient and totally unmotivated. "They are simply not up to the task at hand," said one observer who had spent time in the region. Privately he told me they were "absolutely bloody useless!"

Part of the problem that was fairly common knowledge, even to the Jihadists, was that many Mozambican soldiers went for months without being paid. The money had been dispatched northwards from Maputo but it often went into the pockets of their officers—and being stuck in a remote region over 1,500km from the capital—compounded the matter still further.

Once Wagner had pulled out, the entire northern region had a security blanket dragged over it by the country's state security forces—the *Forças de Defesa e Segurança* (FDS). Journalists covering the story who tried to enter the area were arrested.

According to John Gartner, a former Rhodesian Special Forces operative and head of OAM-I [OAM International]—a Dubai-based private military company that originally tendered for the security contract but lost out to Wagner—Mozambique's military was not the only participant at fault: the Russians too were totally "out of their depth" in fighting Jihadis in Mozambique, "and that in spite of being completely air dominant," he told a colleague.

Earlier, after Wagner had arrived in East Africa, veteran African mercenary aviator Neall Ellis told me that he doubted whether the Russians would be able to cope in Mozambique's harsh environment, where flying is often fraught by weather, bad communications and lack of basics, like fuel.

"The Russian force arrived with a lot of good military equipment, but they obviously knew very little of actual conditions in the field. Also, the terrain in northern Mozambique presented a new set of problems … it's a totally different kind of warfare to what they've experienced in their other wars further north." His immediate perception was that their commanders had done very little groundwork.

The main problem faced by the mercenary forces was that they were totally unfamiliar with what became a series of tough encounters against an enemy that is thoroughly familiar with conditions in its own backyard. Most contacts followed ambushes laid by the insurgents in culverts or approaches to water crossings, the route taken by Wagner's soldiers having been monitored on one of thousands of granite high points scattered throughout the region.

Sources indicate that the rebels were equipped with an array of good Eastern European and Chinese weapons, many of them "out of the box," as well as radio communications equipment. Also, they knew how to make good use of it all.

More salient, Ellis suggested, any outsiders are unlikely to get on with local folk who are largely Muslim with a long history of antagonism towards foreigners that goes back centuries: "The belligerent Makonde tribe, in particular, gave the Portuguese Army a lot of grief while they still ruled."

As for air cover, he declared after their combatants had pulled back to Nacala, "the impression I got from some of my people who were on the ground there, was that Wagner operatives displayed little understanding how such things operate in that part of Africa."

For instance, a journey from Pemba, the oil and gas port on the coast (to the immediate east of the area where much of the fighting had taken place) to the Lugenda River, a tributary of the Rovuma which forms the border with Mozambique (a distance of roughly 350km) can take between 10 and 12 hours in an SUV in the dry season and twice that when it is wet.

Also, the entire region is dotted with tall granite outcrops, some more than a thousand feet high and used by the insurgents to keep track of movement on the ground, sometimes over scores of kilometers. Exactly the same situation held during Lisbon's colonial war in the south-east African territory almost half a century ago.

Ellis added that since the insurgents were Muslim, it was not difficult to imagine where the sympathies of the local population would lie. "And that," he added, "puts paid to any reliable intelligence likely to emerge from the jungle interior."

The truth is that the majority of northerners regard the Mozambican Army, most of whom are southerners, with suspicion, and in some areas populated by the Makonde tribe, with undisguised hostility, especially since President Filipe Nyuti has Makonde tribal roots, as has his chief of police.

Similarly, the northerners tarred the Russian newcomers with a distinct colonial brush, many of the locals outspoken about having "a bunch of foreigners" subjugate them, as did the Portuguese before they were driven out in 1974.

Russian casualties in the insurrection did not go unnoticed, either in Moscow or Maputo. Within a week of arriving in the region early in October 2019, seven Russian Wagner Group mercenaries were killed in two separate incidents. Soon afterwards, in the region's Macomia district, more Wagner soldiers were killed after their group had been caught short in a road ambush. Five more Russian mercenaries were ambushed on October 27, 2019, in the region's Muidumbe district, a reliable Mozambican Army source disclosed.

According to several sources in Pemba, the biggest town in the area, four of the Russians were shot dead at the scene of one attack and then beheaded; the fifth was wounded and later died at the local Mueda District Hospital. "The attackers first set up barricades along the road, and when Mozambique Army vehicles arrived with the Russians in tow, they began firing and then beheaded some of the soldiers," Pjotr Sauer of *The Moscow Times* (with whom I exchanged notes and photos) told me.

Significantly, there was helicopter "top cover" available for all these actions, but as subsequent events proved, heavy jungle overgrowth limited the efficacy of the helicopter gunships to provide any kind of support whatever, except to haul out the casualties.

Notable too, was that the Russian Embassy in Mozambique did not respond to a request for comment from Sauer, though the embassy did advise *Sputnik*, a news agency established by the Russian government-owned *Rossiya Segodnyait*, that it had no knowledge of the incidents. It pleaded total ignorance, which, under the circumstances, was absurd.

One must also ask what Putin hoped to get out of the deal by committing his Wagner Group to a war in a remote part of Africa where communications were lacking and, as his intelligence might already have been aware, was fraught with numerous imponderables. The answer, essentially, is money—enormous amounts of it. President Nyuti had told him that if the Russians were able to suppress the revolt and drive the Islamic rebels out of the country, he would get access to some very substantial gas deposits, of which Mozambique has some of the biggest on the planet.

By the time that Wagner went in, there was almost US$100 million in investments linked to the Cabo Delgado gas fields in place in the north; the biggest single project involving natural resources in Africa, almost all of which has been put on hold because of the insurrection.

Commodity assets include the Mozambique Liquid Natural Gas (LNG) Project, owned largely by France's Total, formerly Anadarko and worth US$20 billion; the Rovuma LNG Project worth US$30 billion and involving ExxonMobil, Italy's ENI and CNPC, and the Coral FLNG Project worth about US$5 billion.

Obviously, the investors who entered the region after gas deposits had been discovered a decade ago were not only alarmed, but most put investments on hold. Among them are several European companies and still more from the United States, China, India, Portugal and elsewhere.

America's ExxonMobil and France's Total—two major players—met in Paris in November 2019 (with French intelligence also in the picture), the intention being to discuss security plans to protect their interests. They could not find common ground to proceed.

Also in the balance is the 15-million-tonne rail project which was to have been backed by ExxonMobil—an investment worth US$30 billion. And had Russia been able to get a foot in the door, as intended, they would have been first in line to claim their dues.

Ongoing hostilities in northern Mozambique make any of these projects not only impractical but economically unfeasible, and they will remain so until the rebels are either defeated or take over the rest of the country. With almost no frontier controls on Mozambique's borders with Tanzania, the insurgents can count on further support from friendly elements who can easily infiltrate southwards across unpatrolled rivers in small boats and pirogues.

The rebels have captured several small ports in the north, quickly put to use to infiltrate men and war materiel into the region from abroad. Drugs are shipped in from Central Asia through Pakistan, the proceeds used to finance the Jihadist war.

Glossary

AAA	Anti-aircraft artillery: also referred to as "Triple-A"
AK, AK-47	*Avtomat Kalashnikova*: 7.62mm (short) assault rifle
Aldeamento	Portuguese protected camp where villagers are gathered together to avoid contact with guerrillas (as with British "protected villages" during the Malayan Emergency)
ANC	African National Congress
Assimilado	Africans in overseas colonies who had "assimilated" sufficiently to earn full Portuguese citizenship rights
AU (African Union)	*See* OAU
Berliet	Heavy French-built transport vehicle in service with the Portuguese Army in Africa
Chefe do Posto	Local Portuguese administrator
CIO	Rhodesian-Zimbabwean Central Intelligence Organization
Congo-Brazzaville	(*République du Congo*): The Republic of the Congo also referred to as Congo-Brazzaville or simply Congo. Not to be confused with Democratic Republic of the Congo (Kinshasa)
DGS	*Direção-Geral de Segurança*: General Security Directorate (Portuguese secret police)
DRC	Democratic Republic of the Congo, formerly Zaire, formerly Belgian Congo, also called Congo-Kinshasa
DShK	*Degtyaryova-Shpagin Krupnokalibernyi*: Soviet 12.7mm heavy anti-aircraft machine-gun

EO	Executive Outcomes: mercenary group that ended civil wars in Angola and Sierra Leone
FADM	*Forças Armadas de Defesa de Moçambique*: Mozambique Armed Defense Forces
FAP	*Força Aerea Portuguesa*: Portuguese Air Force
FAPLA	*Forças Armadas Populares de Libertação de Angola*: People's Armed Forces for the Liberation of Angola (now *Forças Armadas de Angolanas*)
FLN	*Front de Liberation Nationale*: National Liberation Front, Algerian liberation group
FNLA	*Frente Nacional de Libertação de Angola*: National Front for the Liberation of Angola
FRELIMO	*Frente de Libertação de Moçambique*: Liberation Front of Mozambique
G3	7.62mm battle rifle developed in the 1950s by the German armament manufacturer Heckler & Koch GmbH (H&K) in collaboration with the Spanish. Adapted by the Portuguese armed forces
Grupos Especiais	Portuguese Army Special Force units
Grupos Especiais de Pisteiros de Combate	Special units trained in tracking
Lourenço Marques	Capital city of Mozambique: renamed Maputo after independence
MANPAD	Man-portable air defense system (like the Soviet Strela SAM-7)
Metical	Post-independence currency: replaced the escudo
MFA	*Movimento das Forças Armadas*: Armed Forces Movement
MK	*Umkhonto We Sizwe* (Spear of the Nation): ANC military wing (South Africa) with strong Tanzanian ties
MPLA	*Movimento Popular de Libertação de Angola*: Popular Movement for the Liberation of Angola
NATO	North Atlantic Treaty Organization

OAU	Organization of African Unity (today African Union)
OZM-4	Metallic bounding fragmentation mine
PAIGC	*Partido Africano da Independência da Guiné e Cabo Verde*: Guerrilla group in Portuguese Guinea. Took power by force after the Portuguese hastily departed in 1974
Panhard AML	*Auto mitrailleuse légère*: French light 4×4 armored car, developed by South Africa into the *Eland*
Pára-Quedistas	Paratrooper Special Groups (volunteer Black soldiers who had paratrooper training)
PIDE	*Polícia Internacional e de Defesa do Estado*: Portuguese International Police for the Defense of the State or Lisbon's equivalent of the secret police
PKM	A Soviet 7.62mm general-purpose machine-gun much favored by anti-government guerrillas
PMD-6	Anti-personnel mine
POM-Z	Soviet anti-personnel stake-mounted fragmentation mine, much used in Africa
Porto Amélia	Mozambican town, renamed Pemba after independence
Puma	French-built troop-carrying helicopter. Also deployed with heavy side guns mounted
RAF	Royal Air Force
RLI	Rhodesian Light Infantry
RPD	Soviet-made light machine-gun, similar to the *Degtyaryov*, 7.62mm caliber
RPG	Rocket propelled grenade—either RPG-2 (used by guerrillas in Portuguese African conflicts), or RPG-7 more recently, with additional variations
RPK	A 7.62×39mm light machine-gun of Soviet design, developed by Mikhail Kalashnikov in the late 1950s, parallel with the AKM assault rifle
SAAF	South African Air Force

SG-43	The SG-43 Goryunov—a Soviet medium machine-gun introduced during World War II and issued to liberation forces in Africa (equivalent to the American M1919 Browning)
Stick	(Rhodesian Army)—usually a small squad four troops on patrol
SWA	South West Africa (now Namibia)
SWAPO	South West African People's Organization
TM-46 and TM-57	Soviet anti-tank mines used by liberation groups
TNT	*Trinitrotoluene*: is a chemical compound best known as a useful explosive material with convenient handling properties
Tropas Especiais	Special Troops, commonly known by the acronym TEs, which came into effect when one of the UPA/FNLA guerrillas defected to the Portuguese with 1,200 of his men
UDI	Unilateral Declaration of Independence (Rhodesia)
UNITA	*União Nacional Para a Independência Total de Angola*: National Union for the Total Liberation of Angola
ZANLA	Zimbabwe African National Liberation Army (guerrilla group)
ZANU	Zimbabwe African National Union

Select Bibliography

David Abshire and Michael Samuels, *Portuguese Africa—A Handbook*. London: Pall Mall Press, 1969

Ian Beckett and John Pimlott, eds. *Armed Forces & Modern Counter-insurgency*. London: Croom Helm, 1985

Marcello Caetano, *Depoimento*. Rio de Janeiro: Distribuidora Record, 1974

John P. Cann, *Counter-insurgency in Africa: The Portuguese Way of War 1961–74*. Warwick: Helion, 2012

John P. Cann, *Brown Waters of Africa: Portuguese Riverine Warfare 1961–1974*. Warwick: Helion, 2014

John P. Cann, *Flight Plan Africa: Portuguese Airpower in Counter-insurgency, 1961–1974*. Warwick: Helion, 2015

John P. Cann, *The Fuzileiros: Portuguese Marines in Africa, 1961–1974*. Warwick: Helion, 2016

Ronald Chilcote, *Portuguese Africa*. New Jersey: Prentice-Hall, 1967

João Paulo Borges Coelho, "African Troops in the Portuguese Colonial Army, 1961–1974: Angola, Guiné-Bissau and Mozambique." *Portuguese Studies Review* 10 (1) (2002): 129–50

Barbara Cornwall, *The Bush Rebels*. London: Andre Deutsch, 1973

Silva Cunha, *O Ultramar a nação e o "25 de abril"*. Coimbra: Atlantida Editora, 1977

Basil Davidson, *The Liberation of Guiné*. Penguin African Library, 1969

Basil Davidson, *In the Eye of the Storm*. London: Longmans, 1972

J. Duffy, *Portuguese Africa*. Harvard: Harvard University Press, 1959

Richard Gibson, *African Liberation Movements*. Oxford University Press, 1972

Colonel T. N. Greene, *The Guerrilla and How to Fight Him. Selections from the "Marine Corps Gazette"*. New York: Praeger, 1967

Kenneth Grundy, *Guerrilla Struggle in Africa*. USA: Grossman Publishers, 1971

Lewis H. and Peter Duignan, eds. L. H. Gann, author, *Colonialism in Africa 1870–1960* (five-volume set). Cambridge: Cambridge University Press, 1969

J. da Luz Cunha et al, *Africa, a Vitoria Traida*. Lisbon: *Intervenção*, 1977

William Minter, *Portuguese Africa and the West*. London: Penguin, 1972

Nguyen van Tien, *Notre Strategie de la Guerrilla*. Paris: Partisans, 1968

Peter Paret and John W. Shy, *Guerrillas in the 1960s*. Princeton: Princeton University, 1962

Réné Pélissier, *Angola, Guinées, Mozambique, Sahara, Timor, etc: Une bibliographie internationale critique (1990–2005)*. Orgeval: Editions Pelissier, 2006

Douglas Porch, *The Portuguese Armed Forces and the Revolution*. London and Stanford: Croom Helm, 1977

Antonio de Spínola, *Portugal and the Future*. South Africa: Perskor, 1974. Originally published in Lisbon under the title *Portugal y el Futuro*, 1974

John Stockwell, *In Search of Enemies: A CIA Story*. London: W. W. Norton, 1984

John Sykes, *Portugal and Africa*. London: Hutchinson, 1971

Robert Taber, *War of the Flea*. London: Paladin, 1970

Robert Thompson, *Defeating Communist Insurgency.* London: Chatto & Windus, 1966

Roger Trinquier, *Modern Warfare—a French View of Counter-insurgency.* Praeger, 1962

Willem S. van der Waals, Brigadier General, *Portugal's War in Angola 1961–1974.* Ashanti Publishing, 1993

Al J. Venter, *Portugal's War in Guiné-Bissau.* Pasadena: Munger Africana Library, California Institute of Technology, 1973. Also published under the title *Portugal's Guerrilla War.* Cape Town: John Malherbe, 1973

Al J. Venter, *Africa at War.* Old Greenwich: Devin-Adair, 1974

Al J. Venter, *Barrel of a Gun—Misspent Moments in Combat.* Oxford: Casemate Publishers, 2010

Al J. Venter, *War Stories by Al Venter and Friends.* South Africa: Protea Books, 2012

Al J. Venter, *Portugal's Guerrilla Wars in Africa.* Warwick: Helion, 2014

Al J. Venter, *The Chopper Boys: Helicopter Warfare in Africa.* Warwick: Helion, 2016

Endnotes

Introduction

1   James Duffy, *Portuguese Africa*. Harvard: Harvard University Press, 1959, subsequently updated.

Chapter 1

1   Sophie Lenz, "A Day in the Life of Someone Out There—in Mozambique."

Chapter 2

1   Filipe Viera de Castro, *The Pepper Wreck: A Portuguese Indiaman at the Mouth of the Tagus River*. Texas: Texas A & M University Press, College Station, 2005.

2   Thomas Packenham, *The Scramble for Africa: White Man's Conquest of the Dark Continent from 1876 to 1912*. Avon Books, 1992.

3   A comprehensive understanding of Mozambique's earliest days comes from a remarkable book, *The Origins of War in Mozambique—A History of Unity and Division*. It is a mammoth and enormously insightful work compiled by Sayaka Funada-Classen. Hardcover edition first published in 2012 by Ochanomizu Shobo Co. Ltd, Tokyo and then under the African Minds imprint in 2013: www.africanminds.co.za.

4   One source described the war against African chiefs in Mozambique as fierce but short. "After achieving pacification in the areas, foreign enterprises were entrusted with controlling most of the areas." This statement was not accurate because the Portuguese did not achieve military control over the whole of Mozambique until 1920, after its military power had been upgraded during World War I.

5   http://www.allworldwars.com/My-Reminiscences-of-East-Africa-by-von-Lettow-Vorbeck.html.

Chapter 3

1   John P. Cann, Portuguese Counterinsurgency Campaigning in Africa—1961–1974: A Military Analysis. Thesis submitted for the Degree of Doctor of Philosophy. London: Department of War Studies, King's College, 1996.

Chapter 4

1   Zambia's copper mines in the north of the country (many South African-owned) were an exception. Without those revenues, President Kenneth Kaunda would have been ousted long before he was trumped in a general election.

2   The name-change to Tanzania followed an attempted army mutiny in 1964, promptly thwarted by quick British Army and Royal Navy intervention.

3   *Osagyefo*, as Nkrumah liked to be referred to by his acolytes, means "redeemer," or someone with great wisdom, while *Uhuru* in Swahili means "freedom."

4   Eduardo Mondlane, *The Struggle for Mozambique*. Harmondsworth: Penguin Books Ltd, 1969.

5   George Roberts, *The Assassination of Eduardo Mondlane: FRELIMO, Tanzania, and the Politics of Exile in Dar es Salaam*. Taylor & Francis Online: November 9, 2016.

6   *Encyclopedia of World Biography*. United States: Gale Group, Inc., 2010.

7   Iain Christie, *Machel of Mozambique*. Harare: Zimbabwe Publishing House, 1988.

Chapter 5

1   João Ribeiro, *Marcas da Guerra Colonial (Marks of the Colonial War)*. Porto: Campo das Letra, 1999.

2   *Estado Novo*, or the Second Republic, was the corporatist far-right regime installed in Portugal by Salazar in 1933. It was deeply rooted in Catholic social thought and highly influential among both liberals and conservatives.

3   João Ribeiro's published report is used in full in my book *Portugal's Guerrilla Wars in Africa (Portugal e as Guerrilhas de Africa)*. Published by Helion in the U.K. in 2013 and five years later by *Clube do Autor* in Lisbon.

Chapter 6

1   Ian F. W. Beckett and John Timplott, *The Portuguese Army in Mozambique 1964–1974*. London and Stanford: Croom Helm, 1985.

Chapter 7

1   "The White Devil of Mozambique," by S. Nielsen, *Soldier of Fortune* magazine. October 1979, 78–83, 87.

Chapter 8

1   Paper presented at Portuguese/African Encounters: An Interdisciplinary Congress, Brown University. Providence MA, April 2002. An earlier version that focused on the Mozambican case was presented at the Second Congress of African Studies in the Iberian World, held in Madrid, Spain, in September 1999 and published as *João Paulo Borges Coelho, "Tropas negras na Guerra colonial: O caso de Moçambique,"* in José Ramón Trujillo, ed., *Africa hacia el siglo XXI*. Madrid: Sial Ediciones, Colección Casa de África 12, 2001. Permission to use this material in this volume granted personally to Venter during a visit to Maputo in March 2012.

2   *Revista Militar* 41 (7), April 15, 1889.

3   John P. Cann, *Contra-insurreição em África, 1961–1974. O modo português de fazer a Guerra.* Estoril: Edições Atena, Portugal, 1998.

4   See David Martelo, *"Pessoal e orçamentos. Esforço de guerra,"* in Afonso and Gomes, *Guerra colonial,* 519–20.

5   According to Ferraz de Freitas, *Conquista da adesão das populações* (Lourenço Marques: SCCIM, 1965), 6, ordering is based exclusively on physical power and provokes the repulsion of culturally different populations, and for this reason its efficiency tends to decrease in proportion to the decline of the physical power of the one who exerts it. On the contrary, commanding requires knowledge and ability to handle the "social forces," is based on participation, and promotes adhesion of the commanded. As to *accionamento,* it was defined as "the set of moves one needs to take to make sure that the population works with us and becomes prejudiced towards the propaganda of the enemy … [Through *accionamento*] we attract the populations into our orbit, integrate them in our environment, in our culture, in our civilisation and nationality… This would be one of our purposes. The other is to make them work actively with us in detecting and combating subversion …" (GDT/*Serviços Distritais de Administração Civil,* 1966:45, *Arquivo Histórico de Moçambique, Secção Especial,* nº 237). For the psycho-social work with local communities in central Mozambique, namely in organising popular operations conducted by traditional authorities to detect guerrilla movements, see João Paulo Borges Coelho, *A "Primeira Frente" de Tete e o Malawi,* Arquivo (15), 1994: 72.

6   João Paulo Borges Coelho, *"Protected Villages and Communal Villages in the Mozambican Province of Tete (1968–1982): A History of State Resettlement Policies, Development and War."* PhD dissertation: Department of Social and Economic Studies, University of Bradford, 1993, 165 and passim.

7   Al J. Venter, *War Stories by Al J. Venter and Friends.* Pretoria: Protea Books, 2011, Chapter 10: Ron Reid-Daly: "A Tribute to the Man and his Scouts," 178–206.

Chapter 10

1   Al J. Venter, *War Dog: Fighting Other People's Wars—The Modern Mercenary in Combat.* Casemate Publishers, Philadelphia, 2011.

2   Robert Craig Johnson, "Coin: The Portuguese in Africa, 1959–1975" (Part 2 in a series): http://worldatwar.net/chandelle/v3/v3n2/portcoin.html.

3   Al J. Venter, *The Chopper Boys—Helicopter Warfare in Africa.* Warwick, Helion, 2016.

Chapter 11

1   John P. Cann, Portuguese Counterinsurgency Campaigning in Africa—1961–1974: A Military Analysis. Thesis submitted for the Degree of Doctor of Philosophy. London: Department of War Studies, King's College, 1996. https://kclpure.kcl.ac.uk/portal/files/2930588/363059.pdf.

2   David Richardson and Filipa Ribeiro da Silva, *Networks and Trans-Cultural Exchange: Slave Trading in the South Atlantic, 1590–1867.* Netherlands: Brill, 2014.

3   Baltazar Leite Rebelo de Sousa, governor-general of Mozambique: July 12, 1968–January 15, 1970; of his testimony, in *"The Last Governors of the Empire,"* 252.

Chapter 12

1   The author deals with this period extensively in *Battle for Angola,* with a new edition published by Helion in Britain in 2021.

2   Hannes Wessels: *A Handful of Hard Men: The SAS and the Battle for Rhodesia.* Oxford: Casemate Publishers, 2015.

3   Ken Flower, *Serving Secretly: An Intelligence Chief on Record: Rhodesia into Zimbabwe, 1964–81.* London: John Murray, 1987.

4   Chris Cocks, *Fire Force—One Man's War in the Rhodesian Light Infantry.* South Africa: 30 Degrees South, 2009.

5   Richard Wood, *The War Diaries of André Dennison.* Rivonia: Ashanti Publishing, 1989.

6   Killing a superior officer in the field because of real or imagined grudges by exploding a grenade in his tent or in his quarters. A fairly commonplace occurrence among disgruntled American troops in Vietnam.

7   This is very much in contrast to today. The author has been on operations with the Portuguese military several times since, in the Jihadist war in Mali in 2021 and in the Central African Republic two years before that. I was to discover that Lisbon's soldiers in the field in Africa currently are among the fittest and healthiest encountered in any of the wars I've covered. This was underscored by Britain's General Sir David Richard when he commanded Coalition forces in Afghanistan some years before. He rated the Portuguese Special Forces contingents under his command as his "favourite troops."

8   Al J. Venter, *Portugal's Guerrilla Wars in Africa – Lisbon's Three Wars in Angola, Mozambique and Portuguese Guinea.* Warwick: Helion, 2013. In Portugal, *Portugal e as Guerrilhas de Africa.* Lisbon: *Clube do Autor,* 2014.

9   Douglas Porch, *The Portuguese Armed Forces and the Revolution.* London and Stanford: Croom Helm, 1977.

Chapter 13

1   RENAMO was founded in 1975 as part of an anti-communist backlash against the country's ruling FRELIMO party. Much of the rebel movement's support initially came from Rhodesia (in the hopes of destabilizing the newly independent Mozambique) and thereafter South Africa, with similar intent. The RENAMO rebellion lasted almost 20 years and the loss of life has been estimated as a dozen times more than during Lisbon's colonial war.

2   Robert Bryce, "Man Versus Mine." *Foreign Affairs*, January/February 2006.

3   John P. Cann, Portuguese Counterinsurgency Campaigning in Africa—1961–1974: A Military Analysis. Thesis submitted for the Degree of Doctor of Philosophy. London: Department of War Studies, King's College, 1996.

4   Human Rights Watch: *The Arms Project Africa Watch*, 1994.

Chapter 15

1   Shortly after Singapore became independent in 1965, the new government implemented stringent laws to combat malaria. The disease was endemic on the island state which lies close to the Equator. The solution was simple: any household found with containers holding open water and left outside was fined. This could soon become crippling if the same household was

punished repeatedly. Though the measure was regarded as draconian and took years to take effect, malaria in Singapore is something of the past.

Chapter 16

1   Charles Guillain was a 19th-century French explorer who reported on his visit to the East Coast of Africa (1846–1848). He produced a magisterial three-volume work, *Documents sur l'histoire, la géographie, et le commerce de l'Afrique orientale* together with an accompanying atlas folio of engravings and maps, *Voyage à la côte orientale d'Afrique*.

2   Douglas Porch, *The Portuguese Armed Forces and the Revolution*. London and Stanford: Croom Helm, 1977.

Chapter 17

1   Douglas Porch, *The Portuguese Armed Forces and the Revolution*. London and Stanford: Croom Helm, 1977.

2   Personal discussions with Brigadier General W.S. (Kaas) van der Waals who actually acted in a civilian role in the Angolan capital because South Africa's official military attaché was based in Lisbon. Also, see his book *Portugal's War in Angola: 1961–1974*, published by Protea Books in South Africa and Helion in the U.K. It was subsequently translated into Portuguese and published in Lisbon.

3   Rene Pelissier, *Les Campagnes Coloniales Du Portugal; 1844–1941*. Editions Flammarion, departement Pygmalion, 2004.